The Films of Vincente Minnelli examines the career of MGM's leading director of musicals, melodramas, and comedies in the forties and fifties. Widely admired for his flamboyant sense of color and camera movement, Minnelli played a crucial role in maintaining the studio's reputation as the "home of the stars." As well as describing the director's contributions to some of the most celebrated works of Hollywood's classic era, this volume includes a close analysis of five important films that represent the full range of Minnelli's career: *Cabin in the Sky, Meet Me in St. Louis, Father of the Bride, The Bad and the Beautiful,* and *Lust for Life.* These lively readings provide commentary on problems of genre, directorial style, cultural politics, and the connection between aestheticism and mass culture during the first half of the twentieth century.

The Films of Vincente Minnelli

CAMBRIDGE FILM CLASSICS

General Editor: Raymond Carney, Boston University

Other books in the series:

Peter Bondanella, *The Films of Roberto Rossellini*
Sam B. Girgus, *The Films of Woody Allen*
Robert Phillip Kolker and Peter Beicken, *The Films of Wim Wenders*
Scott MacDonald, *Avant-Garde Film*
James Palmer and Michael Riley, *The Films of Joseph Losey*
Scott Simmon, *The Films of D. W. Griffith*
David Sterritt, *The Films of Alfred Hitchcock*
Maurice Yacowar, *The Films of Paul Morrissey*

The Films of
Vincente Minnelli

JAMES NAREMORE
Indiana University

CAMBRIDGE
UNIVERSITY PRESS

Published by the Press Syndicate of the University of Cambridge
The Pitt Building, Trumpington Street, Cambridge CB2 1RP
40 West 20th Street, New York, NY 10011–4211, USA
10 Stamford Road, Oakleigh, Victoria 3166, Australia

First published 1993

Printed in the United States of America

Library of Congress Cataloging-in-Publication Data
Naremore, James.
The films of Vincente Minnelli / James Naremore.
p.   cm. – (Cambridge film classics)
Filmography: p.
Includes bibliographical references and index.
ISBN 0-521-38366-8 (hc). – ISBN 0-521-38770-1 (pb)
1. Minnelli, Vincente – Criticism and interpretation.   I. Title.
II. Series.
PN1998.3.M56N37   1993
791.43'0233'092 – dc20   92-39912
                                                      CIP

A catalog record for this book is available from the British Library.

ISBN 0-521-38366-8 hardback
ISBN 0-521-38770-1 paperback

For Darlene J. Sadlier
and in memory of Arthur G. Keller

Contents

Acknowledgments   *page* ix

Introduction: Why Minnelli?   1

1   The Aesthete in the Factory   7
     From Shops to Palaces / *Dandyism, Modernism, and*
     Entertainment / *On Broadway* / *Inside the Factory* /
     Minnelli's Genres / *Notes on Style* /
     The Critic as Producer

2   Uptown Folk: *Cabin in the Sky* (1943)   51

3   Third Nature: *Meet Me in St. Louis* (1944)   71

4   Comedy, Patriarchy, Consumerism: *Father of the Bride*
     (1950)   90

5   Citizen Shields: *The Bad and the Beautiful* (1952)   112

6   Vincente Meets Vincent: *Lust for Life* (1956)   135

     Notes   154

     Chronology   166

     Filmography   168

     Selected Bibliography   187

     Index   193

Acknowledgments

For advice and help on this project, I owe thanks to several individuals and institutions. Robert Lang, Jonathan Rosenbaum, and François Thomas gave me important bibliographic information; Robert B. Ray talked with me at length about Minnelli; Christopher Anderson and Barbara Klinger shared their knowledge of fifties Hollywood; and a number of people – including Manthia Diawara, John Fell, Gloria Gibson-Hudson, John Hess, Phyllis Klotman, and Cary Wolfe – made useful suggestions about *Cabin in the Sky*. My research was assisted by the talented staff at the Margaret Herrick Library of the Motion Picture Academy, the Lilly Library, and the Indiana University Fine Arts Library. I was also given opportunities to present lectures based on my work: Robert Stam enabled me to participate on a panel he organized at the Society for Cinema Studies; Lesley Brill, Robert Burgoyne, and Cynthia Erb honored me with the chance to deliver the Dennis Turner Memorial Lecture at Wayne State University; and Bill Paul and the film faculty at the University of Michigan invited me to speak at an interdepartmental "Comedy Semester" in Ann Arbor.

Chapter 2, in slightly different form, appeared in the Winter 1992 issue of *Arizona Quarterly*. I am grateful to Susan White and the editors of that journal for their support. Ray Carney, general editor of the Cambridge Film Classics series, and Beatrice Rehl, arts and media editor at Cambridge University Press, were unfailingly cheerful and intelligent collaborators. Mary Racine and Cary Groner greatly assisted with the work of copyediting. As usual, Darlene Sadlier was near my side throughout, helping in more ways than I can count.

Introduction
Why Minnelli?

In 1945, after viewing a premiere of Eisenstein's *Ivan the Terrible* sponsored by the United Nations in San Francisco, Orson Welles wrote a lengthy and amusing commentary on the different styles of Soviet and American movies. Soviet montage, Welles argued, had developed out of economic necessity: "Because of the inferiority of Russian film stock, lenses, and other equipment, the camera must assert itself by what it selects, and by the manner of selection." Meanwhile, the more lavishly appointed, technically advanced Hollywood cinema had developed a "merchant's eye," devoting itself to "star-hogging closeups" and to "lovingly evaluating texture, the screen being filled as a window is dressed in a swank department store."[1]

Welles was speaking about Hollywood in general, and he was neither the first nor the last critic to equate American cinema with a shop window.[2] But suppose we wanted to choose a single filmmaker of the period who most exemplifies the "swank" tendency he was describing: who among the many possible candidates would be the most intriguing selection? It seems to me that the best answer would be Vincente Minnelli, who began his long career at MGM in 1943 and became one of the most successful and admired workers in what Max Horkheimer and Theodor W. Adorno termed the "culture industry." Over the next two decades, Minnelli made important contributions to some of the most celebrated entertainments in history, including *Meet Me in St. Louis, Father of the Bride, An American in Paris, The Bad and the Beautiful, The Band Wagon, Lust for Life,* and *Gigi.* Ultimately recognized as a Hollywood auteur, he won several awards and exerted a modest influence on the Italianate strain of contemporary cinema, especially on the films of Bernardo Bertolucci and Martin Scorsese. Ironically, however, Minnelli's first professional employment, long before coming to Hollywood, was as a designer of display windows for the Marshall Field

1

department store in Chicago. Significantly, he once directed a charming comedy entitled *Designing Woman,* and one of his melodramas, *The Cobweb,* involves a crisis that breaks out in a mental institution when new drapes are selected for the common room.

Minnelli was born into a theatrical family that toured the Midwest in the first decade of the century. His first ambition was to paint, but he worked by turns as a department store decorator, an assistant to a portrait photographer, and a designer of stage settings for the Balaban and Katz chain of movie palaces. He then moved to New York, where he created sets and costumes for Radio City Music Hall, soon becoming a designer-director of Broadway shows. Cosmopolitan in his tastes, he made friendships with George and Ira Gershwin, S. J. Perelman, Oscar Levant, and many of the cleverest talents who worked in the heyday of American musical comedy. Eventually he was brought to Hollywood by former songwriter Arthur Freed, who had assembled a remarkable unit for the production of musical films at MGM. He remained at that studio until the sixties, specializing in musicals, domestic comedies, and melodramas, while growing increasingly famous. He seems to have been happy with the studio's many big-budget producers, designers, and stars. Essentially a *bricoleur,* he kept files of clippings showing different styles of paintings or illustrations, which he liked to go through for inspiration. Like many commercial artists, he particularly admired the surrealists and was among the first Hollywood directors to use their motifs in a self-conscious way. "The accidental juxtaposition of people and things makes for surrealism," he told a *Time* magazine interviewer in 1945. "The surrealists are the court painters of the period. They sum up an age which is at best utter confusion."[3]

Minnelli's interest in painting is evident throughout his career, but part of the drive and brio of his work came from his awareness that movies are a temporal as well as a spatial medium. He loved flamboyant color, costume, and decor, but he never allowed these things to freeze into static compositions. A master of changing patterns and complex movements, he filled his pictures with swooping crane shots, voluptuous plays of fabric, and skillfully orchestrated background detail. Among his contemporaries, only Roubin Mamoulian was his equal at making films in which characters passed so effortlessly from speech into song, from walking into dancing.

Stylistically and thematically, Minnelli's films might be described as late, commercialized expressions of romantic idealism – an attitude born of a culture that had fully assimilated the nineteenth century's striving for "autonomous" art into a capitalist mode of production. Repeatedly he operated on the fault line between bourgeois ideology and extreme aestheticism, making the MGM motto – *Ars Gratia Artis* – sound almost plausible. In fact, the imagination, or one of its surrogates, such as show business or dreaming, was Minnelli's favorite subject. His central female characters – Jennifer Jones in *Madame Bovary*, Judy Garland in *The Pirate*, and Lana Turner in *The Bad and the Beautiful* – were women who lived in fantasy worlds, finding happiness only when they exchanged dreams for self-conscious artifice. Meanwhile his leading men – Kirk Douglas in *Lust for Life*, Fred Astaire in *The Band Wagon*, and Frank Sinatra in *Some Came Running* – played writers, painters, or performers. (If they were not artistic types by profession, they were usually dandies or sensitive youths, like Louis Jourdan in *Gigi*, John Kerr in *Tea and Sympathy*, and George Hamilton in *Home from the Hill*.) By the same token, Minnelli's films generally took place in exotic or studio-manufactured settings, where the boundaries between fantasy and everyday life could easily be transgressed. Most of his pictures – including his most brightly colored musicals – had vaguely "Freudian" overtones, and even when they were set in small-town America, they tended to burst into remarkable oneiric passages, such as the terrifying Halloween sequence in *Meet Me in St. Louis,* the berserk carnival in *Some Came Running,* and the mythic boar hunt in *Home from the Hill.*

Although Minnelli was sometimes preoccupied with a kind of vulgarized psychoanalysis that could be adjusted to the demands of the Production Code, he was among the least macho or phallic of directors, and, together with several of his collaborators in the Freed unit, he brought a rarified sense of camp to musical numbers, making several pictures that were adventurously stylized and ahead of popular taste. To a degree, such films ran against the grain of dominant attitudes, establishing Minnelli as what French critic Louis Marcorelles would later describe as an "Oscar Wilde of the camera." In the last analysis, however, Minnelli's sophistication belongs to the world of *Vogue, Harpers,* and *Vanity Fair.* His musicals are always hymns to entertainment, and his movies about artists never abandon MGM's plush standards of glamour and style.

To study Minnelli's work is therefore to examine the relationship between dandyism and mass culture, or between aestheticism and consumer society. Another way of stating the issue would be to say that his films are a mixture of *Kunst* and kitsch. At every level, they problematize the old and perhaps never valid distinction between authenticity and commercialism, reminding us that the Kantian aesthetic faculty was born during the industrial revolution.[4] Consider, for instance, a famous scene from *The Bad and the Beautiful,* a movie about movies whose very title is symptomatic. Anyone who has seen that film will remember the moment when the actress Georgia

Lorrison (Lana Turner) drives to the home of her producer-lover, Jonathan Shields (Kirk Douglas), hoping to celebrate a film they have just made together. Swathed in mink and bearing champagne, she enters Shields's mansion only to find that he is spending the evening with a starlet (Elaine Stewart). The dialogue between the three characters is only slightly better than a contemporary soap opera, but the scene is nonetheless indelible. Its special power has something to do with the grand staircase in the hallway of the mansion, with the hysterical pitch of the acting, and with the subtly vertiginous movement of camera and players. It also derives from the vivid contrasts of the black and white photography: Douglas's blond hair echoes Turner's, but he moves in and out of inky shadow while she stands in light, her mink stole radiating whiteness. Above these two, at the top of the Gothic stairway, stands Elaine Stewart, dark tresses spilling over her bare shoulders, garbed in a skin-tight, black velvet gown that makes her breasts look like the bumpers of a fifties Cadillac.

Here, in all its erotic fascination and dramatic extravagance, is the perfect instance of what Welles described as a "loving evaluation of texture, the screen being filled as a window is dressed in a swank department store." And Welles's comment seems even more scathing when we note that *The Bad and the Beautiful* explicitly invites comparison with *Citizen Kane*. Produced by Welles's former associate John Houseman, it takes the form of a biographical narrative that is told from the point of view of several characters who once knew a "great man," and it contains numerous scenes that are directly parallel to *Kane*, Welles's most famous achievement. Unfortunately, a straightforward comparison between the two films shows how much Houseman and Minnelli were willing to serve their masters. Like Minnelli's musicals, *The Bad and the Beautiful* is intended to glorify Hollywood (especially producers), forgiving the sins of its central character because of his supposed devotion to artistic "quality." Unlike *Kane*, it is an exemplary studio movie – a sumptuous, stylish entertainment, and the kind of thing critics feel superior to even while they enjoy it.

I would nevertheless insist that *The Bad and the Beautiful* is some kind of masterpiece, perfectly keyed to Kirk Douglas's stardom, and filled with cinematic invention; in fact, few films have given me more pleasure. The larger purpose of my book is to explain this paradox, showing how it affects my response to several of Minnelli's best-known pictures. At the same time, I want to demonstrate a kind of symbiosis between Minnelli's artistry and a rationalized, midcentury entertainment industry.

Given my general aims, I have not attempted a film-by-film account of Minnelli's considerable output. Instead, I offer a comprehensive opening chapter that provides a commentary on several important matters: the director's cultural environment, the institutions where he worked, the generic and stylistic qualities of his films, and the critical discourse surrounding his career. This chapter forms the background for an analysis of five movies, representing a cross section of his work. For some of Minnelli's admirers, the five examples I have selected will be disappointing. I confess that two of his most successful pictures – *An American in Paris* and *Gigi* – leave me relatively cold. Despite a great many incidental virtues, the first of these films is a somewhat leaden spectacular, and the second strikes me as a patently sexist fantasy about "little girls." By the same token, I have forsaken discussion of several titles I wanted to say more about, including *Designing Woman* and *Home from the Hill*. I console myself for such losses with the thought that most of the pictures I have chosen would appear on anyone's list of favorites. I hope my observations will quicken the reader's curiosity and stimulate more writing about Minnelli. One of my purposes, however, is to extend the implications of my remarks beyond the director himself, providing insights into the romantic imagination, American show business, and commodity culture in general.

Figure 1. Vincente Minnelli as a designer at Radio City Music Hall. (Photograph courtesy of Lee [Mrs. Vincente] Minnelli.)

I

The Aesthete in
the Factory

On the facing page is a publicity photograph of Minnelli, circa 1934, in his office at the newly constructed Radio City Music Hall, where he had recently become a designer of "presentation shows." Nearly everything here is sleek and *moderne,* in keeping with the atmosphere of Rockefeller Center. The office furniture was probably created by Donald Deskey, who was described in advertisements for the Music Hall as "the first American-born designer in the modern field,"[1] and the glossy, black-and-white decor suggests the Astaire–Rogers musicals at RKO, a studio partly owned by Rockefeller interests. Like those musicals, Minnelli's work at Radio City offered the Depression years a dream world of sophistication and streamlining; gone forever was the pseudo-Gothic, Victorian past and, with it, most traces of the factory system. Notice, however, that the sense of modernity depends on a mix of styles, some of them aggressively futuristic, others drawn from "primitive" society and slightly earlier times. At the upper left of the frame, two small pieces of African statuary stand next to a contemporary, art deco sculpture, and Minnelli himself looks like a fin-de-siècle painter transported to Metropolis.

The African motif can be found everywhere in Minnelli's early work, and I plan to discuss it later in this chapter. For now, I am more interested in his elegant attire, his liquid eyes, and his pale wrist supporting his cheek. Some viewers of the photograph may ask themselves whether Minnelli was gay. By his own account, he was a heterosexual who disliked crude American notions of masculinity. His films tend to confirm this attitude, although he worked in a milieu where "backstage" homosexuality was fairly common, and his best pictures – all of them made during the most restrictive era of the Production Code – are marked by the sort of "excess" that could not speak its name. Whatever his sexual inclination, his public image offers an answer to a well-known problem posed by Susan Sontag in *Against Interpretation* (1966): it shows us how to behave like a dandy in the age of mass culture.

Actually, Minnelli's rather aestheticized pose recalls a tradition that dates back to Paris in the 1820s – a period when entertainment first became big business, and when Theophile Gautier announced the doctrine of *l'art pour l'art*.[2] Aestheticism and commodification are in fact two of the interdependent "faces" of modernity, and Minnelli often appeared to recognize their ironic relationship. His pictures frequently offered art as a refuge from bourgeois prejudice and industrial alienation; but they also suggested, however inadvertently, that every art is compromised and impure, a product of the very forces it tries to escape. This implicit awareness of a tense affinity between art and commerce may account for the particular tone of his work. Andrew Sarris has noted that Minnelli had an "unusual, somber outlook for musical comedy,"[3] and many critics have commented on the dark spirit in his nonmusical films. In this respect as in others, he resembled the original French dandy, who was both elegant and prone to melancholy.

From Shops to Palaces

Before commenting further on such matters, it may be useful to glance briefly at Minnelli's early life, showing how his career was influenced by the growth of commercial modernity. For a man who became an important force in musical theater and the most flamboyant stylist in Hollywood, he had relatively humble beginnings. The fifth child of a French mother and an Italian father, he was born soon after the turn of the century in the American heartland. (Christened "Lester Anthony Minnelli," he later adopted his father's name, "Vincent," as a *nom du théâtre,* adding the final "e" at the advice of a numerologist.) His parents were itinerant vaudevillians who, during the summer months, helped operate the Minnelli Brothers Tent Show, a touring company that brought middle-class culture to the provinces, playing small towns in Ohio, Illinois, and Indiana. The movable tent seated five hundred patrons, offering music, dances, and pirated versions of Broadway melodramas. Minnelli's father conducted the orchestra, played French horn, and composed Sousa-like marches; his mother, who was the daughter of Parisian circus performers, worked reluctantly as a dancer, singer, and actress.

As a child, Minnelli acted with his mother in *East Lynne,* although in some ways his upbringing was untheatrical. In the winter months, he usually lived with relatives in Chicago or in Delaware, Ohio, where his paternal grandfather, "Professor Minnelli," headed the music department at Ohio Wesleyan University. He attended various schools and was frequently moved from place to place, but his life was never truly chaotic. His devoutly Catholic mother disliked small-time show business, and the tent theater was soon killed off by competition from movies. In 1915, the family settled in Delaware, a college town pervaded by down-at-heels Victorian gentility. The typical household decor, Minnelli later recalled, consisted of "bilious green overstuffed sofas, tiny rosebuds in its ceilings and wallpaper, and pongee curtains which were serviceable year round."[4]

This environment held no charm for the young Minnelli, who, like Emma Bovary, was a dreamer, troubled by what he called a "vague hunger for sophistication."[5] In his autobiography, he says that he once became violently ill after helping a local farmer slaughter a cow and wash maggots from the carcass. (One thinks of George Hamilton in *Home from the Hill,* almost retching when he finds the disemboweled body of a dog lying in the woods.) Understandably, Minnelli much preferred reading in his father's library, acting in school theatricals, and painting pictures in the "studio" he had fashioned in a backyard chicken coop. At one point he obtained a job with a local sign painter, designing show cards for shop window displays, and he was ultimately hired to paint the advertising curtain for a Delaware movie house.

After graduation from high school, Minnelli thought of attending a university, but because his family had little money, he moved to Chicago instead, where he lived briefly with his maternal grandmother and sought work as a commercial artist. Not long after arriving in the city, he found an opportunity:

> Equipped with my portfolio of watercolors, I set out one morning. As I approached the intersection of Washington and State, I was seduced by an elaborate window display. The background was a Florence garden; in the foreground stood some merchandise, artfully arranged. I looked up at the store sign: MARSHALL FIELD.[6]

Minnelli became the fourth assistant decorator at Chicago's leading department store. The Marshall Field windows were "considered the finest in the country, looked up to even by New York," but Minnelli, who was already inspired by the stage designs of Hardin Craig and Robert Edmund Jones, saw them as a theatrical space and hoped to bring them "into the twentieth century."[7] Unfortunately, much of his work was routine. He was never assigned to the high-fashion State Street store, but he soon took charge of the Wabash Avenue branch, which displayed furniture, antiques, and decorative accessories. As in *Meet Me in St. Louis,* the windows in this store changed with each season. Minnelli and his crew would sometimes spend all night arranging the furniture just so, and then draw back the curtains suspended over their work to reveal a dramatic setting appropriate to the time of year.

If, as Walter Benjamin once remarked, "the department store is the *flâneur*'s last practical joke," Minnelli must have been amused. His regular income enabled him to wander the city, sampling jazz and night life. For a while he took classes at the Art Institute, where he saw a fine collection of impressionist paintings. He attended the theater regularly, viewing all the major shows from New York, and at one point he played a role in an amateur production of a Eugene O'Neill one-act drama, which was sponsored by a radical bookshop on Clark Street. Eventually, he began taking a sketch pad along to the theater, visiting backstage and making drawings of the actors and costumes in the manner of Ralph Barton in *Vanity Fair.* On one of these occasions, when he was peddling watercolors based on his drawings, he met the society photographer Paul Sloane, who hired him as an assistant.

In Sloane's work, the worlds of fashion, theater, and painting coalesced. Sloane specialized in glossy portraits of actors or celebrities – pictures that could be reproduced in newspapers or magazines without losing their aura of glamour and refinement. Following a practice dating back to sixteenth-century aristocratic portraiture, he placed figures against drapery and sometimes costumed them in theatrical or period dress. He expended considerable effort on lighting and camera angles, and he employed painters to subtly retouch the photos in his laboratory. Minnelli was good at the retouching process, and even though he claimed to have no special aptitude for cameras, he knew how to control the photographic mise-en-scène, arranging subjects in artfully relaxed poses. Like Guys, Sargent, Charles Dana Gibson, and other illustrators of turn-of-the-century sophistication, he could make clothed figures seem both à la mode and casual, both idealized and empirically true.

The job in the photographic studio brought Minnelli into contact with an influential world of theatrical personalities and Chicago socialites, and it fueled his artistic ambitions. He still harbored a desire to become a painter (in Paris, if possible), and he was increasingly alive to the fashionable intellectual movements of his day. He was particularly intrigued by Freudianism and the surrealists, including Duchamp, Ernst, Dali, Cocteau, and Buñuel; his deepest affinities, however, were always with prewar art. In Paul Sloane's library, he encountered a biography of James McNeill Whistler, and he immediately recognized a kindred spirit. Whistler was an American, a dandy, a wit, a protoimpressionist painter, and a famous interior designer; as Minnelli put it, "Here was a man – and an artist – with whom I could identify."[8]

Inspired by his reading, Minnelli decided to apply for a job more worthy of his talents. He took his portfolio of drawings and watercolors to the head office of the Balaban and Katz chain of picture palaces, where he interviewed for the position of chief costume designer at the Chicago Theater. Given his youth, his move was somewhat daring, but it was consistent with his theatrical interests and his previous experience at Marshall Field. The leading theater owners of the twenties tended to model themselves on the big department store chains; like other merchants, they sought the growing population of urban, middle-class customers, and they constructed baronial edifices in which to display their wares. No one was better at the new type of theater than Balaban and Katz, who had pioneered a management style and a form of "horizontal integration" that was the envy of the business. Taking advantage of urban mass transit and the growth of prosperous suburbs, they built four massive auditoriums – a flagship, the Chicago, in the center of the business district, and three satellites on the north, east, and south sides. By 1926, they had obtained a virtual monopoly on motion picture exhibition in the city. Soon afterward, they merged with Famous Players-Lasky, and then with Paramount Pictures, to become a giant, vertically integrated corporation. (At the time of these mergers, according to film historians Robert C. Allen and Douglas Gomery, 3 to 5 percent of the revenue from every film shown in the United States went into the B&K coffers.)[9] Meanwhile, they also pioneered a special form of exhibition. Each theater was designed to resemble a cross between an amusement park, an opera house, a bank, and a cathedral. Inside, patrons saw not only first-run films, but also spectacular live shows featuring vaudeville stars and synchronized dance numbers, backed by a full orchestra and a battery of complex lighting effects. (*Gold Diggers of 1933*, the Busby Berkeley movie starring James Cagney, was intended as a nostalgic tribute to this style of entertainment, which vanished with the Depression.)

Strangely, B&K had never employed a costume designer. Minnelli seemed a promising young man with the right sort of background, and he was hired on the spot. He immediately began creating costumes for stage extravaganzas of musical and specialty acts at the biggest showplace in Chicago's Loop, supervising a small factory of women who worked at sewing machines in the basement. He was required to develop an entirely new production every week, ultimately designing the sets as well as the costumes, concocting boffo displays for the climactic dance numbers. Every Monday, he traveled with his bosses to the suburban theaters, where he supervised touring companies; then, after each production had completed its run, his costumes, drapes, and settings were disassembled and recycled. His "custom" touch, together with his sophisticated awareness of current trends in art and theater, was noticed in *Variety* and other trade journals, and he soon became a leading figure in the twenties version of the "society of the spectacle." As a favored employee of B&K, he also gained privileged entree to show business and art salons in Chicago, and when B&K was absorbed into Paramount, one of his dreams came true: he was moved to New York, where the Paramount-Publix corporation was administered from a resplendent building on Times Square.

The ground floor of the Paramount Building housed the Paramount Theater, which was the centerpiece of a national chain of picture palaces similar to the ones in Chicago. In 1931, Minnelli began designing costumes for stage shows that opened on Times Square and then toured big-city palaces around the country. (In New York, he was required to join the Society of Painters and Paper Hangers, a guild that administered an entrance exam; according to Stephen Harvey, every applicant was asked to name "two modernistic painters.")[10] Accustomed to the rigors of creating multiple shows, he also found time to moonlight on several Broadway productions. For the 1931 version of Earl Carrol's *Vanities,* he devised a "show curtain" based on Erté's famous decorations for the Folies Begère; in the next year, he designed both sets and costumes for the new edition of Carrol's revue, plus a "book" musical entitled *The DuBarry,* starring opera star Grace Moore. As a lark, he also executed a set of Beardsleyesque illustrations for *Casanova's Memoirs,* a volume of semierotica published in Greenwich Village.

Minnelli had arrived in New York just as the Depression hit the entertainment industry. At first Paramount ignored the bad news from Wall Street, pursuing an aggressively expansionist policy that led the company straight into receivership. By 1933, the expensive stage shows at the Paramount Theater were brought to a halt. Fortunately, however, Minnelli had acquired impressive credentials, and after a brief unemployment he received an offer to become the chief costume designer at the largest indoor theater in the world – the recently constructed, 6,200-seat Radio City Music Hall.

This fabulous showcase had failed miserably as a vaudeville theater, and had recently come under the direction of S. L. "Roxy" Rosenthal, who was turning it into the last of the great picture palaces. Rosenthal brought in a troupe of precision dancers called the "Roxyettes" (descendants of the Tiller

Girls and contemporaries of Busby Berkeley's chorines), plus a glee club, a full ballet company, and a series of specialty acts. The stage show and its accompanying movie changed weekly, and Minnelli was hired to design hundreds of costumes for each new production. Eventually, he was promoted to art director and was allowed to conceive and direct whole shows. Here is Stephen Harvey's description of "Coast to Coast," the first of the Radio City extravaganzas mounted under Minnelli's name:

> Music Hall patrons [were taken] on a fanciful tour of the Mediterranean (the Cote d'Azur), the races at Ascot (the Gold Coast), Africa (the Ivory Coast), and honky tonk San Francisco (the Barbary Coast), to words and music by such notables as Duke Ellington and lyricist "Yip" Harburg. Having visited none of these places except via books, paintings, and travelogues, Minnelli imagined them with the sort of wide-eyed chic ideally suited to the Music Hall stage. His Ascot revellers were orange-feathered Rockettes in white attended by chorus boys in grey morning suits; the Ivory Coast number featured the looming totems of moderne Africana he favored in one set after another during the thirties. But it was the Riviera set that really put them breathless. Punctuated by white cut-out palm trees, the Dufyesque set anticipated the look of his *American in Paris* ballet by fifteen years.[11]

Shows of this type helped Minnelli become a widely publicized figure, the subject of profiles in the *New Yorker* and *Esquire,* and a member of Ira Gershwin's circle of theatrical wits. Then, in 1935, he left Radio City to design and direct the Shubert production of *At Home Abroad,* a musical revue based on a concept similar to "Coast to Coast." Starring Beatrice Lillie, Eleanor Powell, and Ethel Waters, the revue was a critical and box-office success, running for nearly six months. It was followed by two equally admired productions, *The Ziegfeld Follies of 1936* and *The Show Is On,* which established his career as a director and eventually made him attractive to Hollywood.

Dandyism, Modernism, and Entertainment

In the next section I will have more to say about Minnelli's early work on Broadway; but first, with the foregoing biographical facts in mind, I want to return to some of the issues I raised at the beginning – especially to the relationship between aestheticism and consumer society. To appreciate the extent of this relationship, it is important to note that Minnelli's first job as a decorator at Marshall Field placed him in company with some of the twentieth century's most famous artists, including such figures as Man Ray, Salvador Dali, Jasper Johns, Robert Rauschenberg, Claes Oldenburg, and Andy Warhol – all of whom were at one time or another designers of shop windows. In fact, Minnelli belongs to a tradition of painters and decorators that extends at least as far back as the Parisian *magasins de nouveauté* of the 1820s, where a booming textile trade originally displayed its luxury goods. The *magasins,* or "arcades," were glass-roofed and windowed malls, cut through whole blocks of houses and supported by iron frames. Miniature cities, they were lit during the evening with theatrical gas lamps, and in their fittings, according to Walter Benjamin, art was for the first time "brought to the service of commerce."[12]

Before the arcades were built, only the extremely wealthy patronized stores; afterward, and particularly after the 1850s, Paris and every other major city in the western world became a carnival of shops. As Rosalind Williams has pointed out, the merchandise displayed in these businesses was by no means available to everyone, but "the *vision* of a seemingly unlimited profusion of commodities... [was] nearly unavoidable."[13] The shop windows were indeed rather like prosceniums or picture frames, fore-shadowing the movie screen, and the fine sensibilities of artists were needed to shape the visions they contained. Meanwhile, the proliferation of con-sumer objects gave painters and designers new materials with which to work, leading to an increasingly "democratized" sense of style. To be sure, the ideology of art in the nineteenth century was created in reaction against this society of consumption; even so, the modern economy, which Williams describes as a "medium where people habitually interact with merchandise," determined everyone's aesthetic strategies.[14]

The paradoxes of the new economy were especially evident in the figure of the dandy, which emerged with Beau Brummell in London and reached an apotheosis in France after the 1830 revolution, when the "aristocratic elite had lost its political predominance and was uncertain of its social role in the face of the newly dominant middle class."[15] In such an environment, the dandy became a spiritual ideal – a "classless" individual, living in *la bohème dorée* (the gilded Bohemian world), who functioned as a sort of aristocrat of taste. French writers from Balzac onward celebrated the mix-ture of subcultural estrangement and conspicuous consumption in the dan-dy's lifestyle, regarding it as a sign of distinction in a society where the barriers of class had become permeable. Baudelaire, however, recognized the essential contradiction on which this lifestyle was founded: the dandy may have been a rebel against both the Philistines and the barbaric remnants of the nobility, but his spiritual superiority was obtained by virtue of money.

"The dandy is not simply a dreamer," Baudelaire wrote, "and his fantasy must be materialized in exterior signs. This is expensive."[16]

By the twentieth century, every artist in the Western world seemed trapped in the contradiction Baudelaire had described, and modernized forms of commerce were capable of absorbing virtually any resistance. The problem is neatly illustrated by a curious incident from literary history, which took place not long after Minnelli left his job with Marshall Field. In London during the late twenties, Harrods department store invited H. G. Wells, Arnold Bennett, and George Bernard Shaw to write essays that could be used in a publicity campaign. The three authors were offered a princely sum if they would describe any aspect of the store that might interest them; they could be critical if they liked, the only proviso being that whatever they said would become the property of Harrods. All three declined, but in letters of such haughty grandiloquence and length that they gave Harrods the last laugh: the store simply printed the responses without payment, as a series of full-page newspaper ads.

Many years later, the British poet Stephen Spender recalled this event, using it to speculate on the difference between the older, Edwardian intellectuals and the modernist generation of the twenties. What would have been the result, he wondered, if Harrods had made the same offer to James Joyce? After all, *Ulysses* was already a sort of literary department store, with an ad man as its hero. To guess what Joyce might have replied, Spender noted, "would make an amusing literary competition."[17] Joyce was, of course, an austere and cunningly silent artist; an apparently autonomous and politically uncommitted figure who worked in isolation from the literary marketplace, he belonged to a group of radicals who departed from the techniques of popular literature, writing in a language that was difficult to appropriate for advertising copy. Spender claims that Joyce and the other great authors of high modernism wholly rejected the idea of "literary consumer goods," and refused to be judged by "their capacity to sell their particular literary article."[18] Even so, Harrods has long since absorbed their rebellion. Today, it regularly stocks "difficult" novelists in the book department.

A Broadway designer like Minnelli hardly seems to belong to the same world; we can easily imagine him designing the Macy's Thanksgiving Day parade, or perhaps directing an MGM musical about characters who work at Harrods. Yet Minnelli, like Joyce, had an aesthete's temperament. His work was shaped by the same historical forces that gave birth to modernist literature; in fact, he obtained his first professional employment in 1921, only one year before the publication of both *Ulysses* and Eliot's *Waste*

Land. He may not have been a revolutionary, but in his own way he helped "make it new." Working as an emissary between the cultural margins and the center, he fed commercial entertainment's need for artistic novelty or "experiment," becoming famous for importing certain motifs of vanguard art into show business.

When Minnelli began his career in the United States during the twenties, a boom economy was producing autos and skyscrapers; capitalist democracy and technology were extending themselves into forms of leisure activity far beyond what the nineteenth century had imagined. The "Fordist" mode of production was evolving into what Peter Wollen describes as "Sloanist" model, in which design and stylistic innovation fuel the production–consumption cycle.[19] In Europe, the term "Americanism" had already become synonymous with a complex array of modern phenomena including assembly lines, chain department stores, jazz music, and the Hollywood cinema. By 1926, advertising had become so important that Calvin Coolidge praised it as "the method by which desire is created for better things."[20] A new class of industrial managers and social engineers were appearing on the scene, and everywhere the skills of artists were being employed to keep the system running.

These developments, together with the turn away from Victorian "innocence" in the wake of World War I, produced a change in style across the whole range of experience. Writing from Chicago in 1923, Ben Hecht noted that even the most clichéd notions about art had been transformed: "In 1913 Americans thought that Art was men who wore long hair and talked like sissies; a Chinese kimono thrown over a chair in a vestibule; something they had in Europe; any statue in a public park. In 1923 Americans think Art is something that doesn't look like a photograph; marrying a negro in the South Seas; anything a Russian does; turning colored lights on the orchestra in the movie palaces; a rape scene in a motion picture."[21] At about this time, Minnelli was using "colored lights" in the Chicago movie palaces. A new sensibility was emerging, affecting not only bourgeois culture (what Hecht called "Art") but also high modernism and the burgeoning forms of mass diversion. In fact, modern art and the leisure industry were developing in tandem, and they influenced one another in certain ways; hence the old mixture of high seriousness, orientalism, and art nouveau gave way to a vogue for Hollywood, primitivism, and futurist abstraction.

Both Hecht and Minnelli, in different ways, were keenly aware of the new sensibility – although, like most other artists in their generation, they inherited certain attitudes from the era of *l'art pour l'art,* which they brought into modern times. Hecht, for example, never lost his taste for the epigrammatic wit and iconoclasm of the 1890s; his early novels, *Fantazius Mallare* and *Count Bruga,* are saturated with Yellow Book affectations, and even *The Front Page* has a vaguely Baudelarian *nostalgie de la boue.* For his part, Minnelli became a more engaging blend of the aesthete and the modern entertainer, working not in words but in clothing and decor. In 1937, *Esquire* described him as "the incarnation of our preconceived notion of a 'Village type' – flat black hat with a wide brim, loose collar and no tie around his thin neck."[22] In publicity releases, Radio City Music Hall emphasized his vangard taste: "Young and, confessedly, a modernist, Minnelli revels in...torch songs, music from the heart of Harlem and picturesque angular funiture."[23]

Looked at together, Minnelli's various occupations – window decorator, fashion photographer, picture-palace showman, Broadway designer, movie director – are symptomatic of an aesthete's progress through the modern economy, and the different stages of his career offer a condensed history of the "visions" offered by industrialized capitalism. As we shall see, his historical importance lies in his ability to modernize entertainment, drawing on both "high class" and bohemian domains of art. He does this, moreover, by repeatedly borrowing ideas from three Parisian artistic formations that have an underlying historical affinity: the decorative art nouveau of the 1880s, the early modernism of the impressionist and postimpressionist painters, and the dream visions of the surrealists. All three of these formations are equally romantic, equally aestheticized, and equally "dreamy." Significantly, too, they would have been unthinkable before the development of consumer society in the nineteenth century. Art nouveau was produced by the dandies themselves – exquisitely fashionable dreamers who were also quintessential materialists. In a more indirect way, impressionism was a celebration of the new Paris, the prototypical city of leisure and entertainment. As for surrealism, it had a double aspect: on the one hand, it used dreams, automatic writing, and various forms of *détournement* to expose the sexual and political unconscious; on the other hand, it was grounded in "thingness" (before the ur-surrealist Lautréamont could imagine "the chance encounter of an umbrella and a sewing machine on a dissecting table," he had to live in a world where such objects could be manufactured). It is therefore not surprising that each of these movements eventually contributed to mainstream commodity culture: the descendants of the aesthetes became fashion designers, the impressionist painters were bought by capitalist investors, and surrealism provided inspiration for television commercials.

In his autobiography, Minnelli notes a connection between the three

17

movements when he says that "there'd already been traces of surrealism in the work of Ronald Firbank and Aubrey Beardsley."[24] One branch of surrealism could indeed be understood as an outgrowth of the aesthetic movement, and the nineteenth century's ultimate aesthete – J. K. Huysmans's character Des Esseintes in *A rebours* – could be seen as a kind of transitional figure between Beau Brummell and André Breton. Minnelli's films often provide concrete demonstrations of this relation: in the "dream ballet" of *An American in Paris,* for example, art nouveau, impressionism, and surrealism repeatedly converge. But of course Minnelli was also different from the artists he admired. Like George Gershwin, he blended the late aesthetic style with an American idiom, drawing on jazz and popular narrative, combining the old world with the new. Stephen Harvey has commented that by the end of the thirties "Minnelli had made a special niche for himself in the tonier reaches of popular entertainment," by virtue of "his penchant for blurring the distinctions between high and low art."[25] Another way of putting this would be to say that Minnelli and his most talented co-workers created a form that was neither high nor low, neither conservative nor vanguardist, but a relatively up-market synthesis of two cultures – one of them aristocratic and European, the other populist and American. Thus the ballet in *An American in Paris* tells a straightforward boy-meets-girl story, and it features a "lowbrow" jazz number danced by Gene Kelly and a white chorus. By this means, low culture and high culture become accessible to the middle class, the perversity and violence of surrealism are tamed, and passionate aestheticism is ruled by heterosexual norms.

On Broadway

According to historian Stanley Green, approximately 175 shows that could be termed "musical" were produced for the New York stage during the thirties – the decade in which Minnelli became a director.[26] The various shows fell into at least five categories, recognized as such by the trade:

1. Sixty-eight "musical comedies," or loosely plotted narratives containing a great deal of comedy and specialty numbers, usually dealing with such themes as show business, gangsterism, college life, and middle-class marriage and divorce.
2. Thirty-two "operettas," or fairy-tale romances set in Ruritanian locales, concerning the lives of aristocrats. These were comic in tone, but were more slowly paced than the musical comedies, with less dancing and a more operatic singing style.

18

3. Fifty-six "revues," consisting of songs, comic sketches, and dance routines, usually organized around a central theme, such as newspaper stories, the history of show business, or tours around the world. In the late thirties some of the revues had a political point of view, but in general they were purely escapist entertainments.
4. Seventeen "all-black musicals," constituting a separate but virtually parallel theater. These were almost equally divided between the comedy and revue formats, but generally they had less unified narratives and less thematic consistency.
5. Two "modern" or "American" operas: Gertrude Stein's *4 Saints in 3 Acts* and George Gershwin's *Porgy and Bess*. (Perhaps Marc Blitztein's *The Cradle Will Rock* and the first U.S. production of Brecht and Weill's *Threepenny Opera* could be added to the list.)

Leaving aside the last category, we can construct a simpler typology, dividing all New York production into two forms, known in the trade as "book musicals" and "revues." The former had grown out of the cycle of Ruritanian operettas, whereas the latter had developed from an older, more popular tradition of music hall or vaudeville. By the mid-thirties, both had evolved distinctive styles. The success of *Show Boat* in 1927 and *Of Thee I Sing* in 1930 had imposed an American tone on Broadway, at the same time encouraging the proliferation of "integrated" musical comedies, in which singing and dancing advanced a narrative. Meanwhile, as vaudeville declined, the revues became more topical, more thematically unified, and more upscale; in contrast to the Ziegfeld productions of the twenties, they depended less on the "glorification of the American girl" and more on elegance, satire, and wit.

Film historians usually think of Minnelli as an innovator of the integrated book musical, but his success in the theater was almost entirely connected with the new kind of revue. Chiefly as a result of *At Home Abroad, The Ziegfeld Follies of 1936*, and *The Show Is On*, he was regarded as a sort of auteur – a man who was bringing sophistication, urbanity, and a personal attitude to variety shows. His productions tended to highlight his "modernistic" designs; but equally important, they fostered a sense of unity and individual expression. By contrast, the older revues had kept the various numbers distinct from one another, like acts in vaudeville or burlesque. The sequence of events was determined on the basis of tempo, mood, or theatrical effect, so that lyric moments alternated with comedy, star turns alternated with chorus numbers, and spectacular routines were placed at climactic moments. The same general rules applied in Minnelli's day, but his shows

19

were also marked by a protonarrative transitivity – what Minnelli himself described as an "idea of production." He was insistent on a feeling of variety-within-harmony, and as a result, his directorial presence was felt not only in the visual effects but also in what we would nowadays call the "concept."

Only a few years after Bertolt Brecht had argued for a "radical separation of elements" in musical theater, the Broadway stage and Minnelli in particular were working in an opposite direction. Minnelli's shows were strongly unified and marked in various ways with his "touch": he chose the themes, he guided the performers, and he designed the sets and costumes. Although he was far from being a true theatrical egotist, his name was featured prominently in the ads, and reviewers consistently praised his sophisticated taste. In 1937, he received the rare tribute of a one-man exhibition at an East 57th Street gallery, featuring his designs for *At Home Abroad*. That same year, *Theater Arts* magazine claimed that he was "intellectualizing the revue," and noted that "in all his future work he proposes to establish an idea of production as the elementary working basis.... [H]e believes that the revue audience has grown to demand a show that has some definite idea behind it; there must be continuity."[27] " 'The time has passed,' " he told the journal, " 'when revue staging needed only to be handsome.... Now the designer must produce something which will complement the material.' "[28] Paraphrasing him, *Theater Arts* remarked, "The comment of the designer as expressed in his decor is the thing which gives personality to his work ... and therefore he always wants to create a scenic background ... that will, in fact, be a comment of his own."[29]

Actually, Minnelli's revues were based on fairly conventional concepts, and his "ideas" were little more than rubrics under which songs and dances could be arranged. *At Home Abroad* was organized around the familiar concept of a world tour; *The Ziegfeld Follies of 1936* was an homage to Cecil Beaton (with whom Minnelli would later collaborate on *Gigi*); and *The Show Is On* was a condensed history of show business. All three shows were filled with topical jokes, but they avoided anything like didactic or political messages. For example, when *At Home Abroad* sent characters traveling to various parts of the globe, it never mentioned the turmoil of mid-thirties Europe or the restrictions on travel and trade that had been proposed in advance of World War II. The theme of travel was used to motivate a simple linking design – a flat setting, like a map, filled with schoolbook colors. Given the general premise, the writers of skits were able to play cultural stereotypes off against one another (New York vs. Paris, England vs. Africa), while Minnelli cleverly deployed chromatic variations in his sets and costumes (dark vs. bright colors, pastels vs. primary shades).

A sense of variety-within-unity was also generated by the manipulation of a highbrow—lowbrow distinction. All of Minnelli's successful revues were composed of performers from different theatrical backgrounds, so that stars like Beatrice Lillie and Reginald Gardner were on the same program with Bert Lahr and Bobby Clark. Meanwhile, the sequence of musical episodes alternated between what was called "rhythmic dancing" or "hot numbers" and elaborate ballets. (Minnelli was particularly interested in ballet, which he told *Theater Arts* " 'should take an increasingly important position in the revue.' ")[30] Sometimes the mixture of high and low became a source of humor; in *The Show Is On*, for instance, one of the sketches was a musical comedy based on *Romeo and Juliet*. ("I'm not the kind of girl for a boy like you. / I'm a Capulet, you're a Montague.")

In addition to his repeated borrowings from highbrow or modernist art, three other aspects of Minnelli's work in this period deserve special consideration, because they figure to some extent in his subsequent films.

1. *Streamlining*. In its 1937 article, *Theater Arts* commented that Minnelli was the product of "an age which has speed, sophistication, and satire as its familiars." A sense of speed was particularly important to the popular culture of the thirties and early forties; it can be seen not only in the style of performers like James Cagney and Bob Hope, but also in the streamlined surfaces of fashionable art deco, in public architecture, and in the structure and pacing of all types of entertainment. On Broadway, thematically unified reviews and integrated musical comedies were designed to move quickly from one episode to the next, cleverly and economically joining disparate elements. (The same feeling of swiftness and snap can be found in the best films of the period, such as *Trouble in Paradise* and *42nd Street*.) Minnelli's revues in particular were rapidly paced and directed with panache. Their themes or "points of view" facilitated smooth transitions between numbers, and within the individual skits performers could segue easily from dialogue into song and dance. Equally important, the dancing sequences were different from the mass-ornament choreography in stage shows of the twenties and in most musical films of the thirties. In place of chorus girls kicking, marching, or arranging themselves in patterns, Minnelli's shows featured Eleanor Powell's tap dancing and Robert Alton's ballets.

2. *Africanism*. This term is intended to suggest something akin to what Edward Said means by "Orientalism" – that is, a European or white American fascination with an exotic cultural "other." The topic is large and complex, and I will have more to say about it when I discuss the first film

Minnelli directed, *Cabin in the Sky*. For the time being, I want to note only that while Broadway theater in the thirties was made by and for whites, it sometimes imagined people from Africa, Harlem, or the Caribbean in a new way, allowing them to signify a certain kind of glamour and sophistication. Blackface entertainers like Al Jolson were still enormously popular, and vestiges of the minstrel show persisted into the forties (in fact, Minnelli himself parodied a minstrel in the 1937 production of *The Show Is On*). Nevertheless, from the twenties onward, blacks in New York were increasingly associated with jazz, modern art, and the writings of the Harlem renaissance.

Minnelli was the leading Broadway proponent of this second image. He was aware of the European modernists's appropriations of African art (as in postimpressionism, in some aspects of early futurism, and in cubism), and he also knew that the most sophisticated forms of American vernacular music, including the best songs of Berlin, Gershwin, and Porter, were deeply indebted to African-American culture. Thus, all of Minnelli's revues featured exoticized Latin or African settings; all of them quoted African tribal motifs in their designs; and all of them starred black women, who were given luxurious roles to play. It is hardly surprising that Minnelli would later direct Lena Horne's best moments on the screen, or that the image of the elegant black chanteuse would recur throughout his movies.

3. Parody, pastiche, quotation. We have become accustomed to thinking of "postmodernity" as a contemporary state of affairs in which images are recirculated and recombined, so that cultural boundaries become blurred and everything is turned into a spectacle without a referent. But this phenomenon has an older history, and is fundamental to modernity itself. Consider the slick-paper magazines created in the thirties, where the ads mingle with the fiction and the artwork on the same pages. Consider, too, the musical revues of the same period, which used every artistic style that came to hand, elaborately reworking and recycling fashions and artistic styles. By their very nature these productions were self-reflexive, frequently using show business as a theme, incessantly quoting or parodying other artists and entertainments, treating history and geography as a sort of costume party.

From at least the time of the Folies Bergère and the Paris cabaret, designers of musical entertainment have tried to give a sense of variety to production numbers by referring to current fashions in entertainment and the arts. The "modern" revues of the thirties accelerated this tendency, and they required audiences who could appreciate a dense intertextuality. Given his firsthand experience of the late Victorian and modern stage and his encyclopedic interest in art, Minnelli was naturally attracted to the form. In the *The Ziegfeld Follies of 1936,* for example, he "updated" the old Ziegfeld musicals by costuming the chorus girls in fin-de-siècle rather than pseudo–Henry XVI fashions; and for a skit entitled "The Reading of the Play," he meticulously arranged everything on the stage to resemble a specific late Victorian photograph. Following a roughly similar logic, his writers and choreographers relied heavily on parody, making fun of virtually every kind of theater. In the *Follies,* Fanny Brice imitated Martha Graham for a skit called "Modernistic Moe," and in *The Show Is On,* the first-act finale was a "Techniscope and wide-screen" send-up of Hollywood, which Minnelli described as follows:

It satirized the Golddiggers' Big Broadcast of the Broadway Melody type of musical, and it incorporated all of the movie clichés of the time. The comedy scenes [written] by David Freedman were played in the jerky rhythm that characterized such films.

The sketches which opened the sequence were a take-off of the Dick Powell–Ruby Keeler musicals. Fanny Brice played the chorus girl who fills in for the star on opening night and Bob Hope was her sweetheart.

The two kids meet in an agent's office. "Hey, you're different," the boy says. "You're different, too," the girl answers. With that, they fall into a passionate embrace. All of these little scenes were mounted in black and white.

They were followed by the full-scale Technicolor production number, similar to the color finales to some of the black and white pictures of the time. A new dance "craze" was being introduced – "The Gazooka" – and it was similar to all the previous ones the public had come to expect: "First you take this step . . . and then you take . . ." And yet nothing ever happened.

To remain true to my inspiration, I decided the color sequence should be as blurred as most Technicolor films of the time. When the triangle discs came together to form the platform for the number, the color came on in the form of sets and dancers covered in colored cellophane, giving them similar blurred edges.[31]

As this description suggests, the "central ideas" of Minnelli's revues and individual numbers were usually derived from preexistent images. Even his later book shows and integrated musical films were based on a kind of parody; again and again, he achieved his most memorable effects from the visible imitation of period styles, and he never seemed interested in a quest for authenticity. To see just how much this approach affected his subsequent work, we need only consider his 1953 film, *The Band Wagon,* which synthesizes and sometimes parodies the two major types of Broadway theater I have been describing. An integrated musical comedy about show business, *The Band Wagon* takes its title, star, and score from one of the most successful musical revues of the thirties. The plot involves an encounter between a pop star (Fred Astaire) and a ballet dancer (Cyd Charisse), and everything is resolved by an elaborate show-within-the-show, consisting of a series of numbers that pay tribute to the variety format. True to the spirit of the original revues, the cast of the film includes black performer LeRoy Daniels and British vaudevillian Jack Buchanan, and its climactic spectacle is a "modern" ballet that satirizes Mickey Spillane.[32] Minnelli was therefore both a creator of a personal style and a clever manipulator of the storehouse of art; and in this sense he was a true modernist, prefiguring the death of romantic expression and the birth of endless quotation.

Inside the Factory

None of Minnelli's work on the New York stage was as successful as his revues of the mid-thirties. Later in the decade he directed two book shows, a topical satire called *Hooray for What* and the last of the Jerome Kern musicals, *Very Warm for May,* both of which had relatively short runs. Two of his most interesting projects from this period, *The Light Fantastic* (a "surrealist" revue starring Beatrice Lillie) and *Serena Blandish* (an "Africanist" musical featuring Ethel Waters and Lena Horne), were never realized. Meanwhile, Hollywood began to show interest in his work. Samuel Goldwyn tentatively approached him as a possible director of a revue entitled *The Goldwyn Follies,* and in 1937 Paramount offered him a producer-director contract.

Minnelli accepted Paramount's offer, but he never made a picture there. In those days, the major film companies could afford to put prospective talent on retainer; for example, both Sergei Eisenstein and Luis Buñuel had previously spent fruitless days at Paramount. We can only imagine what Minnelli's image as a filmmaker might have been like had he been able to begin directing movies at that studio earlier in the decade. During much of the thirties, production chief Adolph Zukor had managed Paramount from New York, leaving the details of major films in the hands of producer-directors like Ernst Lubitsch, Josef von Sternberg, Rouben Mamoulian, and Michel Leisen — an elite corps of stylists that was famous for its sexiness and continental sophistication. Minnelli, who was a great admirer of Mamoulian's *Love Me Tonight* (1932), might have flourished in such an atmosphere. In the late thirties, however, both Paramount and the picture business had changed, and Minnelli was neglected. The most fully developed of his unrealized ideas was *Times Square,* which he described as a "mystery chase" set on Broadway, featuring production numbers from shows that were currently running. He also proposed a surrealist ballet starring several of Paramount's biggest names, and he had conversations with Kurt Weill about collaborating on a musical film. In his spare time, he contributed a title to an Astaire-Rogers vehicle at RKO (*Shall We Dance*), and he worked as an "adviser" to Raoul Walsh on *Artists and Models* (1937). For the latter film, he and Harold Arlen devised a number entitled "Public Melody Number One" – a parody of gangster pictures, featuring Louis Armstrong and Martha Raye. "As filmed," Minnelli later wrote, the number was "a full scale mess, missing all the nuances we'd supplied."[33]

After six frustrating but well-paid months, Minnelli bought up his contract and returned to New York. He directed a couple of shows on Broadway, then went to Hollywood again in 1940, arranging a more flexible and less lucrative contract with Arthur Freed at MGM. For a while he served as Freed's idea man, contributing suggestions for musical numbers while he learned the studio system. The terms of his employment were renegotiated at short intervals, and within two years, when both he and the studio decided that his apprenticeship was complete, he was assigned a project to direct.

It should be remembered that this was the most repressive, regularized, but generally prosperous era in the history of cinema. All of the major Hollywood studios belonged to vertically integrated corporations, and throughout World War II a captive audience could be relied upon to see whatever was offered. Except for westerns, movies were usually made indoors or on the back lots. Control was in the hands of studio production executives, and from 1934 until the mid-fifties, the Breen Office regulated the sexual and political content of films. Of all the dream factories, MGM was the most artistically empty, although it was also the most substantial and prestigious.[34] It controlled the New York and east coast market through the theaters of its parent company, Lowe's, Incorporated, and during the Depression, under central producer Irving Thalberg, it was the only major studio to consistently show a profit. Thalberg, who specialized in hollow, somewhat pretentious movies with big stars and high production values, gave MGM its regal image; after his death in 1936, however, the studio increasingly reflected the sensibility and management style of L. B. Mayer – a bullying sentimentalist who loved operetta, Andy Hardy, and the Republican party.

Mayer vastly expanded the studio bureaucracy, establishing a nine-member "Executive Committee" and a small army of midlevel producers who saw to it that the typical product was both aesthetically and politically conservative. At the same time, he encouraged a policy of "strength in depth," acquiring as much talent as he could find. In the early forties, MGM employed more than 4,000 people at its grandly appointed Culver City facilities, and it bristled with activity. Here is Hugh Fordin's description of a typically surreal day on its sound stages in 1941:

> On Stage 18, Greta Garbo and Robert Alton [were] dancing the "Chica Chica Rhumba" for *Two-Faced Woman;* W. S. Van Dyke was directing William Powell and Myrna Loy in *The Shadow of the Thin Man* on Stage 16; King Vidor was directing Hedy Lamarr, Robert Young, and Charles Coburn in a scene for *H. M. Pulham, Esq.* on Stage 22; Spencer Tracy and Katharine Hepburn were rehearsing *Woman of the Year* for George Stevens on Stage 3; in their first scene in *Johnny Eager* were Lana Turner and Robert Taylor on Stage 4, Mervyn LeRoy directing; on Stage 10 Walter Pidgeon and Rosalind Russell in *Miss Achilles Heel;* Nelson Eddy and Rise Stevens prere-cording *The Chocolate Soldier* on Stage 1; Wallace Beery and Marjorie Main on Lot 2 in *The Steel Calvary;* Norma Shearer in Rehearsal Hall A taking dancing lessons; Edward G. Robinson taking off in an air-plane on Stage 30 for *Unholy Partners;* on Stage 12 Johnny Weiss-muller swinging from tree to tree; and Eleanor Powell rehearsing a tap-dance for *I'll Take Manilla* in Rehearsal Hall B.[35]

MGM was the last place on earth where an auteur might feel comfortable. Even so, it employed some impressive house directors (including King Vidor, George Cukor, and the underrated Victor Fleming), together with a few producers who brought distinction to their work. Among the latter group was Arthur Freed, who had begun his career as a lyricist, moved up to associate producer on *The Wizard of Oz,* and then become head of his own unit. Freed and his associate, Roger Edens, assembled a formidible array of artists from Broadway and Tin Pan Alley, as well as the biggest library of scores and show tunes in Hollywood; they soon established a relatively open and congenial atmosphere in which New York artists could collaborate, and because they operated under few budget restrictions, they became the world's preeminent source of musical films.

Minnelli made a dozen movies with Freed, and as their collaboration developed, he was given increased authority. He also worked regularly with other producers on nonmusical films, and by the early fifties his screen credits included three of the most successful pictures in the studio's history: *Meet Me in St. Louis, Father of the Bride,* and *An American in Paris.* In the early sixties, looking back over a twenty-year association with MGM, he told a British interviewer:

> Nearly always I have had the opportunity of working with the writer more or less from the beginning. In cases where the script has not been completed, I generally work with the writer for at least five or six weeks. In some cases I haven't had that time for giving directions; in that case it's been done as we go along.... Cutting has never been a problem because I've always worked on it in harmony with the producer and the studio. There are compromises, of course, but I've always been quite satisfied with the cutting in the end.[36]

These are the words of an artist whose taste and temperament were not in substantial conflict with the studio. Nevertheless, like any director, Minnelli experienced struggles and disappointments. Until fairly late in his career, he did not originate the films to which he was assigned, and in many cases he began work only after the first draft of a scenario had been constructed. During editing and postproduction, he usually functioned in an advisory role; thus a scene showing Lena Horne in a bubble bath was omitted from *Cabin in the Sky,* and the Halloween sequence in *Meet Me in St. Louis* nearly suffered a similar fate. When L. B. Mayer was replaced as production chief by the liberal Dore Schary, things were not much better: an important episode involving the most interesting character in *An American in Paris* was dropped from the film; Minnelli lost a bitter quarrel with John Houseman over the cutting of *The Cobweb;* and before the studio would assign him to *Lust for Life,* he had to direct a formulaic adaptation of *Kismet.* In the sixties, as the old system crumbled and MGM underwent rapid changes of management, the situation grew even worse: *Two Weeks in Another Town* was recut in such arbitrary fashion that Minnelli almost disowned it.

Despite these conflicts, Minnelli was always valued by MGM, not only for the high quality of his films, but also for his devotion to work and his ability to compromise. In certain periods – especially after his biggest box-office successes – he had great influence, and his interest in a project meant that it would be given special attention. Several of his more unorthodox and interesting films, such as *Yolanda and the Thief, The Pirate,* and *The Bad and the Beautiful,* belong to these periods. In every circumstance, however, the quality of his work depended on the whim of executives and the vagaries of big-budget production. He was a specialist in glamorous, grandly designed films that needed the special talents of singers, dancers, and a large technical staff; and because he and MGM were committed to the star system, his pictures often succeeded or failed on the basis of how well they suited their celebrity players. Gene Kelly was crucial to *The Pirate,* just as Fred Astaire was crucial to *The Band Wagon.* On the other hand, *The Four Horsemen of the Apocalypse* badly needed a younger, more romantic leading man than Glenn Ford, who was forced on the project by producers; and *Goodbye, Charlie,* one of the few movies Minnelli made outside MGM, would have been vastly more intriguing had it starred Marilyn Monroe (who died just as the production began) instead of Debbie Reynolds.

Even though Minnelli was a fastidious stylist, he was limited to the paints, canvas, and brushes supplied by the studio. MGM had its own writers, composers, costume designers, sound recorders, photographers, and graphic artists – to say nothing of a specific range of film stocks, a standardized lab technique, and a huge property storehouse. Within the limits of the system, Minnelli was able to say a good deal about sets and costumes (departments that could be intractable), and he usually influenced the overall visual conception of his films, working closely with designers prior to the beginning of photography. Sometimes his own hand is visible in background details, as in his murals for the nightclub in *Cabin in the Sky,* and in his show curtain for the "Be a Clown" number in *The Pirate.* His chief job, however, was to act as artistic supervisor during shooting. He peered obsessively through the viewfinder of the camera (a practice frowned upon in the industry at the time), worrying a great deal about sets and performances; and he kept the overall shape of the movie in his head, visualizing how the complex mosaic of shots would eventually fit together. Fictional director Max Von Ellstein in *The Bad and the Beautiful* is speaking for him (and for every other director in Hollywood) when he insists on the importance of guiding the film carefully through this stage of production. Von Ellstein tells an interfering producer that a picture full of climaxes "is like a necklace without a string. It falls apart. You must have light and shade . . . acceleration and retard. . . . You must build to your big moment."

Minnelli had several "big moments," but the important point to remember is that his technique developed within the constraints of an institution. He never challenged the underlying assumptions of classic cinema, and in many ways the look and feel of his films are indistinguishable from those of MGM in general. Perhaps for that reason, the pictures he made at the end of his career, when the studio system was ending, are rather like visual and cultural throwbacks. In the last analysis, he seems to have needed the factory as much as it needed him.

The philosopher Max Black once remarked that all human thought begins in metaphor and ends in algebra. Black's observation ought to be kept in mind whenever we employ "genre" as an artistic term. The word derives by metaphoric association from the Latin root *genus,* meaning race, gender, or biological category. At one level it seems useful to discuss works of art in the scientific manner of a biologist, but we also need to recognize that art is born from a social rather than a natural process. Genre, like language, is shaped by practice, and film scholars can no more fix the limits of a specific type of film, such as the western, than lexicographers can fix the limits of a word. A filmmaker like Minnelli obviously depended upon formulas and conventions, without which he could never have seemed novel or innovative; in a sense, however, genre is always "emergent," formed at the intersection between the habitual expectations of audiences and the movie industry's need to maintain a sense of variation-within-consistency.

I offer this caveat because Minnelli is one of the few auteurs in classic Hollywood whose name is regularly associated with more than one genre. Critics usually divide his work into three categories: musicals (mostly produced by Arthur Freed), comedies (many produced by Pandro Berman), and melodramas (several of the best produced by John Houseman). But each of these categories is large and baggy, capable of including different sorts of films. For example, Rick Altman has argued that the classic Hollywood musical can be divided into three important subgenres: the "fairy tale" musical, the "folk" musical, and the "show" musical.[37] Minnelli made all three types, but even within these useful and relatively manageable subdivisions his projects varied considerably, leaving room for debate about how we ought to describe individual pictures. Is *The Pirate* a fairy tale musical, a show musical, or a hybrid form? And what should we call *Ziegfield Follies?* Altman lists it as a "fairy tale," but it could also be regarded as a folk musical, since it offers a nostalgic re-creation of the Ziegfield era; in my own view, it clearly belongs to the show musical category – although it seems different from *The Band Wagon* and more like an actual revue.

The huge area of comedy is even more bewildering. Comedy has a long, complex history; in classical Greece and Rome it was divided into "old" versus "new" forms, and in the movies it has such different manifestations as *Abbot and Costello Meet Frankenstein, She's Gotta Have It, Pride and Prejudice,* and *Bringing Up Baby.* Meanwhile, the genre known as melodrama covers almost everything. Some critics use the term in relatively narrow fashion, to indicate what Hollywood once called the "woman's weepie" or the "magazine picture." In one sense, however, every Hollywood movie is melodramatic. (Notice that the etymology of the word – *melos* + *drama* – points us back in the direction of the musical, which might be regarded as the basis of theater itself, or, to use a Paterian formulation, as the condition toward which all art aspires.) Even if we were to try to situate melodrama somewhere between its narrow and broad meanings, describing it as a noncomic narrative that deals with psychological traumas in the patriarchal family, our problems would not disappear. Such a definition, which would more or less fit such different films as Minnelli's *Undercurrent, Tea and Sympathy, Lust for Life,* and *Home from the Hill,* would be too capacious to have much utility.

Another problem is that the three basic divisions and their potential subcategories contaminate one another. The Freed-Minnelli musicals, for example, are also *comedies,* as distinct from a picture like *Torch Song,* or from later musical films like *Cabaret, Nashville,* and *New York, New York.* Hence the George Cukor version of *A Star Is Born,* which Altman describes as a "show musical," has more in common with nonmusical melodramas like *The Bad and the Beautiful* than with a comic picture like *The Band Wagon.* Indeed most Hollywood movies, like most novels or plays, are mongrelized forms. The list of such films directed by Minnelli alone would certainly include *I Dood It* and *The Clock.* The first is partly a "crazy comedy" derived from a Buster Keaton picture and rewritten to fit Red Skelton, and partly a show musical built around Skelton's costar, Eleanor Powell. The second, which Stephen Harvey calls a "melodrama," could just as easily be termed a sentimental comedy of marriage.

Faced with Hollywood's tendency to meld or combine generic conventions, we might do better to behave like Polonius, who describes a traveling band of players as "the best actors in the world, either for tragedy, comedy, history, pastoral, pastoral-comical, historical-pastoral, tragical-historical, tragical-comical-historical-pastoral, scene individable, or poem unlimited" (*Hamlet,* II, ii). Adopting a similar procedure, we could say that *Lust for Life* is a biopic-melodrama; *Meet Me in St. Louis* is a folk-musical-comedy with traces of Victorian Gothic horror; and *Madame Bovary* is a woman's weepie–costume picture–literary adaptation. On the other hand, we could avoid the problem altogether by demonstrating that all the Hollywood genres are alike. They are all illusionistic, goal-driven narratives that work toward a strong closure; they are often boy-meets-girl or "buddy" stories that use a romantic couple to synthesize contrasting values; and they usually justify themselves as entertainment rather than high seriousness. Minnelli's films as a group have all these features in common, and they sometimes look like attempts to explore different facets of a single idea. Thomas Elsaesser points to a fundamental connection between them when he suggests that the dramas and the comedies are *"musicals turned inside out."*[38] Considerable evidence could be produced to support his contention: what is *Father of the Bride* if not *Meet Me in St. Louis* minus the songs, placed in a contemporary setting, and told from the point of view of the paterfamilias?

Like every creation of modern society, the cinema is a profoundly eclectic medium, combining features from widely different cultural domains, responding to changes in the marketplace, and constantly spinning its products off into cycles or subgenres. In Minnelli's early career, when the studios were prosperous and the audience was conceived as a mass public, Hollywood evolved a relatively stable set of genres; nevertheless, the thirty-three feature films signed by Minnelli are difficult to group in ways that will satisfy the critical rage for order and algebra. As a result, unlike virtually every other writer on Minnelli, I have chosen to discuss his films chronologically rather than generically, emphasizing their historical context and the general features they have in common. At the same time, I want to acknowledge that a concept of genre was important to Minnelli's work. His different films may have been capable of transformation and combination, but the basic distinction between comedy and drama, as well as the distinction between films with or without songs, seems inescapable. Following, then, are some tentative observations about the three large categories of movies in which he specialized.

With the qualified exceptions of *Home from the Hill* and *Some Came Running*, Minnelli never worked in the area of "male" action films. (In this respect, the etymological relation between "gender" and "genre" is significant. Like the distinction among genres, the boundary separating male and female is in many ways socially conditioned, and it controls meaning.) Minnelli is most famous for integrated musical comedies that exemplify the classical semantic/syntactic features described in Altman's *The American Film Musical*. Furthermore, all his pictures in this vein were related to contemporary developments on the Broadway stage: they were loosely based on Broadway shows (*Cabin in the Sky*), they were tributes to Broadway songwriters (*An American in Paris*), or they were straightforward adaptations of "presold" Broadway hits (*Bells Are Ringing*). Minnelli and Arthur Freed often used writers, composers, and stars from New York, and in one instance – *Gigi* – they produced an original Lerner and Lowe book show that functioned as the cinematic equivalent of *My Fair Lady*. Sometimes, as in the case of *Meet Me in St. Louis,* their ideas, scripts, and music were created almost entirely within the walls of MGM; but even their most innovative pictures were influenced by what audiences recognized as a well-established theatrical form.

If Minnelli's musicals were related to Broadway's golden era, most of his nonmusical comedies seem to belong to the age of television. Hollywood in general had moved in this direction after World War II. The baby boom, the postwar economic growth, and the migration to suburbia led to a spate of "realistic," gently satiric films dealing with married couples in relatively pastoral settings – among them, *The Egg and I* (1947), *Apartment for Peggy* (1948), *Sitting Pretty* (1948), and *Mr. Blandings Builds His Dream House* (1948). *Father of the Bride* was produced in the wake of these protositcoms, and it was so popular that it led to a sequel, *Father's Little Dividend*, and then to a short-lived television series. Most of Minnelli's subsequent comedies followed a similar pattern. *The Long, Long Trailer* was a vehicle for Lucille Ball and Desi Arnaz; *The Courtship of Eddie's Father* became a successful ABC show in 1969–72; and *Designing Woman* influenced the title, if not the basic situation, of a hit series on CBS in the late eighties.

Perhaps because they were made at MGM, none of these films can be described as sex farces or verbal comedies in the manner of Sturges, Lubitsch, or Wilder. (*Goodbye, Charlie*, which was produced at Twentieth Century Fox, is a striking exception, and a relative disappointment.) In most cases they depict conventional family life in middle-class consumer culture, and even when they take place in high society – as in the case of *Designing Woman* and *The Reluctant Debutante* – they contain very little witty dialogue. They depend heavily on slapstick or sight gags, but these gags are plausibly motivated and are usually performed by dramatic or "legitimate" actors like Spencer Tracy, Gregory Peck, or Rex Harrison, rather than by vaudevillians or clowns. In a very general sense, therefore, the relation of gag to narrative in Minnelli's comedies is similar to the relation of song to narrative in his musicals: laughter rises out of plausible domestic circumstances, helping to define character or advance the story. The result is a bourgeois or "integrated" form, mixing broad physical comedy with sentimental situations, centering on characters who resemble a relatively large and prosperous segment of the moviegoing audience.

Minnelli's twelve dramatic films can also be positioned historically, as a symptom of Hollywood's turn toward psychological or quasi-Freudian themes in the years during and after World War II. (By the fifties, the influence of Freud on pop culture was so strong that a comic book called *Psychoanalysis* was widely available on newsstands.)[39] But if Minnelli followed the general trend, he also showed a particular interest in a subcategory of psychological fiction that might be termed the "art melodrama." As we-have seen, he was deeply attracted to stories about artists of one kind or another, and both his musical and nonmusical films often deal with the relationship between neurosis and artistic imagination. The typical plot situation in his melodramas is therefore vaguely reminiscent of *Madame Bovary:* the protagonist is caught between an imaginary world of beauty, romance, and erotic fulfillment and a real world of money, bourgeois convention, and sordid sexuality. (When the protagonist is not literally an artist, she or he tends to be a "feminine" personality in conflict with patriarchy and crude provincialism, as in *Tea and Sympathy* and *Home from the Hill.*) The distinctive tone of Minnellian melodrama arises out of the central character's frustrated effort to transform the real world with the imaginary one, thus sublimating desire into art. This project is doomed to failure, but it provides the films with an impressive atmosphere of stylistic "excess" or melodramatic delirium. It also makes the artist-hero a quintessentially neurotic and lonely figure. We can sense this loneliness even in Minnelli's relatively optimistic musicals, which momentarily transform the world through song and dance. In the melodramas, however, Minnelli's characters never reconcile life and art; they only veer back and forth between a passionate, colorful anguish and a momentary calm, when their work provides refuge from the storm. Again and again in these films, Minnelli suggests that the artistic drive results from a deep-seated psychological trauma. He represents art as a utopian force, but he seems to recognize that it can never transcend its rather bleak social and psychological circumstances; consequently, the melodramas are the most revealing of his genres – the place where he nears a crisis, and where the contradictions and paradoxes of his aestheticism become most evident.

Notes on Style

It is easy to see how Minnelli's work in movies was affected by his early experiences as a designer in Chicago and New York. Some of the classic Hollywood directors began as writers, others as actors, still others as photographers or painters; Minnelli contributed something to all these crafts (and was a fairly accomplished pianist), but he had a special interest in showy costumes, furnishings, and accessories. Many of his films could be understood as what Stephen Harvey calls "a kind of display art at its most glorified."[40] In *The Four Horsemen of the Apocalypse,* for example, Glenn Ford and Ingrid Thulin enjoy a romantic evening in Paris, first visiting an elegant restaurant, then a nightclub, and then the banks of the Seine. Each setting is spread before us in a Cinemascope panorama, and the changes of locale provide Minnelli with an opportunity to play with variations of color, tempo, and mood, in much the same way as when he directed Broadway revues. The restaurant is decorated in green, gold, and blue, and is accented with huge sprays of white flowers; the nightclub is earth-colored, filled with Spanish bullfight posters and couples dancing beneath red lights; the street outside is dark and wet, with red neon illuminating damp cobblestones; and at the riverside, where Minnelli's camera rises slightly above Ford and Thulin, we see only moonlit water and gray pavement.

I have argued that this sort of art is an inevitable outgrowth of consumer culture, but I do not want to suggest that Minnelli was simply a salesman. On the contrary, his films were relatively free of commercial tie-ins, and they often dealt with the sort of period subjects in which contemporary goods couldn't be shown. As Jane Gaines has noted in a valuable essay on movie costuming, the better Hollywood directors in Minnelli's day were actually fearful that extravagant dresses and sets might seem merely commercial. No matter how glamorous a film might be, its designs were never supposed to distract us, having "no other purpose than to feed a visual appetite."[41] True, the stars and costumers promoted consumer goods in advertisements or in publicity stills, but the feature film itself was regarded as an uplifting entertainment, above the vicissitudes of mere fashion, and its sets and costumes were supposed to serve purely narrative functions.

Minnelli clearly thought of his work in these terms; at the same time, however, he used the screen as a window onto a colorful, expensive, and slightly heightened world. Even when he made films about working-class characters, he was unusually attentive to women's dresses, hairstyles, or accessories, which he used theatrically, enhancing characterization but also stimulating the audience's desire. Judy Garland's shop girl outfit in *The Clock* was praised by James Agee for being "the most appropriate prop I can remember since McTeague's checked cap in *Greed*,"[42] but it also makes Garland look sexy and subtly glamorous. Similarly, Minnelli made Lena Horne in *Cabin in the Sky* and Shirley MacLaine in *Some Came Running* look rather like Sternbergian floozies – and when his daughter Liza starred in *Cabaret,* he suggested that she ought to wear her hair like Louise Brooks.

Unlike Sternberg or many other costume fetishists in Hollywood, however, Minnelli seldom posed women as if for a still photograph. He was supremely aware of how clothing behaves in motion, and some of his most dynamic visual ideas depended upon a glamorous dress sweeping or whirling across the screen: thus we have Jennifer Jones in *Madame Bovary,* waltzing around a ballroom in a ravishing white gown with a slightly vulgar, neurotic bird perched atop its bodice; Leslie Caron in *Gigi,* stopping conversation in Maxim's as she removes a cape to reveal a seductive, over-the-shoulder creation; Kay Kendall in *The Reluctant Debutante,* bursting into Rex Harrison's sedate offices wearing a flamboyant red hat and coat; and Lana Turner in *The Bad and the Beautiful,* spinning through a maelstrom as bright lights flash across her mink stole. Minnelli's best-known "surrealist" moments are designed in a similar way. In the dream sequence in *Yolanda and the Thief,* for example, Fred Astaire finds himself surrounded by a group of washerwomen who trap him in a maze of colorful, billowing sheets; when he dances free, he encounters a Daliesque figure emerging from a lake, covered by ghostly, windswept veils. Referring to such numbers, Joel E. Siegel has observed that an "abstract vision of swirling forms and colors ... seems to haunt the best and worst of [Minnelli's] films."[43] But notice that the abstract feeling is often generated through a manipulation of *fabric,* as if Minnelli were fascinated by the action of pure drapery.

This store-window sensibility extends to every aspect of Minnelli's mise-en-scène. He may have been capable of directing painful or disturbing subjects, but his style was always "against nature," making everything on the screen look dressed and artificial. In his hands, even sordid or provincial material became decorative. Lana Turner's sleazy apartment in *The Bad and the Beautiful,* the Boenerge coal mines in *Lust for Life,* the backwater Texas town in *Home from the Hill,* the impoverished black community in *Cabin in the Sky* – all these settings provided him with an opportunity to create patterns of light or color. When he worked on location, as in parts of *Gigi* and in *Some Came Running,* his films looked hardly less stylized than a pure fantasy like *The Pirate.* Usually he took inspiration from specific artists or period styles: *Meet Me in St. Louis* evoked the paintings of Thomas Eakins; *Yolanda and the Thief* quoted the children's illustrations of Ludwig Bemelmans; *The Bad and the Beautiful* alluded to Garbo's historical pictures; *Lust for Life* turned the French landscape into a copy of Van Gogh; and *Gigi* occasionally looked like a drawing by SEM.

Of course Minnelli's films were very much a contemporary decorator's idea of an artist or a period, and they were always kept within the bounds of MGM's high-gloss taste. Within these limitations, however, he was a fastidious handler of dress extras (as in the Pennsylvania Station sequences of *The Clock* and in the Maxim's episode of *Gigi*), and he sometimes used set decorations in an almost Brechtian way, to "narrate" or explicitly comment on the action. In *The Bad and the Beautiful,* for instance, we see Fred Amile pacing around a Hollywood producer's outer office, anxiously awaiting Jonathan Shields, who is inside pitching a script. On the wall behind Amile is a poster for a movie entitled *Money Talks.* After a few moments,

35

Shields emerges from the conference to announce cheerfully that he will be allowed to produce the film on a major budget, but without Amiel. Minnelli cuts to a new angle, framing Amiel's reaction against a poster for a horror movie.

Partly because of Minnelli's interest in sets and costumes, most of his films contain scenes that take place at parties or festive celebrations — for instance, the ball in *Madame Bovary,* the wedding reception in *Father of the Bride,* the carnival in *Some Came Running,* and the birthday party in *The Courtship of Eddie's Father.* In this respect he makes an interesting contrast with a director like John Ford, who also tended to show his characters at social occasions. In Ford's films, the atmosphere is rustic and communal; the characters often wear uniforms or traditional garb, and the celebration resolves dramatic tensions through order and ritual. Minnelli staged more colorful, decadent affairs, and their effect was centripedal rather than centrifugal. The brilliant fabrics and moving bodies were always in danger of spinning out of control, as if some underlying tension were expressing itself in a dizzy, churning display of unbound energy.

In quieter, more conventional scenes, Minnelli typically placed two or more figures together in a shot, framing them in a *plan américain* and allowing us to glimpse their environment. He used shot/reverse-shot combinations sparingly, and, except in isolated moments of comic subjectivity, he avoided extremely short or long lenses. Critics frequently describe him as a leading exponent of the long take, and in fact the average shot length in his films is slightly longer than the industry standard. But statistical measurements of this sort can be misleading. Minnelli seldom photographed whole sequences in a single shot, and he never experimented with the ten-minute take. His nonmusicals rarely involved extensive panning movements or tracking shots in the manner of Renoir or Ophuls, and they never staged sequences in extreme depth, which would have allowed figures to move back and forth through different planes of the composition.

Actually, some of Minnelli's most brilliantly constructed shots could have run a bit longer. Near the beginning of *Cabin in the Sky,* the camera rushes alongside Ethel Waters for a considerable distance down a crowded street, and then rises on a crane to show her arrival at the entrance of the "Club Paradise." When Waters pauses in front of the saloon doors, Minnelli cuts to a closer view, looking over her shoulder and tracking forward as she moves into the room. The shot would have been more effective had the camera craned down to the close angle, but Minnelli (or his cameraman, Sidney Warner) seems to have preferred the slightly more conventional technique of intrasequence cutting.[44] Much the same thing happens in the famous "putting out the lights" sequence of *Meet Me in St. Louis*. Set designer Jack Smith and cameraman George Folsey went to great pains constructing movable walls and an array of complex lighting tricks because Minnelli wanted to stage the action in a single, extended shot. As Judy Garland and Tom Drake move slowly through three rooms, the camera follows them, at one point rising to the level of a chandelier and then slowly descending. "I want to tell you," Folsey said to Hugh Fordin, "that was about as tough a job as I've ever had to do."[45] "Everything was in one shot," Minnelli claimed, "because I felt intuitively that it was wrong to break it up – we rehearsed this a whole day."[46] But Minnelli is inaccurate when he recollects that *everything* was in one shot. Unfortunately, just as Judy Garland is about to extinguish the last light, we cut to a new angle. Formal logic dictates that the shot ought to have ended a moment later, when all the lights are dimmed and we see a lovely closeup of Garland on the stair, saying goodnight to Drake; as the sequence now stands, it's as if a beautifully sustained rhythm had broken off too soon, before being punctuated by the final close-up.

Whatever one might say about the structure or duration of these shots, they at least help to illustrate Minnelli's eloquent use of the boom-mounted camera. With the possible exception of Max Ophuls, no Hollywood director was more closely associated with spectacular crane movements. *Time* magazine once reported that Minnelli was "boom happy," and that "his love of mobility, of snooping and sailing and drifting and drooping his camera booms and dollies, makes *The Clock,* largely boom-shot, one of the most satisfactorily flexible movies since Fredrich Murnau's epoch-making *The Last Laugh*."[47] Film historian Barry Salt echos this sentiment when he writes that *The Clock* used a crane to cover long takes, "possibly for the first time in a non-musical film."[48] Although Salt's claim is doubtful (especially considering the ballroom sequences in Welles's *The Magnificent Ambersons,* which was made three years earlier), the crane was without question a hallmark of Minnelli's style. Significantly, when Minnelli depicts fictional directors at work in *The Bad and the Beautiful* and in *Two Weeks in Another Town,* he shows them atop gigantic Chapman booms, guiding the action like Napoleonic generals.

European directors had experimented with complex airborne movements of the camera in dramatic films throughout the twenties, but according to Salt, Hollywood did not begin to use especially constructed camera cranes until fairly late in the decade, for the purpose of photographing musical sequences. The bird's-eye view of an elaborate production number was *de rigeur* in the classic musical, and when Minnelli joined the Freed unit, it was inevitable that he would be assigned a crane. He immediately showed his fondness for shots that arched high above a scene, gliding toward or away from a group of figures – as in the opening number in *Cabin in the Sky,* where an aerial camera zigzags down the full length of a church auditorium, picking up units of the Hall Johnson choir. Probably he influenced the style of all the MGM musicals, which never used the rapid, kaleidoscopic montages of the earlier Busby Berkeley pictures done at Warner's; notice, for example, how Stanley Donen and Gene Kelly skillfully manipulate a tracking and craning camera in the famous title number of *Singin' in the Rain* (1952).

Minnelli was a pioneer of this technique, even if he was not unique. His graceful camera movements enhanced the lighter-than-air feel of dance sequences, and at the same time indicated his respect for the skill of performers like Kelly and Astaire. One of the few major directors in the history of the genre who didn't begin life as a choreographer (in a list that includes not only Berkeley and Donen, but also Charles Walters and Bob Fosse), he remained a distant observer, never splintering a dance number into closeups of gyrating torsos or flying feet. Unlike the postclassical Bob Fosse, who used every dance as an occasion for Eisenstenian montage, he relied upon the simultaneous movement of his camera and players through a carefully designed setting, using alternating tracks and crane shots to emphasize the spatial and temporal unity of a world constructed in the studio. (To some extent his influence lives on in contemporary rock video, as in Janet Jackson's "All Right," which was intended as an homage to the MGM style.) In *Ziegfeld Follies,* for instance, the camera tracks with Fred Astaire along the full length of a dark, foggy set designed to represent the Limehouse district of London in the 1890s. Astaire wanders past costermongers, prostitutes, sailors, and assorted denizens of the slum, each of them costumed with a lively eccentricity. When he crosses in front of a crowded pub, warm light spills from the windows, revealing Harriet Lee inside, singing the "Limehouse Blues"; then, as he moves a bit further down the street, he encounters Louise Bremer, who suddenly emerges from the gloom wearing a tight yellow dress. In the dream sequence embedded within this number, the camera is mounted on a crane, and the color values change dramatically. Astaire and Bremer perform a balletic dance against a vast yellow and red set designed by Irene Sharaff in the style of Louis XVI chinoiserie; we view the scene from the roof of a sound stage lit brightly enough to illuminate a small city, floating down to a medium shot and following the dancers across a stylized garden.

Several of the auteurist critics in the sixties wrote about Minnelli's gliding camera as if it confirmed André Bazin's preference for "realist" mise-en-scène over "manipulative" montage. But perhaps a better way of understanding the impulse behind his work is to recall the much earlier photographic "panoramas" of nineteenth-century Paris, in which, according to Walter Benjamin, "the city dilates to become landscape, as it does in a subtler way for the *flâneur*."[49] Benjamin remarks that the panoramas "point ahead, beyond photography, to films and sound films,"[50] and Minnelli's pictures could be seen as the culmination of their underlying logic. Consider the opening and closing shots of *The Clock,* where MGM's stage 27 has been turned into a replica of New York's Pennsylvania Station, and where the camera executes a slow craning and tracking movement down on an amazingly lifelike crowd. Rather like C. B. DeMille, but in much more sophisticated fashion, Minnelli exploits Hollywood's godlike ability to create a world on a stage; he uses his camera crane not only to preserve the unity of the mise-en-scène, but also to show off big sets filled with costumed figures, giving the audience a vision of plenitude and a sense of dominion.

It is important to remember, however, that Minnelli's work involved more than the costumes, the sets, and the camera. Like any director, he supervised the acting. Where dance numbers were concerned, he relied upon choreographers, but in all other cases he controlled the movement of figures on the screen and the emotional tone of the performances. Perhaps because of his background in theater, he tended to compose shots that ran on at considerable length, showing actions and reactions within a single frame. In *Father's Little Dividend,* for example, five characters crowd together in a hospital corridor to view a newborn baby through a pane of glass. The sequence contains some amusing offscreen narration, and at one point Minnelli gets a laugh by cutting to a low-level, wide-angle shot from the infant's point of view; for the most part, however, the comedy derives from nothing more than people pressing against one another, responding in different ways to what they see. Framed as a group, they look wildly animated, and the scene is funny even when the sound is turned off.

In the course of a detailed and intelligent commentary on *The Courtship of Eddie's Father,* V. F. Perkins has noted that critics often fail to notice this sort of work. The director's role as "governor of the action" is neglected, Perkins says, because most people "tend to see direction exclusively in terms of the camera and the cutting bench."[51] The point is worth emphasizing, because even under the most regularized forms of studio production, directors have always influenced the tone and meaning of films by virtue of their collaboration with the actors. During performance, a line or a speech that might have worked on paper sometimes falls flat and needs to be revised;

and when characters are embodied by specific persons, they can change in unexpected ways, opening up new dramatic possibilities. Minnelli was able to seize these opportunities, and although he didn't create unorthodox performing styles or fresh ways of blocking a scene, his work with actors is consistently excellent.

As an example, consider a relatively minor scene in *The Bad and the Beautiful,* when James Lee Bartlow (Dick Powell) and his wife Rosemary (Gloria Grahame) return to their Beverly Hills bungalow after a Hollywood party. She has been flirting with another man, and Bartlow is angry. In a single shot, the two characters move about their bedroom in sullen silence, break into a subdued quarrel, then make up. Bartlow, who is approaching middle age, is fascinated by his wife's mixture of gentility and sexual guile; she plays on this image, manipulating it cleverly but at the same time making us feel her vulnerability. The psychological dynamic of the marriage is revealed largely through Minnelli's choreography, which gives the actors small bits of business to perform, keeping them distant from one another until they embrace at the end. Throughout, the tone of the dialogue has been skillfully modulated, and the unobtrusive framing enables us to view everything with a mixture of ironic detachment and sympathy. Near the end of the scene, Rosemary looks down at the floor and remarks, "I dare say I *am* gettin' too big for my britches." Bartlow, who has been removing his tie and cufflinks, crosses and takes her into his arms. "They're pretty britches," he murmurs. She looks up in mock embarrassment: "James Lee! You have a very naughty mind!" Sliding her arms around his shoulders, she adds, "I'm happy to say." He bends toward her, but she teases him, turning her face aside. Releasing herself, she walks a few paces across the room, turns, and gives him a sultry look. She then walks slowly back into his arms, running her fingers through his hair and giving him a frank, openmouthed kiss.

None of Gloria Grahame's behavior in this scene is suggested in Charles Schnee's script, which simply notes that Bartlow and his wife embrace. The actors and the director added the details, relying upon a formalized, somewhat pantomimic style that resembles a dance. And given his preference for this style, it is not surprising that Minnelli felt more at home with dancers or old-fashioned movie stars than with Method actors. He and George Peppard reportedly had difficulty adjusting to one another during the filming of *Home from the Hill,* and Ellen Burstyn, who starred in *Goodbye, Charlie,* has complained that "Mr. Minnelli's way of directing is to do the scene and then you imitate him – not one of the most stimulating ways of working."[52] Probably Minnelli didn't "do the scene" for players like Fred

Astaire or Spencer Tracy, but he had learned his craft in a comic Broadway theater that valued crisp, ostensive rhetoric over naturalism and spontaneity, and he thought of actors as personalities or specialists in movement who could be fitted into his visual designs.

Minnelli also favored actors who could embody certain character types. From the time he met Judy Garland until the end of his career, he was intrigued by the image of a child-woman, dressed in a highly artificial fashion. He also worked repeatedly with "feminine" males, such as Louis Jourdan, John Kerr, and George Hamilton, who functioned rather like romantic versions of himself. Interestingly, however, the actor with whom he had the richest, most impressive collaboration was Kirk Douglas. In certain ways Douglas prefigured the Method stars, who were somewhat scary, oscillating between morose anguish and extreme violence; as a character on the screen he was maimed more often than Brando, and he was often rough with women. But no actor of his day was less "cool." A robust, athletic, sometimes explosive player, Douglas loved stagy rhetoric, and he did everything passionately. This made him an easy target for impersonators, and for the *Harvard Lampoon,* which once offered a "Kirk Douglas Award for the Worst Actor of the Year." He might have earned more respect in classic comedies or musicals, where an air of exhuberant artificiality is required; but as it happens, he became the perfect exponent of Minnellian melodrama, specializing in neurotic-artist roles.

To see how effectively Douglas and Minnelli worked together, we need only recall the moment I have already noted from *The Bad and the Beautiful,* when Georgia Lorrison discovers Jonathan Shields spending the night with another woman (Figure 2). Behaving like a silent movie star or a slightly hammy thespian, Douglas wallows in old-fashioned histrionics. "Shut up! Shut up and get back upstairs!" he seethes to Elaine Stewart, speaking through clenched teeth and grasping a banister in his fists. He slumps forward, his face in shadow, breathing like a soul in torment. Suddenly he wheels around to confront Lana Turner, and we cut to a close-up in which his hair has become inexplicably but expressively disheveled. "Maybe I like to be *cheap* once in a while," he snarls, his features lit from below like the villain in a horror movie. Seizing Turner by the hair, he pulls her head back and glares menacingly down at her. "How do you know how I feel about you, how deep it goes?" he moans. Then he pushes her away, stepping back into the shadows. "Maybe I don't want anybody to own me.... Get out! Get out! *Get out!*" The last of these commands is voiced in one of Douglas's favorite mannerisms — a piercing scream, almost like an animal in pain.

Douglas's flashy, full-bodied intensity is a perfect complement to Minnelli's own bravura technique. In fact, this scene exemplifies all the stylistic features I have been attempting to describe. Notice the luxurious contrast between the gowns worn by Elaine Stewart and those of Lana Turner. Notice, too, the way Minnelli keeps everything in motion, relishing the opportunity to photograph a Gothic stairway with a camera crane: early in the sequence, the shadow of a banister slashes diagonally across the foreground, separating Georgia from Jonathan; she crosses eagerly to him, and the camera moves forward urgently, as if to share in the closeness; he withdraws, crossing into a shadowy area, and the camera pulls back; when she moves forward again, the camera rises, swinging in an arc around the banister and framing the action tightly. Finally he grasps her by the arm. "I want you to go back!" he says, and as he tries to lead her off, the camera follows, craning upward to view her face as she turns in the doorway and faces him. Nothing here constitutes a departure from the norms of classic Hollywood, but the setting, the costumes, the camera, and the performances all help to create a Minnellian "world," filled with glamorous surfaces, theatrical intensities, and excited movements. Artificial as this world might seem, its narrative power and strange beauty are undeniable.

The Critic as Producer

In the remaining chapters of this book, I discuss a cross section of Minnelli's films, beginning with his debut, *Cabin in the Sky,* and ending with his favorite picture, *Lust for Life.* Prefatory to this discussion, a few comments about the reception of his work and about my own role as critic seem in order. First let me note that I saw pictures like *The Bad and the Beautiful, The Band Wagon, Lust for Life,* and *Home from the Hill* when they were originally released in theaters. I probably think of Minnelli differently than do most people under forty, who have seen him only on television, in classrooms, or in revival houses. Of course, I can never recapture my initial experiences, which are mediated by my subsequent life. Today, I belong to what Barbara Klinger calls an "academic reading formation," and many of my observations are keyed to the debates that have animated film studies in the past two decades.

But if I have changed, so have Minnelli's films, which were designed to be shown on big screens. Minnelli holds the all-time record among movie directors for premieres at Radio City Music Hall, and yet his work survives chiefly on television or videotape. *Father of the Bride* has been colorized, and very few of the later films are available in their original Cinemascope format. Prints of the best-known titles can be obtained through 16mm

Figure 2. Kirk Douglas and Lana Turner in *The Bad and the Beautiful*. (© 1952, Turner Entertainment Co., all rights reserved.)

collectors and rental agencies, but most show signs of deterioration: *Meet Me in St. Louis* has lost its sensual blacks, mahoganies, and flesh tones (although a new print has recently been shown by the British Film Institute); and *Lust for Life,* which was made in a less durable color process, has begun to turn orange. Perhaps the only way to view Minnelli in something close to his original circumstances is in the rarified, somewhat artificial context of museum retrospectives, such as the one organized by MOMA and AT&T in 1989. No matter how we watch him, however, his films have acquired a certain air of nostalgia and mystery, simply because they are old.

Minnelli did most of his work in a period before rock and roll, before videocassette recorders, and before cineplexes; he was a product of modernity, but we cannot help seeing him through a "postmodern" lens. In the age of electronic reproduction, his surviving pictures begin to seem like found objects, washed up on the shores of history, possessing implications that neither he nor MGM intended. We know, for instance, that *The Pirate* was one of Hollywood's first self-conscious exercises in camp. Speaking of the S. N. Behrman play upon which the film was based, Minnelli has remarked, "It was great camp, an element that hadn't been intentionally used in films . . . I say intentionally."[53] But when we look at *The Pirate* today, we cannot tell exactly how much of its effect was deliberate. The film was made by the old studio system (or by what Andrew Ross describes as a "disempowered mode of production"), and it automatically invites a later audience to engage in a whole new range of ironic readings.[54]

Critics need to be aware of these problems, but they can never transcend them. Criticism is always governed by a fluctuating consensus about what artistic texts signify. For example, the most intelligent American reviewers of Minnelli's early films, who were guided by the dominant critical values of their day, tended to describe Minnelli as a poetic humanist. James Agee and Manny Farber, writing respectively for the *Nation* and the *New Republic,* were attracted to the passionate heightening of sentimental, "everyday" situations in *Meet Me in St. Louis* and *The Clock;* at the same time, they were put off by the studioish look of both films. Farber noted that *The Clock* was "dominated with the desire to be neatly pleasant and pretty," and he completely dismissed the story as the kind of "sensation-filled, laugh-hungry, coincidence-ridden affair a gag writer would invent."[55] For his part, Agee speculated that "Minelli [*sic*] does not discriminate very clearly between the good in his work or the not-so-good or the downright bad which in part he puts into it and which is in part forced on him."[56]

The British critics who wrote for *Sequence* during the late forties and early fifties saw Minnelli differently: for them, he represented the height of

sophistication in the filming of popular song and dance. Lindsay Anderse
declared that *Cabin in the Sky* was "miles removed from the slick unei
terprise of the current musical fashion," and paid special tribute to *Th*
Pirate, which he described as a "daring experiment in artifice" and a film
of "unrivalled *chic*...studded with numbers of the most polished bril-
liance."[57] Even so, Anderson was disappointed with Minnelli's most recent
movies. *An American in Paris* struck him as a weak derivation of Donen
and Kelly's *On the Town* and a "relapse into the conventions of old-time
musical comedy." At bottom, he claimed, the film offered "a Paris firmly
in the Culver City tradition of ebullient, gesticulating bistro-proprietors, and
their huge wives who love nothing better than to mother these so-gay, so
irresponsible young Americans (Gene Kelly and Oscar Levant, if you
please!)."[58]

As we might expect, the French in the fifties and sixties debated about
whether Minnelli was an auteur or simply a *metteur-en-scène;* in fact, a
controversy over this issue, centering chiefly on *Lust for Life,* provoked
André Bazin into writing a famous rebuke of his younger colleagues, where
he pointed to the "genius of the system."[59] Even the most devoted of the
auteurists were divided over Minnelli. For some, he was a sly satirist of the
"American way of life"; for others, he was a talented hack. One proponent
of the former view was Jean Domarchi, who described *The Bad and the
Beautiful* as an attack on American capitalism, directed by a sort of latter-
day Balzac: "If the Hollywood un-American Activities investigation had had
any sense," Domarchi wrote, it would have put Minnelli on the blacklist,
rather than "those admirable but infinitely less dangerous directors like
Dassin, Losey, or Berry."[60] During a 1961 roundtable discussion at *Cahiers,*
Jacques Rivette took an opposite position: "When you extend the *politique
des auteurs* to people like Minnelli or ten other American filmmakers, it
becomes an abberation. ... When you talk about Minnelli the first thing to
do is talk about the screenplay, because he always subordinates his talent
to something else."[61]

Only a few months after Rivette's statement, Jean Douchet responded
with an elaborate, protostructuralist interpretation of Minnelli's entire
ouvre. According to Douchet, "Each Minnelli character pursues, in effect,
an inner dream. ... Each one wishes to surround himself [*sic*] with a set
which bears the mark of what he is, what he loves, what he desires. ... But
when the dream assumes a body, it finds itself for this very reason subjected
to contingency."[62] The key to Minnelli's world, Douchet argued, was the
way sets or "dreams" came into conflict. In a subsequent article for *Objectif,*
he claimed that *The Long, Long Trailer* was an "exemplary" case in point:

"Our heroes realize their dreams of conjugal felicity by buying a mobile 'home,' an immense trailer painted an aggressive yellow. How this itinerant touch of yellow clashes with the decor of the landscape; how the external world penetrates this home and ravages everything."[63] Despite Douchet's analysis, however, other cineasts (including François Truffaut) remained unimpressed. Jean-Louis Comolli charged that Minnelli's attention to sets and art direction was "only an effort at *mise-en-scène*";[64] and in 1965, Jean-Andre Fieschi commented, "When you read an interview with Minnelli – a nice man, but he doesn't have much to say – and then an interview with John Houseman, who produced Minnelli's films, its obvious that the *auteur* is not Minnelli but Houseman."[65]

Jean-Luc Godard "quoted" Minnelli throughout this period, most notably in *Le Mepris* (1963) and *Pierrot le Fou* (1965), where Minnelli seems to represent a pop sensibility toward which Godard feels a certain ambivalence. At about the same time, coincident with a growing academic interest in film, the Anglo-American auteurists began to discuss Minnelli in somewhat Arnoldian fashion. In 1962, the first issue of the British journal *Movie* published a chart showing the editorial board's estimation of living British and American directors: Minnelli was placed in the "brilliant" category, just behind Howard Hawks and Alfred Hitchcock, who were the only two figures ranked as "great." *Movie* eventually devoted a special issue to Minnelli, and regular contributors to the journal, including Ian Cameron, Paul Meyersberg, V. F. Perkins, and Mark Shivas, wrote New Critical explications of such films as *Two Weeks in Another Town*, *The Courtship of Eddie's Father*, and *The Four Horsemen of the Apocalypse*.

In the United States, Albert Johnson had already published a two-part essay in *Film Quarterly* describing Minnelli as "the master of the decorative image."[66] But the most influential judgment from this side of the Atlantic came in 1968 with the publication of Andrew Sarris's *The American Cinema*. Sarris placed Minnelli on the "far side of paradise," just beyond the pantheon of Hollywood's greatest artists. "If he has a fatal flaw," Sarris wrote, "it is his naive belief that style can invariably transcend substance and that our way of looking at the world is more important than the world itself."[67] Sarris's argument depended upon a romantic faith in "the world itself," but it confirmed a view among some auteurists that Minnelli's work, for all its importance, lacked a certain high seriousness. As Sarris put it, "Minnelli believes implicitly in the power of his camera to transform trash into art, and corn into caviar. [He] believes more in beauty than in art."[68]

The French and Anglo-American debates over Minnelli in this period were part of a larger critical discourse that had both conservative and transgressive implications. On the conservative side, auteurism was designed to establish a canon of artists. As Michel Foucault has shown in his well-known essay, "What Is an Author?" (1969), all forms of author criticism, in their desire to "recover" the creative individual from a body of texts, tend to duplicate three techniques of early Christian exegesis: first, they postulate the author as having a standard level of quality, so that certain texts associated with his name can be set apart on the grounds of inferior workmanship (or studio interference); second, they define the author as "a field of conceptual or theoretical coherence," demonstrating a theme running through various of his works; and third, they identify the author with a specific historical figure "in which a series of events converge."[69] Once the name of the author has been certified in this fashion, it can establish a system of ownership (as in copyright). It can also provide a means of classification for a heterogeneous mass of texts, specifying certain items that are "not to be immediately consumed and forgotten."[70]

In my own study of Minnelli, I employ techniques similar to the ones Foucault describes – although I also try to show that Minnelli's identity was shaped by a complex of institutions and artistic formations and that the authorship of his films was in the last analysis multiple or collaborative. Elsewhere I have written about the "survival of the author" in contemporary film criticism, arguing that some notion of personal agency is necessary to any cultural politics.[71] Without repeating my argument, let me simply observe that the radical or transgressive element in early auteurism lay in the fact that traditional forms of literary interpretation were being applied to mass-cultural texts – in other words, to precisely those objects that had been designed to be "consumed and forgotten." The auteurists, like the earlier French surrealists, were trying to bestow what Roland Barthes would describe as a "writerly" quality on an ostensibly "readerly" set of movies. At one level the auteurists were profoundly unreasonable, but their discussions of Minnelli and several other "assembly line" directors still carry an exhilarating charge.

Where academic criticism was concerned, all this debate was swept away by the events of 1968 in Paris and by successive waves of radical film theory. During the seventies, a conjunction of Althusserian Marxism, Lacanian psychoanalysis, and Saussurian linguistics led to a preoccupation with the "subject in the text," and, in a manner reminiscent of the Frankfurt School's most pessimistic analysis of mass culture, commercial cinema was depicted as a vast "apparatus" for molding consciousness. When directors were mentioned, they were subordinated to a typology of narrative modes. Movies were scrutinized for internal "cracks" or contradictions, and they became

47

interesting only when they were judged to have a critical or ambiguous relation to the dominant ideology.[72] Of course, discussions of Minnelli's art did not completely disappear in the seventies and eighties. Nonacademic monographs on his work were published in Paris, Rome, and New York, and Stephen Harvey completed *Directed by Vincente Minnelli*. Elsewhere, however, scholars had relatively little to say about the ideolect or style of Minnelli's individual pictures; instead, they concentrated on genres and institutional practices. Probably the last important attempt to discuss Minnelli in auteurist terms was an insightful 1970 essay by Thomas Elsaesser in the *Brighton Film Review*. Elsaesser's paper, which set out to reveal "the fundamental *unity* of Minnelli's vision,"[73] was in some ways reminiscent of Jean Douchet's earlier work. When it was reprinted in a BFI anthology on musicals in 1979, however, Elsaesser added a partial disclaimer, noting that "the auteur is the fiction, the necessary fiction one might add, become flesh and historical in the director, for the name of a pleasure that seems to have no substitute in the sobered-up deconstructions of the authorless voice of ideology."[74]

The new breed of academic historians was interested chiefly in genre, and when it evoked Minnelli's name in this context, it treated his musicals somewhat differently than his melodramas. The musicals were regarded as conservative entertainments (especially by Jane Feuer), but the melodramas were often viewed as potentially "subversive" expressions of a political unconscious. One reason for the difference of emphasis was that academic work on melodrama had been prompted by a feminist interest in "women's pictures" and by theoretical arguments such as Paul Willeman's 1972 essay, "Distanciation in Douglas Sirk." Willeman claimed that expressionist style or flamboyant mise-en-scène could be used to "intensify" the family melodrama and thereby subvert its manifestly conservative ideology.[75] Along similar lines, Thomas Elsaesser's influential "Tales of Sound and Fury" (1972) offered a structuralist/psychoanalytic reading of the genre, placing strong emphasis on the "interiorisation" of ideological conflicts in middle-class domestic settings. Geoffrey Nowell-Smith's "Minnelli and Melodrama" (1977) took the psychoanalytic argument still further, suggesting that the emotional and stylistic excess of typical melodramatic scenes could be likened to what Freud had called "conversion hysteria." According to Nowell-Smith, "the undischarged emotion [or forbidden discourse] which cannot be accommodated within the action, subordinated as it is to the demands of family/lineage/inheritance, is traditionally expressed in the music and, in the case of film, in certain elements of the mise-en-scène."[76]

Nowell-Smith's analogy between the body of a film and the body of a patient might seem tenuous; nevertheless, he was pointing to a stylistic trait we can sense everywhere in Minnelli, and his paper led to an extended debate over the ideological effects of melodrama.[77] Critics have disagreed about whether such films have a conservative or a critical function, but during the eighties they tended to offer counter-cultural interpretations of directors like Sirk and Minnelli, who heighten or "musicalize" the cinematic mise-en-scène. Consider Robert Lang's *American Film Melodrama* (1989), which takes Nowell-Smith's essay as a starting point. Lang concludes that "Minnelli manages to be powerfully subversive and mainstream at the same time. . . . [He] took the formula and exaggerated its structures to the point of their subversion."[78]

One problem with these arguments is that we have no evidence that popular audiences (or MGM executives) ever found anything subversive in Minnelli's films. The artificiality of Minnelli's style and the "distanciation" created by the passing of time have undoubtedly opened a space for critics to engage in ironic or subversive readings, but such readings usually involve a willingness to suspend historical knowledge. The fact is, all mass-cultural texts are riddled with contradictions at every point of the production-consumption cycle; their ideological meaning depends ultimately on who reads or views them, under what circumstances, and from what angle. In a sense, Hollywood's ability to posit contradictions is precisely what enables its products to continue functioning in the discursive economy; as Stuart Hall has put it, "This year's radical symbol or slogan will be neutralized into next year's fashion; the year after, it will be the object of a profound cultural nostalgia."[79] In certain isolated cases, we can also reverse the process, making last year's conservative object into this year's radical text.

Partly for such reasons, recent theorists have become skeptical of any interpretation that infers ideological effects from textual evidence alone. "Excess," too, has become a dubious term, since it often functions as a name for anything that cannot be subsumed under a narrowly Aristotelian poetics. Nevertheless, all the writers mentioned above have important things to say about Minnelli, and I hope my indebtedness to them and others will be clear in the chapters that follow. I should also note that despite their differences, most of the critics agree about certain points. Virtually everyone who has written about Minnelli describes him as a paradoxical phenomenon, partly a servant of the industry and partly an unorthodox stylist. Some writers explain the paradox as a "deep-structural" effect of American ideology, and others as a sign of the director's own divided attitude toward his material. In either case, Minnelli is usually regarded as both a conformist and an individual, both a company man and an artist.

Like every other celebrated American director, Minnelli was an "author" or creative agent who sometimes had a good deal of power within the studio system; at the same time, he was created by a variety of cultural, historical, and social forces. Analysis of his work must therefore take into account all the factors I have been trying to describe, including the division of labor in the film business, the contradictions in the worldview of individual artists, and the multitude of uses consumers can find for what they see. We should not ignore the nuances of Minnelli's style or the ideological aims of Hollywood, but we should remember that aesthetic pleasure is negotiated at a social level, and that meaning is always up for grabs. In what follows, therefore, I can only try to give a reasonably accurate account of the circumstances under which Minnelli's pictures were made, speculating about how they functioned at specific moments. In the process, perhaps I can do honor to his artistry, and offer ways of looking at him that will be useful for our own point in time.

2

Uptown Folk

Cabin in the Sky (1943)

Between 1927 and 1954, the major Hollywood studios produced only six feature films that took place in an all-black milieu: *Hallelujah!* (MGM, 1929), *Hearts in Dixie* (Fox, 1929), *The Green Pastures* (Warner Brothers, 1936), *Cabin in the Sky* (MGM, 1943), *Stormy Weather* (Twentieth Century Fox, 1944), and *Carmen Jones* (Twentieth Century Fox, 1954).[1] The period in question is bounded at one end by the introduction of sound and at the other by a shift toward a decentered, "package unit" mode of production.[2] More important, 1954 was also the year in which the Supreme Court ordered public schools desegregated, paving the way for a civil rights movement that would have a lasting effect on all the media. Until then, any studio film purporting to deal exclusively with black experience was truly exceptional and controversial. The six films just listed are therefore among the most unusual products of "classic" Hollywood. No proper history of the movies should ignore them, and they deserve far more intensive study than they have received.[3]

Minnelli's first project – MGM's *Cabin in the Sky,* starring Ethel Waters, Eddie Anderson, Lena Horne, and a host of black performers – is one of the best of the "all-Negro" productions. It warrants special attention, not only because of its entertainment value, but also because it appeared at a crucial juncture in the series, when African Americans were increasing their demands for better treatment from the movie industry, and when the federal government was engaged in a semiofficial drive to encourage pictures with black casts. A transitional work, *Cabin* reminds us of the many ways in which the art of minorities has been coopted by show business, but at the same time it reveals a potentially affirmative or progressive tendency in Hollywood. Ultimately, it enables us to understand the complicated and

51

troubled relationship between ethnicity (or "difference") and modernity (or "massification").

In certain respects, of course, all the "classic" films about blacks were alike. They were all products of a segregated society; they were all written, produced, and directed by whites; and they were all musicals or melodramatic narratives that made extensive use of song and dance, thus reinforcing the white culture's perception of African Americans as a fun-loving, "rhythmic" people. As a group, the six films also intensified the opposition between city and country that structured classic Hollywood movies and many aspects of the culture at large.[4] Notice, for example, how a similar opposition functioned in early uses of "jazz," a term that had been appropriated by white songwriters from Tin Pan Alley and turned into a vague signifier, indicating popular music as a whole. On the one hand, jazz was associated with flappers, skyscrapers, and the entire panoply of twentieth-century modernity; on the other hand, because it originated with African Americans who migrated to the northern cities, it suggested agrarian or precapitalist social relations, and it could be linked to a pastoral myth. Thus Kern and Hammerstein's *Show Boat* (1927) and Gershwin's *Porgy and Bess* (1935) – two celebrated "modern" stage musicals – were grounded in folkloric treatments of blacks. Even Warner Brothers's *The Jazz Singer* (1927) evoked both the city and the country. Throughout most of the film, jazz represents a force of modernization that disrupts a conservative Jewish household; but when the protagonist enters show business, he reasserts old-fashioned values by donning blackface and singing "Mammy."

The same contrasts can be observed everywhere in *Cabin in the Sky*, which uses black-influenced popular music to tell a story about a rural community threatened by a world of gamblers and nightclubs. But *Cabin* creates a different effect from earlier pictures of its type. Whatever its artistic merits (and these are far from negligible), its treatment of the country–city theme is ironic or insincere, signaling an important change in mainstream cinema's negotiation of racial issues. Viewed in retrospect, the film might be described as a fulfillment of capitalist progress: it participates in the breakdown of a pastoral, the death of a certain kind of folkloric "authenticity," and the growing urbanization of black images in Hollywood.

My own response to this tendency of the film is similar to the one suggested by Richard Dyer's frequently cited essay "Entertainment and Utopia," which contends that even though movies (especially musicals) usually give us conservative messages, they do not unproblematically reproduce a dominant ideology. Dyer notes that workers in the entertainment industry have a good deal more influence over the production of cultural forms than do the factory employees who manufacture other types of commodities; he also points to the "important role of structurally subordinate groups in the society – women, blacks, gays – in the development and definition of entertainment."[5] In his opinion, classic Hollywood delimits its treatment of social issues and tries to "manage" contradiction, but at the same time it provides an imagery of energy, abundance, intensity, transparency, and community – a utopian vision of how things ought to be, or of "something we want deeply that our day-to-day lives don't provide."[6] On all these points I would strongly agree. I would disagree, however, when Dyer lists *Cabin in the Sky* among a group of well-known musicals that "point back to a golden age," as if they were being "bought off by the nostalgia or primitivism which provides them with a point of departure."[7] In my view, *Cabin's* nostalgia is superficial, and its primitivism has been turned into the sign of a fashionable modernity. Although the film is never free of racism, the mere presence of its black cast makes it in some measure a contribution to widespread discussion of an otherwise hidden social reality. Moreover, as I hope to show, its potentially reactionary content is "saved" or "made progressive" by the very forces of aestheticism and commodification that leftist critics usually condemn.

The broad theoretical position for which I feel the greatest affinity has recently been articulated by Robert Stam, who uses Mikhail Bakhtin's ideas about literature to address ethnic and racial representations in the cinema. Stam argues that every film is a "mediated version of an already textualized and discursivized socio-ideological world," and that critics ought to be less concerned with a picture's "fidelity to a preexisting truth or reality" – that is, with the supposed accuracy of its images – than with its "specific orchestration of voices in relation to a theme."[8] Such an approach would reveal that movies are "deeply immersed in historical circumstance," and would enable us to see fictional characters as "discursive constructs advanced by one group ... for the consumption of a variety of audiences."[9] My work has similar aims in mind, and I would also call attention to Bakhtin's claim that all art operates in a "dialogically agitated and tension-filled environment."[10] For obvious reasons, the environment surrounding a film like *Cabin in the Sky* was especially agitated, and I propose to give it careful scrutiny.

As a way of organizing my discussion, I shall argue that *Cabin* was situated uneasily among at least four conflicting discourses about blackness and entertainment in America during World War II.[11] The four discourses were composed of a variety of texts, including speeches, newspaper items, critical and theoretical writings, and artistic representations; for the most part they were generated outside of Hollywood, and they tended to cut across the usual political divisions between right and left, affecting both the production and the reception of the film. By examining each in turn, I hope to recover *Cabin*'s historical specificity, showing how Minnelli and several artists at MGM responded to the racial dialogue of their day.

Cabin was shaped first of all by a vestigial "folkloric" discourse having to do with poor blacks in rural southern communities. I hasten to emphasize that nothing in the film was generated by an indigenous, agrarian culture, and that folklore itself is a relatively modern phenomenon, born of late-eighteenth-century attempts to distinguish between the learned and the popular. We should remember, however, that "the folk" can have different uses. For the most part, the childlike mammies and pappies who once populated our songs, stories, and movies were figments of a reactionary white imagination – embodiments of what Peter Burke describes as everything "natural, simple, instinctive, irrational, and rooted in the local soil."[12] But another kind of folklore has been important to the historical consciousness of African Americans, and during the thirties folkloric images of black people were frequently used by the Works Progress Administration (WPA) and the Popular Front on behalf of a progressive social agenda. The entire artistic culture of the Depression was in fact somewhat "folksy" in tone, ranging from public murals to Leadbelly recordings, from the American Communist Party's folk song movement to John Steinbeck's *The Grapes of Wrath,* and from off-Broadway theatrical productions like *Mule Bone* to Pulitzer Prize–winning hits like *The Green Pastures.*

Cabin in the Sky has an ancestry in this mostly liberal, thirties-style folkloricism. The film was based on a 1940 Broadway musical by Lynn Root concerning an impoverished Georgia laborer named "little Joe" who is wounded by gunfire during a dice game. Joe's devout wife, Petunia, prays for his recovery, and black emissaries of God and the Devil are sent to earth to do battle for his soul. Joe is given a short reprieve so that he can mend his ways, but the Devil complicates matters – first by allowing Joe to win the Irish sweepstakes, and then by sending a temptress to lure him away from home. In the end, Petunia's faith wins out, and she and Joe ascend into heaven. Root's quasi-allegorical plot was rendered in the form of a colorful, mainstream spectacular, but many of the black performers, including such figures as Rex Ingram and Katherine Dunham, were associated in the public mind with a kind of folkloric art; indeed the show's lyr-

54

icist, John Latouche, had worked with the WPA and had written a famous Depression-era cantata entitled "Ballad for Americans." Not surprisingly, when MGM purchased the property, it conceived the forthcoming film as a substitute for *Porgy and Bess* (which was unavailable for purchase), and it hired Marc Connelly, author of *The Green Pastures,* to work on the screenplay.[13]

By the time *Cabin* went into production, however, African Americans had enlisted to fight in a war against fascism, and a second discourse about race was emerging, foreshadowing the civil rights movement of the next decade. Immediately before the war, Walter White, executive secretary of the NAACP, had met with a group of Hollywood executives and stars – including Walter Wanger, David Selznick, Daryl Zanuck, and James Cagney – to discuss "the limitation of the Negro to comic or menial roles."[14] Then in 1942, the NAACP held its national convention in Los Angeles, where White called for an end to racial stereotyping and greater participation by black workers in Hollywood craft unions. Later that same year, at the invitation of Wendell Willkie, White made a similar speech to the East Coast Committee on Public Relations of the Motion Picture Producers Association, which promised him it would "effect as rapid a change as possible in the treatment of Negroes in moving pictures."[15]

Not coincidentally, *Casablanca* and *In This Our Life* were released by Warner Brothers in 1942, and several of the subsequent wartime pictures, including *Sahara* (1943), *Bataan* (1943), and *Lifeboat* (1944), showed urban blacks pitted against Nazi or Japanese antagonists. Equally important, the Office of War Information financed a series of documentaries about black participation in combat, among them Carleton Moss and Stuart Heisler's *The Negro Soldier.* During the same period, black musical performers, some of them bearing flamboyantly aristocratic names, were featured in movies about contemporary show business: Count Basie, Duke Ellington, and Nat "King" Cole worked at Republic Pictures in 1942–3, as did Louis Armstrong and Dorothy Dandridge; and in 1944, Fox produced *Stormy Weather,* starring Lena Horne and a virtual pantheon of jazz entertainers. Meanwhile, as Thomas Cripps has pointed out, the sentimental depictions of plantation life in Julian Duvivier's *Tales of Manhattan* (1942) and Walt Disney's *Song of the South* (1946) were denounced by black organizations – this despite the fact that both films "might have been lauded for efforts in social progress" only a few years earlier.[16]

When *Cabin in the Sky* and *Stormy Weather* went into production, *The New York Times* reported that both pictures had been given the explicit encouragement of the Roosevelt administration:

Two major studios, Metro-Goldwyn Mayer and Twentieth Century-Fox, in producing pictures with all-Negro casts, are following the desires of Washington in making such films at this time. Decisions to produce the pictures, it is stated, followed official expression that the Administration felt that its program for increased employment of Negro citizens in certain heretofore restricted fields of industry would be helped by a general distribution of important pictures in which Negroes played a major part.[17]

But even though Hollywood and Washington seemed to be collaborating in an effort to employ minorities, many black leaders were dismayed by the idea of MGM's musical about rural colored folk. *Cabin* had never been the sort of picture to appeal to most white southerners, but it also threatened to offend its more liberal audience in the predominantly urban centers where Lowe's, Inc. owned theaters. One sign of the trouble the film might encounter was a letter from Hall Johnson, the conductor of a black choral group hired to perform in *Cabin,* to associate producer Albert Lewis. Johnson (who had also worked on the 1935 adaptation of *The Green Pastures*) warned that "Negroes have never forgiven the slanderous misrepresentations of [Connelly's play], and when after five successful years on the stage it was finally made into a picture, they did not hesitate to express their opinion."[18]

Almost concurrently, an influential group of white intellectuals was voicing a quite different complaint, growing out of what might be termed the discourse of critical modernism. Some participants in this third discursive activity believed in an indigenous folk culture that could be captured on film, but they argued that the black folk and jazz music in particular had been commodified, controlled, and transformed by the media and the WPA; as a result, important local differences were being erased, and America was moving ineluctably toward a one-dimensional society. A *locus classicus* of such reasoning was James Agee's "Pseudo-Folk," published in the *Partisan Review* in 1944, less than a year after *Cabin in the Sky* was released. Agee was especially disturbed by the "decadence" of swing music, and he worried that the latest fashion in pop tunes would have a bad influence "among Negroes, . . . our richest contemporary source of folkart, and our best people en bloc."[19] To his ear, swing was a corruption of true jazz, which had been produced "where the deep country and the town have first fertilized each other."[20] As examples of the fake, mass-cultural populism that was destroying jazz and overtaking America like a "galloping cancer,"[21] he cited the declining quality of Louis Armstrong's most recent work; the sleek, big-band arrangements of Duke Ellington; the "pseudo-savage, pseudo-

'cultured' dancing" of Katherine Dunham and her troupe; and Paul Robeson's performances of John Latouche's "inconceivably snobbish, esthetically execrable 'Ballad for Americans.' "[22] Although he never mentioned *Cabin in the Sky,* he could hardly have come closer to describing it. Both Armstrong and Ellington were featured in the movie, and, as we have seen, both Dunham and Latouche had contributed to the original Broadway show.

Interestingly, Max Horkheimer and Theodor W. Adorno's *Dialectic of Enlightenment* was roughly contemporary with Agee's essay. (The book was published in 1947, but it was written during the war, largely in California, and it carries a 1944 copyright.) In making this connection, I do not mean to suggest an influence or equivalence. I am simply trying to describe a widespread intellectual critique of the media that took several forms. Unlike Agee, Horkheimer and Adorno came from a European Marxist tradition; they were never preoccupied by the folk (understandably so, since in Germany *völkish* theory had long been appropriated by the fascists), and for the most part they regarded jazz as a pernicious outgrowth of the culture industry.[23] Nevertheless, like many intellectuals of the left, right, and center, they believed that industrialized capitalism of the interwar years was standardizing and reifying social relations, and they shared Agee's distaste for tendentious, fake, or "inauthentic" art. In 1941, Adorno had described the "utopian" element in American life as a "desperate attempt to escape the abstract sameness of things by a kind of self-made and futile *promesse du bonheur.*"[24] For his part, Agee remained a lover of movies; he was, however, an equally fierce critic of "sameness." In fact, when he claimed that a valuable "folk tradition" was being "thoroughly bourgeoizified" by the media,[25] he was responding to the same rationalization and commodification that had given rise to the Frankfurt school's pessimistic, somewhat Weberian analysis of "late capitalism."[26]

Arthur Freed, the producer of *Cabin,* was oblivious to such critiques; as a leading executive in America's most prosperous movie studio, however, he was sensitive to charges of racism. In an attempt to avoid controversy, he gave interviews to the black press in which he addressed "the Negro problem," committing himself to a "dignified presentation of a peace-loving and loyal people," and promising to "spare nothing" on the production.[27] The last of these pronouncements was disingenuous, since *Cabin* was the lowest-budgeted musical in the history of the Freed unit ($700,000). Photographed in a sepia-tinted black and white, it borrowed its most spectacular visual effect – a tornado that destroys a nightclub – from *The Wizard of Oz.* Even so, the studio made a considerable investment in the picture: it hired Elmer Rice and Joseph Schrank to assist Connelly with the adaptation

(Schrank wrote the first draft and received the sole credit); it commissioned Harold Arlen and E. Y. Harburg to supplement the original John Latouche–Vernon Duke score; and it selected the popular radio personality Eddie Anderson to replace Dooley Wilson.

MGM's production resources, the cast of star performers, and Freed's efforts at public relations all helped the film to earn a modest profit at the box office. According to Thomas Bogle, *Cabin* was received enthusiastically by black audiences in the South, and was widely shown at U.S. Army camps, where Lena Horne was a special favorite.[28] But tensions were evident during the shooting, and the old guard of directors and cameramen were not especially hospitable to a newcomer like Minnelli. Fortunately, a small picture with an all-black cast was not likely to make insiders excessively jealous, and Freed eased Minnelli's way by giving him technical help: Roger Edens and Busby Berkeley supervised the songs and dances, and Andrew Marton gave advice about positioning the camera in ways that would preserve continuity from shot to shot. Meanwhile, everyone had to cope with segregation in Hollywood. When Minnelli took Horne out to dinner, he needed to obtain the permission of resturant owners, and until midway into the production, when studio executives ordered the commissary integrated, the players were required to eat their lunches in L. B. Mayer's private dining room.[29]

Upon the film's release, certain reviewers were highly critical of the results. Although *Cabin* received good notices from the *New York Times* and the *New York Daily News* (the latter of which had a substantial black readership), David Lardner of the *New Yorker* scoffed at MGM for trying to produce a "lovable ol' folk fantasy,"[30] and the anonymous reviewer for *Time* – none other than James Agee – charged that the studio had treated its fine cast as "picturesque, Sambo-style entertainers."[31] *PM Magazine* remarked that the film was an example of "how *not* to fulfill a pledge such as Hollywood made to Wendell Willkie last year, to treat the Negro as a first-class citizen in films."[32] At least one review in the African-American press was even more scathing. Writing in the *New York Amsterdam News* two weeks after *Cabin* had opened its successful run at the Criterion Theater on Broadway, Ramona Lewis described the film as "an insult masking behind the label of folklore. . . . It pictures Negroes, heads tied up, with crap shooting inclinations and prayer meeting propensities at a time when [they] are daily proving their heroic mettle in battle and defense plant. . . . Since box office returns convince Hollywood more than anything else that it is in the right, it's too bad the actors didn't have the courage to refuse to make the film in the first place."[33]

In different ways, each of these negative reactions was appropriate. There can be little doubt that *Cabin* was a Hollywoodish depiction of black "folk-lore," saturated with inferential forms of racism; nor can there be any doubt that it represented a carefully managed style of mass entertainment, designed to serve the interests of a white corporation. Nevertheless, the film has a paradoxical effect, as if it wanted to dissolve binary oppositions between the town and the country, thereby unsettling the strategy of containment that usually operated in Hollywood's folkloric narratives. Placed alongside earlier pictures in the same vein, such as King Vidor's sincere but no less racist *Hallelujah!* or Warner Brothers' adaptation of *The Green Pastures*, it seems distinctly urban in spirit, keyed to the talents of Ethel Waters, Duke Ellington, and Lena Horne. In true Hollywood fashion, the performers are treated as celebrities, so that they take on a glamorous aura and sometimes appear in cameo roles as "themselves." And because these performers have a spacious, handsomely mounted vehicle (staged on the visibly artificial, "utopian" sets that were a hallmark of the Freed unit during the forties), they are able to behave like something other than minstrel-show caricatures.[34]

Let me make clear that I am not trying to excuse MGM's racism. The studio was responding in certain ways to potential criticism from its black audience, but it was also attempting to preserve the image of cheerful, plantation-style darkies. My point is simply that the film's folkloric project was vitiated – partly by the black critique of Hollywood, partly by the Roosevelt administration's desire to integrate certain aspects of the wartime economy, and chiefly by the growing commodification and modernization of American life. In this last regard, I would also argue that *Cabin*'s strong feeling of urbanity and sophistication derives in great measure from a fourth discourse about blackness, different from the ones I have described thus far: a chic, upscale "Africanism," redolent of cafe society, Broadway theater, and the European avant-garde.

As I indicated in the previous chapter, the term "Africanism" should be understood in a limited and stipulated sense, describing a cosmopolitan artistic sensibility that pointed away from the American provinces – usually toward Harlem, Paris, French colonial Africa, and the Caribbean. This sensibility was prompted indirectly by developments within black culture itself, especially by the black internationalism described in a founding document of the Harlem renaissance, Alain Locke's "The New Negro" (1925).[35] It also has something in common with "Negritude," a word coined by the poet Aimé Césaire in 1939. But the particular attitude I am trying to identify was chiefly a white mythology, with distant origins in the artistic and intellectual revolutions that had swept Europe during the early twentieth century. Its progenitors would include Conrad's *Heart of Darkness* (1902), Picasso's *Les demoiselles d'Avignon* (1907), Fry's exhibition of the post-impressionist painters (1910), Freud's *Totem and Taboo* (1913), and the dadaist experiments with "Negro poems" or *Negergedichte* (1916).[36]

Throughout the twenties and thirties, as European high modernism became institutionalized, African motifs found their way into "classy" forms of decoration and entertainment, operating in almost dialectical relation with narratives about the pastoral southland. (Meanwhile, in Germany, the Nazis branded both modernist art and the newer types of black entertainment as "degenerate.") This chic, highly commodified style – raised to delirious excess by Josef von Sternberg in the "Hot Voodoo" number of *Blonde Venus* (1932) – offered a "savage" urbanity in place of a "childlike" pastoralism. It was already present to some degree in the original Broadway production of *Cabin in the Sky*, where the two primitivisms seemed to combine. It could also be heard in the work of songwriters employed by the Freed unit; for instance, Cole Porter had written a series of Africanist numbers for Broadway shows like *Jubilee* (1935) and *Panama Hattie* (1940), both of which were purchased by MGM. As we have seen, however, one of the leading exponents of the style was Minnelli – and he, more than anyone else, was responsible for *Cabin*'s distinctly urban tone.

A devoted student of jazz and modern art, Minnelli was valuable to the film because, in Geoffrey Nowell-Smith's well-chosen phrase, he furthered MGM's policy of bringing "refinement to the popular."[37] He was undoubtedly offered the chance to supervise *Cabin* because during the mid-thirties he had become famous as a director-designer of sophisticated Broadway reviews featuring black performers. Ethel Waters had starred in two of his most successful New York shows, including *At Home Abroad* (1934), where she was cast as the "Empress Jones," a potentate of the Belgian Congo who travels to Harlem and brings the latest styles back to her subjects. ("Cartier rings they're wearin' in their noses now," she sang.) Minnelli had also created settings for Duke Ellington's big band at Radio City, and was responsible for the extravagant and erotic costumes Josephine Baker wore in *The Ziegfeld Follies of 1936*. Robert Benchley of the *New Yorker* snidely accused him of having a "Negroid" sense of color,[38] but in his authorial signature and personal style, Minnelli continued to exploit what Stephen Harvey has called "the totems of Africa *moderne*."[39] In 1937, *Esquire* magazine praised his personal clothing style as "a perfect marriage of Harlem and the Left Bank."[40]

An example of one of Minnelli's set designs for the unproduced S. N. Behrman musical *Serena Blandish* (1939) is shown in Figure 3, illustrating

60

Figure 3. Minnelli's set design for the unproduced S. N. Berhman stage show *Serena Blandish*, 1939. (Photograph courtesy of Lee [Mrs. Vincente] Minnelli.)

Figure 4. MGM's promotion for *Cabin in the Sky*. (© 1943, Turner Entertainment Co., all rights reserved.)

his tendency to blend surrealist motifs with an *au courant* Africanism. It should be emphasized that this style is no less racist than high modernism itself, and no more progressive than much of the commercial folklore of the thirties. Like the folkloric artists, Minnelli relied on a kind of primitivism, explicitly associating blackness with sexuality, instinctiveness, and the Freudian subconscious. At the same time, however, he promoted an uptown face of jazz, tied to contemporary fashion and big-time entertainment. In this context, blackness began to signify both wildness and sophistication. The African imagery was as "stereotypical" as any other cultural code, but it seemed attractive and denatured by parody or playful quotation; moreover, because it was regarded by audiences as in the vanguard, it tended to problematize the distinction between the savage and the cultivated.

However one might describe the political effect of such designs, the important point about Minnelli's work is that he was far more attuned to contemporary New York than to the Old South, and in a picture like *Cabin* his aestheticism tended to undermine the conservative implications of the original material. This is not to suggest that he was an artistic subversive. On the contrary, his elegance and "exoticism" were perfectly in keeping with the institutional needs of MGM in 1943 – as we can see from the studio's promotion of the picture, which tried to deemphasize the story's rural atmosphere. Consider the lobby card from the original release, reproduced in Figure 4, showing Lena Horne, Eddie Anderson, and Ethel Waters gathered around a picket fence. The artwork and promotional copy are appropriate to a big-city nightclub, promising "entertainment galore" and "gorgeous girls," while depicting two richly costumed figures strutting off to a dance. Although the film is less brazenly "citified" than this ad, MGM's publicity department was being reasonably faithful to the values Freed and Minnelli put on the screen.

If we now turn to the film itself, we will find that most of the historical forces and discursive categories I have been describing – the vestigial folklore of the thirties, the NAACP's mounting criticism of Hollywood, the increasing collaboration between mass entertainment and government, and the posh Africanism of high-toned Broadway musicals – have left their mark, producing a kind of ideological schizophrenia. At the beginning of the credit sequence, for example, a title card announces "The Broadway Musical Play *Cabin in the Sky*," as if MGM wanted to legitimize the project by pointing to refined origins. When the credits end, however, a "crawl" moves across the screen, informing us that "throughout the ages, powerful thoughts have been handed down through the medium of the legend, the folktale, and the fantasy. . . . This story of faith and devotion springs from that source and seeks to capture those values." Here the film seems to be claiming a different lineage, even though the word "fantasy" mingles ambiguously with appeals to patriotism, folklore, and religion, opening the possibility for a more playful reading.

To be sure, *Cabin* continues to exhibit halfhearted concern with the religious beliefs of a "simple" couple who live outside the corrupting reach of modernity, together with a pervasive nostalgia for a lost home life. As Rick Altman has pointed out, the Hollywood "folk musical" is defined by these two qualities, especially by its preoccupation with "family groupings and the home."[41] Such films often involve both a desire for adventure and a recurrent homesickness, and they tend to be resolved by a *nostos* after a period of wandering. In *Cabin*, for example, Joe is torn between the artificial "Club Paradise" and the genuine paradise of a community church; between a sexy, brown-skinned mistress and a somewhat mammyfied wife; between a fast life of wine and easy money and a domestic life of lemonade and productive labor. He strays from home in order to find excitement and pleasure; but he yearns for what he has left behind, and his return (or more precisely, his recovery after a fevered, guilty dream) is essential to the happy ending.

As we have seen, *Cabin* is based on a paradigmatic tension between city and country. Ultimately, the film gives the tension a conservative resolution, making the town lead to Hell and the country lead to Heaven, and its racist implications become especially apparent when we realize how often the two opposed realms are depicted respectively in shades of blackness and whiteness. The nightclub is situated in a noirish street, whereas the cabin is often flooded with light; Joe wears black tie and tails when he spends the Devil's money, and a white robe when he ascends a stairway to paradise; the Devil's henchmen (costumed as big-city elevator operators), are dressed completely in black, in contrast with the soldiers of the Lord, who wear uniforms of glowing white.

But the town is nonetheless an attractive place, and the real story is elsewhere – largely in the photography, the art decoration, the costuming, the performances, and the musical numbers. In fact, in order to achieve a satisfying conclusion, *Cabin* finds ways to pull its two worlds into a kind of synthesis.[42] Thus the domestic woman moves briefly into the nightclub, wearing a shiny dress, performing a spectacular and amusing dance, and beating the siren at her own game. More importantly, the cabin becomes a performing space, where tap dancing and lively pop tunes bring sexuality and entertainment under the benign influence of spirituality and married love. One of the best numbers in the picture, Ethel Waters's superb rendition of "Takin' a Chance on Love," is staged in the family kitchen, and it uses the metaphor of gambling (Joe's major vice) to speak about monogamous romance.

Here as elsewhere, *Cabin* simply borrows a few stock images from a folkloric code, putting them in the service of a new form of musical theater. In the opening credits, it makes a patriotic appeal to folklore, but then it uses jazz and jitterbug to perform the function of hymns and work songs in earlier movies of the type. As a "folk musical," it therefore differs sharply from *Hallelujah!*, where, according to Altman, "the tempered rhythms of the spiritual, sung in unison by the gathered community" are set off against "the syncopated rhythms of jazz and the chaotic sexual drive which they invoke."[43] Unlike King Vidor, Freed and Minnelli have utterly secular imaginations, and their film contains no Manichean musical oppositions. In fact, the only religious song heard in *Cabin* is a snippet of "Old Ship of Zion," which is immediately preceded by "Little Black Sheep," an ersatz hymn written by E. Y. "Yip" Harburg.

Cabin might be properly described as suburban rather than folkloric, because it blends MGM's middle-class values with the Freed unit's relatively elite Broadway ethos. To see just how much it tilts toward the city, however, one needs to step far outside the studio system, viewing it alongside Spencer Williams's *Blood of Jesus* (1941), an independent film directed by a black man and aimed at an audience of southern black churchgoers. Williams's film, which has none of the production values of MGM, was designed, in Thomas Cripps's words, "to mourn the passing of the great days when Afro-Americans were embraced by a familial certitude that would later be shattered by the great black diaspora from Southern farm to Yankee city."[44] Williams portrayed the devil in the style of *aesthetique du cool,* and he made urban jitterbug seem a lurid music, appropriate to a world of crime and prostitution. In *Cabin,* Freed and Minnelli were able to use the same fundamentalist semantics, yet their tone was completely different. For example, in one of the most exhilarating sequences of the picture, a high-stepping couple, dressed in the latest fashion and moving to the beat of Duke Ellington's "Goin' Up," enter the swinging doors of the Club Paradise; the camera dollies backward as the couple glides onto the dance floor, and then, as a crowd of neatly dressed men in zoot suits and women in bobby socks gathers around, it cranes high above the room, drifting across the scene to close in on the bandstand. A publicity still reproduced in Figure 5 shows the performers in the sequence and suggests the ambience of the

Figure 5. Duke Ellington and dancers in the Paradise nightclub sequence of *Cabin in the Sky*. ()

Figure 6. Eddie Anderson, Ethel Waters, and Kenneth Spencer in *Cabin in the Sky*. Notice the "Africanist" design on the wall at the left. ()

room. Clearly, this is no smoky den of iniquity. It seems more like a show-case for a famous orchestra, and the lovely collaboration among Elling-ton's music, Busby Berkeley's choreography, and Minnelli's camera crane amounts to a kind of celebration.[45]

It follows that if the nightclub is treated as relatively innocent fun, religion is depicted in perfunctory or comic ways. Unlike Williams's *Blood of Jesus*, *Cabin* imagines the afterlife whimsically, in a style similar to Lubitsch's *Heaven Can Wait* (also released in 1943). It never mentions Jesus, it never shows a crucifix, and it barely alludes to Scripture; instead, it offers a nonsectarian God who behaves rather like a cosmic cost accountant, and it proffers a few simple edicts against gambling and adultery. The Devil's henchmen do their work from the "Hotel Hades," which resembles the office of an MGM producer during a story conference; and the entrance to Heaven – a vast, cloud-covered stairway flanked by black cherubim – seems to have been derived from a Ziegfield production number.

By the same token, the quotidian, earthbound scenes in *Cabin* resemble a pure dream world. Most Hollywood movies about "the folk" at least claim to represent a specific place, but here the characters inhabit a poor but utopian black universe, structured by the absence of white people and decorated with an odd mixture of artifacts. Indeed one of the major dif-ferences between the Broadway show and the film is that in the film the battle between God and the Devil turns out to be something Joe *dreams*. This change gave the picture a happy ending, and at the same time enabled Minnelli to invest the mise-en-scène with an Afro-Caribbean look that fore-shadows his subsequent work on *Yolanda and the Thief* (1945) and *The Pirate* (1948). In his autobiography, he claims that he struggled with MGM's art department in order to keep the cabin from seeming "dirty" or "slov-enly,"[46] but his dreamy settings also tended to aestheticize poverty, moti-vating some condescending jokes. At one point, for example, Joe uses earnings from a local feed mill to buy Petunia a washing machine; because there is no electricity in the cabin, he places the gleaming white appliance on his porch as a symbol of prosperity. In this context, the washer becomes a surrealistic image – a bizarre *objet trouvé*, rather like the mobile home in *The Long, Long Trailer*, which both satirizes and validates the society of consumption.

Not only the settings, but also the manners and accents in the film are heterogeneous and fantastic. Hall Johnson had written to the producers advising them to use "an honest-to-goodness Negro dialect,"[47] but the script was rendered in a series of excruciatingly condescending white versions of demotic, southern-black English. Here is the way Joseph Schrank and Marc Connelly imagined Petunia praying for Joe's recovery:

> If yuh lets him die de debbil gonna git him fo' sho'. An' he aint wicked, Lawd — he jus' weak, dat's all. He aint got no powah to resis' de debbil lest Ah watches him.[48]

And here is Joe when he discovers a pair of dice in his bedroom drawer:

> Right now I'm wrestlin' wid de devil. When I was lookin' for de necktie in de bureau drawer, I also found two clamity cubes. I aint throwed 'em away yet. If I been redeemed, why don't I pitch 'em right in de stove?[49]

Fortunately, little of this language survives in the performances — an effect that becomes especially evident in the case of a minor player, Butterfly McQueen, who never uses the spacey singsong that audiences (even audiences of films produced by blacks) had come to expect of her.[50] Petunia's prayer has been completely revised for the completed film, and Eddie Anderson delivers the speech about "calamity cubes" in the same gravelly, urban accent he used on the radio, so that it hardly sounds like the same language. At one point, Ethel Waters sings a few lines of "Happiness is a Thing Called Joe" in a fake dialect ("He gotta smile dat make de lilac wanna grow"), but everywhere else, she sings in crisply enunciated standard English, using the slightly elocutionary vocal technique of her best-known recordings.

Where the design of the film is concerned, Minnelli seems to have taken pleasure in making a southern locale look like the big city. In one of the most revealing comments in his autobiography, he remarks that the set he liked best was "a southern ghetto, with a warm, golden look, created from a permanent version of a New York street."[51] He also tried to glamorize the featured players: whenever Ethel Waters is seen in a bandanna, she wears fashionable earrings reminiscent of the Cartier jewelry she had sung about in *At Home Abroad;* and when Lena Horne dresses up as a temptress, she exchanges her pillbox hat for a magnolia, pinning the visibly artificial blossom to her hair like Billie Holiday.

Much the same thing could be said about the dressing of the sets. Minnelli painted his own "Africanist" murals on the walls of the Paradise nightclub, (see, e.g., the design on the wall at the left of Figure 6), and he turned the cabin into a spacious interior, accented with reproductions of Victorian art. He gave Joe and Petunia an elaborate, wrought-iron bedstead, and in each of their rooms he placed white wicker chairs designed in a lacy, roccoco filigree. (The same chairs show up again in 1944, helping to furnish Judy Garland's bedroom in *Meet Me in St. Louis;* in 1950, they reappear in MGM's *Two Weeks with Love,* a Jane Powell–Debbie Reynolds musical set in a fashionable Catskills resort.) To grasp the full implications of this style, we need only glance at the stills reproduced in Figures 7 and 8. The first comes from Williams's *Blood of Jesus,* where a black household has been decorated with a single picture – a dime-store image of Jesus exhibiting his bleeding heart, visible at the upper left of the frame. The second still comes from *Cabin,* and helps to indicate the comparative opulence of MGM. Notice especially the framed picture at the upper right of the frame, showing a white cherub kissing a sleeping boy.

Largely because of this elaborate, exquisite decoration, *Cabin* seems remote from anything we commonly associate with folkloric movies. A deliberate exercise in *faux-naïveté,* it has more in common with what Rick Altman has called "fairy tale musicals," in the sense that it elicits identification "with fantasy, with the far away, with the imaginary."[52] Generally speaking, of course, all of the classic Hollywood musicals were fairy tales; but *Cabin*'s oneiric quality has an odd relationship to its ostensible subject, making its folkloric setting seem a mere pretext. The deeper purpose of the film becomes evident when we consider two rhyming camera movements, one near the beginning of the story and one near the end: in the first, Joe stands looking at a lottery ticket he has fastened to his bedroom mirror; as he leans forward in a trance, the camera cranes up and over his shoulder, moving toward the tilted surface of the glass as if to plunge him and us into an imaginary world. In the second, Petunia looks into a mirror that has survived the devastation of the Club Paradise; she notices something reflected there, and the camera cranes downward to share her viewpoint, revealing a studio-manufactured stairway leading off through the clouds. These shots contrast Joe's dream of riches with Petunia's dream of Heaven, but they also serve as metaphors for two aspects of the Hollywood cinema. Like the movies, they appeal both to our desire for luxury and to our desire for a magical, nonmaterial existence. They invite the audience to form a subjective bond with a poor black couple, but in the process they make Joe and Petunia seem like ideal consumers of entertainment – a pair of restless American dreamers caught up in a world of music, light, and dance.

Like virtually all of the Freed unit musicals, *Cabin in the Sky* involves a good deal of what Jane Feuer has termed "conservative self-reflexivity"; it banishes every social contradiction, first by appealing to its own status as entertainment, and then by presenting "a vision of human liberation which

Figure 7. Set decoration in *Blood of Jesus*, directed by Spencer Williams, 1941. (Courtesy the Black Film Center/Archive, Indiana University.)

Figure 8. Set decoration in *Cabin in the Sky*. (Rex Ingram and Lena Horne; © 1943, Turner Entertainment Co., all rights reserved.)

is profoundly aesthetic."[53] Notice also that the aesthetic sensibility (as Baudelaire observed) is always expensive, dependent on signifiers of material abundance and rarified taste. Thus when Waters, Anderson, and Horne play the roles of folkloric characters, they do not look poor; and because they are treated as stars, they induce a feeling of playful masquerade. In a strange way, this transformation of blackness into a commodity on display has a salutory effect. We might say, echoing Richard Dyer's formulation, that the film gives us the feeling of "what utopia would feel like rather than how it would be organized."[54]

Clearly, the makers of *Cabin* were taking care to keep too much social reality from intruding on the attractive surroundings. Their strategy may seem offensive when so much of the actual experience of African Americans has been suppressed or driven into a political unconscious, but *Cabin* has a complex ideological potential. From the point of view of many social critics of the time, its Hollywood surrealism and freewheeling, commodified treatment of folklore were irredeemably decadent and false; yet its design runs against the grain of a repressive and no more "true" set of conventions. After all, there is no such thing as an "authentic" folk movie, and *Cabin* may have been better off for its evident artificiality. Freed and Minnelli were hardly social activists, but by imbuing their film with a dreamy atmosphere and an urban Africanism, they and the performers turned it into what is arguably the most visually beautiful picture about black people ever produced at the classic studios. We might say that during the early forties in Hollywood, their aestheticism amounted to a modestly positive gesture.

Perhaps a better way of making the same point would be to repeat the familiar Marxist axiom that capitalism represents a progressive stage in history. Unfortunately, such progress always involves injustices and ironies. As I have already observed, *Cabin* and every other studio film about blacks simply reinforced the hypocritical, separate-but-equal policies of a segregated society. This injustice was compounded because whites were in charge of every behind-the-scenes aspect of the production, and because much of the debate over the film's merits was framed and conditioned by a white cultural establishment. It is ironic that *Cabin* can nonetheless be described as a step forward in the democratization of show business, and that a film containing so much nostalgia and bogus folklore should have provided a showcase for some of the most witty and talented entertainers of the period. But the greatest irony of all is that the black performers, who were at last becoming full-fledged stars, were merely gaining membership in a conservative enterprise – a system devoted to praising the American way, and to promoting the values of glamour, charm, and illusion.

3
Third Nature

Meet Me in St. Louis (1944)

The folkloric tradition described in the preceding chapter did not end with the war, but it began to assume a different setting and a much more sumptuous form. During the thirties, folk narratives usually involved southern black or northern working-class characters who came from what FDR had called the bottom of the "economic pyramid." In the forties, the middle class was increasingly folkloricized. The aura of remoteness and simplicity crucial to this process was achieved by situating narratives in a not-too-distant past, among pioneer and especially western communities.

The shift from a north–south to an east–west geography brought with it subtle changes in ideological emphasis, as we can see in Rogers and Hammerstein's *Oklahoma!* (1943), an enormously successful Broadway musical that influenced the postwar decade in much the same way *Porgy and Bess* influenced the thirties. The protagonists of *Oklahoma!* may look like cowboys, but they are also the ancestors of modern Americans. Would-be suburbanites, they grow corn in order to purchase fancy surreys, and they live within a train ride of Kansas City, where, as the song tells us, everything is "up to date." Although they inhabit quaintly simple times, they have left behind an old world (represented by the overpopulated East) and brought progress to the plains. Above all, they represent the power of capitalism to remake the land; and because they are closely associated with the frontier earth, they make commodification and industry seem as natural as the passing seasons.

Minnelli's third film, *Meet Me in St. Louis,* was directly inspired by the success of *Oklahoma!,* a show in which MGM had a large financial investment, and it tells a similar kind of story. Set in the "gateway to the West" at the turn of the century, it celebrates the foundation of an urban Eden in the wilderness – a place where capitalism makes the lawns spacious and the weather perfect, and where a giant exposition of commodities has been built on a swamp. ("They're going to have a fashion pavillion at the fair," Judy Garland happily proclaims.) This theme would recur with only minor variations in several postwar musicals, including *State Fair, Centennial Summer, Summer Holiday,* and *In the Good Old Summertime;* none of these later pictures, however, were able to suggest so many ironies and ambiguities while sustaining an air of lighthearted simplicity, and none were so formally elegant or artful.

In some ways, *Meet Me in St. Louis* could also be seen as a prosperous, "all-white" counterpart to *Cabin in the Sky.* Budgeted at almost three times the cost of the earlier picture, its only vestiges of blackness are a couple of Moorish statues in the Smith family hallway and a cakewalk to the tune of "Under the Bamboo Tree." Meanwhile, like *Cabin,* it has a dreamlike narrative that confirms Arthur Freed's favorite motto from *The Wizard of Oz:* "There's no place like home." Commentators usually emphasize this sense of nostalgia, pointing to the film's sweetly colorful evocation of family life.[1] Wartime audiences must have been particularly drawn to its comforting, maternal atmosphere, and to its many scenes of festive holidays and home cooking. But for all these traditionalist values, *Meet Me in St. Louis* is also a streamlined spectacle that treats the past in the manner of a sophisticted tourist, viewing it as *style.* Its real purpose is to celebrate the convenience and supposed bounty of modern life, and to reinforce the American dream of having your cake and eating it.

The screenplay for the film, by Irving Brecher and Fred Finklehoffe, is based on Sally Benson's understated, semiautobiographical sketches of her childhood, which were originally published in the *New Yorker.* But MGM's production is aimed at making Benson's portrait of everyday life in the age of innocence seem exceedingly luxurious; moreover, as Robert Ray has pointed out, the resolution of the film's tenuous plot depends on the "ideological translation of the frontier mythology into promises of unlimited opportunities for economic growth."[2] In effect, Minnelli and the other artists at MGM were contributing their expertise to a vast transformation that has been analyzed by William Cronon in his economic history of Chicago, *Nature's Metropolis* (1991). Cronon speaks of a "second" or "artificial" nature that resurfaces wildness, so that rivers, lakes, and flatlands can do service for commerce.[3] The term "second nature" appears also in the writings of George Lukács and Theodor W. Adorno, who constantly remind us of how the given biological world is mapped and developed through technology.[4] St. Louis, which was built to support trade along the Mississippi River, is a textbook case of such development, and MGM's movie about the city could therefore be described as a kind of "third nature" – a simulacrum constructed in a studio, designed to glamorize and commodify an already artificial landscape.

Not surprisingly, the narrative in *Meet Me in St. Louis* is organized around the passing seasons, with each new episode introduced by a tintype drawing that dissolves into live-action Technicolor. In these picture-postcard views, nature becomes a fashion plate; and in the four dramatic episodes, clothing and furniture are carefully selected to suggest what Roland Barthes might call "season-ness." Minnelli's skill as a colorist (to say nothing of his experience designing seasonal windows for a Chicago department store) was never put to more effective use, and in some cases George Folsey's photography is almost tactile, evoking precise changes of air and light. As a result, the film continually demonstrates how industry can make "improvements" on biology. St. Louis seems a better place than New York precisely because it achieves more success as a "natural metropolis" – a commercial center where art produces verdant lawns and perfect weather, preserving the middle-class family and effacing any memory of either wildness or industrial blight.

This idealization of progress is apparent from the opening shot, in which Minnelli's boom-mounted camera moves at a leisurely pace down MGM's elaborate outdoor set of Kensington Avenue, showing us the Smith house on an archetypal June day in 1903. Suddenly, amidst the pedestrians and horse-drawn wagons, a red motorcar appears, honking its horn cheerfully as it whisks past and speeds off at the right of the screen. The automobile helps date the story and, equally important, shows how progress harmonizes with the pastoral surroundings. Unlike the Orson Welles adaptation of Booth Tarkington's *The Magnificent Ambersons* (1942), this is not a film about relentless historical change and social dissolution; and unlike the Howard Lindsay–Russell Crouse adaptation of Clarence Day's *Life with Father* (a long-running Broadway show that influenced MGM's project), it never looks back to the elite, Anglophile east, where everything is steeped in tradition. Tarkington and Day, in different ways, had written about conservative patriarchs who resist any change in their well-ordered existence. By contrast, *Meet Me in St. Louis* deals sympathetically with women in the heartland, who are seen as representatives of an emerging consumer society and who have a much more flexible attitude toward modern life.

Far from being opponents of change or progress, most of the characters in the film are civic boosters and optimists who are at their happiest when the city shows signs of bustling enterprise. Hence they seem only mildly inconvenienced when newfangled devices intrude on their familar routine.

In the opening episode, for example, a telephone figures prominently in the action. The maid Katie (Marjorie Main) complains that she "wouldn't marry a man who proposed over an *invention*," and Mr. Smith (Leon Ames) grumbles that ever since the apparatus was installed it has regularly disturbed his peace. For Mrs. Smith (Mary Astor) and her daughters, however, the telephone is a welcome addition to the family dining room, bringing romance and adventure into the home. The long-distance conversation between Rose (Lucille Bremer) and her boyfriend at Princeton turns out to be comically embarrassing and unromantic; but at the same time it draws the family closer together, prefiguring countless scenes involving telephones and adolescent girls in the television sitcoms of the fifties.

Although the film ultimately confirms patriarchal values, it consistently makes women the active agents of the narrative, and it links the sense of progress and happiness with a "feminine" point of view. The males tend to be mannequins, like the boy next door (Tom Drake, who was chosen after Van Johnson was drafted into the army), or insensitive businessmen, like Mr. Smith. Indeed, Mr. Smith is so insistent on being treated like the lord of the manor that he often seems boorish and frightening. When he returns home after a hard day at work and expects his cool bath and hot dinner exactly on time, a ripple of anxiety passes through the women in the house; and later, when he announces that everyone is going to move to New York, the family shrinks away from him, gathering in silent, protective groups at opposite sides of the dining table. Mr. Smith obviously feels affection for his wife and daughters, but he is dismally ill-informed about such things as romance and housekeeping, which are the really important matters in this film. He is also wrong about where one can find progress or modernity, which lie in the new west.

The glorious vision of domestic economy in *Meet Me in St. Louis* hardly looks like an economy at all. Catsup making is a communal activity, and the various parties, meals, or celebrations that mark different stages of the narrative seem to emerge effortlessly out of the round of seasons. Clearly, MGM was imagining a peaceful time before the two world wars, when women were not yet fully socialized into politics and the work force. Just when these women were entering public life in greater numbers than ever before, the film suggested that old-fashioned domestic labor was more natural and far less boring than shopkeeping or business. In the same breath, it depicted the Smith women as ideal consumers of fashion and spectacle and as harbingers of the postwar movement to suburbia.[5]

The look of the film is consistent with these complex purposes. Minnelli and set designer Lemuel Ayres (who was hired because of his work on

Oklahoma!) fill the screen with authentic, turn-of-the-century artifacts, but at the same time they update the mise-en-scène, making it seem harmonious with contemporary fashions in entertainment. We can learn something about bygone local customs from *Meet Me in St. Louis* (e.g., that women bottled their own catsup and that kids threw bags of flour at grownups on Halloween), but the picture never tries to be "realistic" in the same way as its source. A masterpiece of Freed-unit fantasy, it allows Judy Garland to sing a perfectly orchestrated rendition of the latest pop tune while supposedly riding across town in an old-fashioned trolley car. Everywhere else, it reconciles contradictions, blending story with musical number and progress with provinciality. (It does all this, incidentally, in much more satisfactory fashion than Fred Zinneman's later adaptation of *Oklahoma!* [1955], in which Method actors and outdoor photography dilute the utopian, theatricalized atmosphere necessary to Broadway's musical style.)

Minnelli contributed significantly to the effect I am trying to describe, using the "folkloric" elements as a starting point for a whimsical exercise in visual technique. Certainly his own childhood in the Midwest was very different from the one depicted in the film, and he seems not to have asked himself what turn-of-the-century St. Louis was actually like. Instead, he asked what *art* in the period was like. He knew that if MGM's settings vaguely resembled paintings by Thomas Eakins, they would seem both authentic and playfully chic; in this and other ways, he created a world in which Judy Garland could suggest a Victorian maiden while still seeming "in character" as a contemporary musical performer.

Minnelli was also a major contributor to a certain air of melancholy and danger that pervades the autumn and winter scenes, helping to countervail an otherwise saccharine tone. Most of the time, *Meet Me in St. Louis* is such a prettified account of growing up WASP that it strongly resembles a big-budget variation of the Andy Hardy pictures. L. B. Mayer approved the production for exactly that reason, and at one point the film was intended to be the pilot for a series of Hardyesque B movies. Arthur Freed and scriptwriter Fred Finklehoff had more ambitious ideas, and they helped preserve the gently ironic, episodic quality of Sally Benson's fiction; like Mayer, however, they were strongly committed to a sentimental vision of the American family. Minnelli did not object to this vision, but for him the chief appeal of the project lay elsewhere, in Sally Benson's brief sketch about Halloween. While the script was being developed, he also suggested ways to exploit the talents of a new child actress, Margaret O'Brien, whom he claimed to have discovered.[6] The scenes involving O'Brien as Tootie Smith, and to a lesser extent the scenes involving Joan Carroll as Tootie's older sister Agnes (the only female in the Smith family who does not look adorably lovely), are in fact the most impressive moments in the film. Without them, *Meet Me in St. Louis* would still be an intelligently designed musical, containing one of Judy Garland's best performances and three memorable songs by Hugh Martin and Ralph Blane; with them, it seems keyed to childhood imagination and to the potentially dark side of Kensington Avenue.

The opening sequence of the film has been much praised for its narrative economy and visual grace.[7] In a half-dozen shots, all of them joined together so smoothly that they seem like one continuous movement of the camera, we are introduced to six characters and taken on a tour of the house where most of the story will take place. The sequence begins and ends in the Smith family kitchen – a locus of female work, providing communal activity, nourishment, and maternal care – and is unified by a "pass along" version of the title song. First we hear the Smith's only son, Lon (Henry Daniels), humming the tune to himself as he brings in the day's mail. Lon's sister Agnes, who has been playing outside with a garden hose, enters from a screen door, slips on an old pair of her father's shoes, and clomps upstairs, singing "Meet Me in St. Louis" at the top of her voice. Cut to the second-floor bathroom, where Grandpa Prophater (Harry Davenport) hears Agnes approaching. As the grandfather exits the bath, he goes singing and waltzing down a corridor to his bedroom, where he tries on an assortment of colorful hats; suddenly we hear other voices, and from over his shoulder we look out a window to see Esther Smith (Judy Garland) and a couple of her friends riding up in a carriage. Brandishing a tennis racket, Esther alights at the front door and joins in a chorus, finishing off the number. She then enters the kitchen, where, like several characters at the beginning of the sequence, she tastes her mother's recipe for catsup and suggests how the seasoning can be improved.

Minnelli's incessantly panning and craning camera takes us on a circular journey that imitates the pattern of the film as a whole. Like this opening sequence, *Meet Me in St. Louis* is a domestic narrative that follows a comfortable round of activity, never going far from home; it emphasizes family rituals, and its only major conflict – Mr. Smith's desire to leave town for a better job – has a powerful impact because it threatens the sense of repetition and continuity. Even this conflict, however, is not introduced until the film is more than half over, and it vanishes fairly quickly. All the other impediments are quite minor: "Summer" is chiefly concerned with Esther's attempts to attract John Truitt, her next-door neighbor; "Autumn" momentarily complicates matters when Tootie tells Esther a lie about John; "Winter" deals with the problem of who will escort Rose and Esther to the Christmas dance; and "Spring" is nothing more than a cheerful coda, in which all the characters meet at the fair. In all four episodes, the father's entry from the outside world operates like a leitmotif, bringing with it a sense of potential disruption or disharmony. Meanwhile, everything we see is cleverly linked or integrated. The narrative centers on a cohesive group, passing easily from one domestic problem to another; the music rises out of everyday situations, unobtrusively blending "folksy" tunes with a newly commissioned score; nondiegetic orchestration insinuates itself into quotidian scenes, as when Joan Carroll sings a nasal rendition of "Meet Me in St. Louis" while sneezing and walking around in wet, baggy underclothes; and within individual numbers, relative amateurs like Carroll work in happy unison with professionals like Judy Garland.

The film carefully avoids Hollywood-style production numbers or settings that connote urban entertainment, and at every level it makes disparate elements cohere. The mobile, middle-distance photography and invisible editing create a seamless visual texture; meanwhile, the slightly heightened performing style gives speech a lyrical quality, and directional microphones enable singers to use intimate or "realistic" phrasing. The sound engineering is particularly important to this process of integration. As Geoffrey Nowell-Smith has pointed out, the Hollywood musical was the first place where "different types and sources of sound had to be merged for presentation in a public space."[8] In such films, musical numbers were prerecorded and then lip-synched – a procedure that facilitated performance and assured perfect continuity between shots. The combination of prerecorded song and post-production mixing allowed technicians to adjust the volume and balance of sounds, masking any contradiction between an intimate dramatic setting and a large performance arena. But another, equally important device for achieving coherence between song and story was the set design, which neatly reconciled the competing demands of verisimilitude and fantasy. In the opening sequence of this picture, for example, the doors and windows of the house look out onto a world of painted greenery, and the actors are costumed rather like figures in a showroom. Together with Lemuel Ayers and costumer Irene Sharaff, Minnelli has given the film what Rick Altman calls a "too good to be true" look, so that nostalgia becomes indistinguishable from fashion.

At times, Minnelli's approach is a bit too colorful and cozy, providing all the sentiment and very little of the emotional conviction we can feel in a nonmusical like Capra's *It's a Wonderful Life* (1946). In the crucial scene in which the Smiths express their solidarity by gathering in the parlor to eat dessert and harmonize around the piano, each member of the cast moves with what critic George Toles describes as "Trapp family prescience," as if Minnelli were less interested in the emotional undercurrent than in "the *pictorial* harmony of the completed tableau."⁹ Except in the episodes involving Tootie, Minnelli seems reluctant to explore the psychic lives of his characters, and he never allows us to sense anything like the Victorian murkiness and chill that sometimes invade Capra's film (not to mention Welles's *Magnificent Ambersons*). Throughout, the Smith house is as comfortable as a climate-controlled movie theater, and the rooms are filled with a Technicolored array of antiques that look as if they had come straight from a shop.

But if, as Toles remarks, the artificial setting gives the film an air of "predigested ritual," it also enables the performers to burst more easily into song. The gap between period realism and contemporary musical entertainment is filled by making the Smith house look vaguely like a consumerist utopia. Consider a few of the artifacts in the opening sequence. When Agnes enters the foyer, pausing to sneeze, we glimpse an oriental rug, a gilded mirror, and a silver water pitcher standing on a tray. As she moves to the left, the camera follows, revealing white drapery, a mahogany stairway, two cushiony red chairs, an ornamental umbrella stand, a white doorway with beveled glass panels, and an ebony bust on an ivory pedestal. When she goes marching and singing up the stairs, the camera tilts and pans along the banister, showing off a mammoth painting in a gold frame, a pair of delicate wrought-iron gas lamps, and a sunny, stained-glass window. Reaching a landing, she is viewed from on high as she passes a handsome grandfather clock; then she steps up to the second floor hallway, where she walks along parquet floors, passing white gauze curtains and household plants standing in pillared vases. Cut to the interior of the large, porcelain-and-wood bathroom, where Grandpa Prophater stands before a semicircular, stained-glass window that admits light through a pattern of blue and gold panes. When he spryly dances into his bedroom, we are confronted with a virtual exhibition hall of Victorian crafts and manufacture, expressive of his boyish fantasies: a pair of crossed duelling swords, a display of antique pistols, a huge painting of a sailing ship, a carved wooden bedstead, a gold spittoon, several mahogany cabinets, an ornamental fireplace with a gilded clock on the mantel, and a mirrored valet covered with eccentric hats.

MGM's decoration was inspired in part by Sally Benson's sketches, which depend a great deal on loving descriptions of late-Victorian furnishings. The film, however, has a different effect. Here, for instance, is Benson's account of Rose entering the house on a day in June:

> She got up and went into the front hall. It was dark and cool and smelled of the wax that Katie used to polish the parquet floor, which was dotted with Oriental scatter rugs. Against the left wall was an upright piano with an elaborately carved front faced with a square of green baize. The baize was punctured with holes where the children had pushed their fingers through it. There was a piano stool covered with green velvet and green-and-rose brocaded satin porters hung in the wide doorway that led to the parlor. Beside the doorway was a heavy, round mahogany table on which was set a Tiffany glass bowl and a silver card tray filled with calling cards. In the back of the hall, on another table, was a Sheffield water-cooler lined with porcelain; a silver goblet was under the faucet.[10]

The house in the story is luxurious, but also dark, heavy, and marked with wear. One detail in the passage above is especially important in securing a realist effect: the green baize on the upright piano, which is "punctured with holes where the children poked their fingers through it." Nothing in MGM's decor corresponds to this technique; on the contrary, the film takes every opportunity to brighten the settings, giving them an almost Venetian sense of color and ornamental flourish. In Benson's stories, for example, we are told that the large front bedroom shared by Esther and Rose "was an elegant room, with pale-blue wallpaper which was striped with silver, and glossy bird's-eye-maple furniture, a chaise lounge, and white ruffled curtains tied with pale-blue bows."[11] In the film, some of this color scheme has been retained, but Esther and Rose have a gilded, wrought-iron bedstead shaped like the curving neck of a swan. Their mirrored dressing table is suitable for a movie star, fringed in blue satin and covered with elegant bottles of perfume. Meanwhile, a couple of delicate, handcrafted lamps in the background (apparently powered by electricity) give off a warm, indirect light.

The Freed unit musicals were, of course, never intended to disguise their origins in a studio, and the shiny commodities visible everywhere in *Meet Me in St. Louis* help to synthesize the ordinary with the extraordinary, assuring that a vision of the past will properly integrate with the musical numbers. To make the fit between setting and music still more coherent, the film cleverly mixes old songs with new, using sleekly modern orchestrations and arrangements to "quote" earlier conventions. A certifiable antique like "Skip to My Loo" is played for an *Oklahoma!*-style square dance in the Smith's living room, but Hugh Martin and Ralph Blane give the song additional lyrics and a swing rhythm, so that it verges on forties-style jitterbug. Conversely, "The Boy Next Door" is performed in waltz time, and "The Trolley Song," which became a major hit in 1944, uses a contemporary musical idiom to nostalgically celebrate an early form of mass transit.

Minnelli's staging of the musical sequences is beautifully appropriate to the film's general aims. He adds a dimension of theatrical self-consciousness or wit, encouraging the audience to suspend disbelief and accept a whole range of implausible effects; as a result, *Meet Me in St. Louis* becomes a kind of masquerade rather than a straightforward attempt to reproduce the past. The set dressings occasionally underline this sense of deliberate artificiality. For example, when Judy Garland and Lucille Bremer sing a duet to the title song, Minnelli composes a tilted, low-angle shot that balances their two profiles against an alabaster sculpture atop the family piano. At the lower right of the screen, Garland leans over Bremer's shoulder to harmonize, and at the upper left we see an art nouveau piece representing the head and shoulders of a pair of androgynous lovers, with the male figure standing behind the woman and bending over to kiss her neck. The sculpture adds a note of eroticism to an already sexy scene (Garland and Bremer have long, elaborately coiffed hair and are costumed in slips and satin smocks, rather like chorus girls of the gay nineties), but it also functions in much the same way as the tintype illustrations that introduce each major episode, showing art in the process of imitating art.

If Minnelli's style makes the old seem playfully modern, it also enables Judy Garland to look mature while she plays an ingenue. This strategy must have pleased Garland, whom the studio was reluctantly allowing to grow up. As Richard Dyer has noted, her "belting" and "torchy" renditions of pop tunes were usually in excess of the small-town values she embodied,[12] and MGM seems to have thought that the key to her stardom lay in this disparity between her looks and her singing style. In *The Wizard of Oz* and throughout the late thirties, she had been required to wear girlish clothes and tight bindings across her breasts. She was understandably reluctant to perpetuate this image, and at first she resisted being cast in *Meet Me in St. Louis;* ultimately, however, the film manages to diminish the contrast between her age and her performance. (One year later, she appeared in "The Great Lady Has an Interview," a song-and-dance number Minnelli directed for *Ziegfeld*

Follies; photographed in a bravura long take, she parodied the studio's most regal actress, Greer Garson.)

The Esther we meet in Sally Benson's stories is still an adolescent, but in the film she is more like a romantic lead. At one point, when Rose remarks that "men don't like the bloom rubbed off," Esther looks wryly into a mirror and complains, "Personally, I think I have too much bloom." Throughout the story, she displays a good deal of self-reliance and pep, together with a serious, rather maternal quality (Dyer calls her the "Miss Fix-It" of the household); and because she performs all the important musical numbers, she is easily mistaken for the oldest of the Smith children. Garland's looks and singing style add to the impression of maturity. Her long hair is dyed a glamorous strawberry blond, and, except in "The Trolley Song," she never belts out a tune. In this context, the somewhat halting vibrato in her bell-like voice signifies an exquisite yearning for an experience beyond the confines of the house. Her rendition of "Over the Bannister Leaning" is a lovely but amusing pastiche (she is singing the man's part of the song), in which she behaves like a modern young woman who is playing a role; meanwhile, "The Boy Next Door" and "Have Yourself a Merry Little Christmas" are wistful, melancholic numbers, performed in a contemplative register. The latter song is in fact the most downbeat, ironic Christmas carol ever written for the movies – and its clever fusion of dramatic dialogue with orchestral melody makes Garland seem almost world-weary.

With Garland, Minnelli puts innocence in quotation marks, employing a stylish *faux naïveté* similar to that in *Cabin in the Sky;* with Margaret O'Brien, however, he problematizes the very idea of innocence. O'Brien is obviously a child prodigy, but her rather mannered, theatrical gestures barely conceal her involuntary emotions and her slightly awkward movements. In the cakewalk number, for example, her cuteness is mixed with uncertainty and overwrought glee, exactly like a child who is showing off for grownups. Here as everywhere else, she is the antithesis of Shirley Temple, not only because she seems less weirdly accomplished, but also because she delights in forbidden games. Robin Wood has observed that her performance foreshadows the demonic children of seventies horror movies; it introduces a certain Freudian element into the film, and it gives the Halloween episode an unusually forbidding quality.[13]

This is not to suggest that O'Brien is destructive of the picture's more general aims. As Altman has noted, the folk musical nearly always has a "melodramatic syntax" and a "residue of uneasiness which cannot be assimilated to the glowing vision of the past."[4] Indeed the classic cinema as a whole (somewhat like Shakespearean drama) depends on a mixture of generic conventions that unsettle without really threatening a sense of dramatic unity. Russian theorist Adrian Piotrovsky, writing at the beginning of the sound period, noticed a similar principle at work in all of the best Hollywood movies: "The combination of melodramatic and even tragic situations and the constant switching from the happy to the serious," he wrote, "constitute such a triumphant denial of sentimentalism and one-track emotion that those of us who are searching for paths toward dialectical form have something to learn from it."[5] Where *Meet Me in St. Louis* is concerned, the movement from musical comedy to Gothic horror actually serves to enhance the emotional, generational, and seasonal rhythm, making the happy ending seem inevitable and appropriate.

Here we might note that Tootie Smith is crucial to the plot of the film at only one juncture, when her attack on a family of "snow people" motivates Mr. Smith to change his plans about moving to New York. Somewhat earlier, she causes a momentary rift between Esther and the boy next door, but most of the time she is neither a protagonist nor an antagonist, neither a hero's companion nor a villain's accomplice. Notice, too, that although her biggest scenes occur in autumnal and wintry darkness, when the Smiths are threatened by devilish anarchy and the possibility of leaving town for good, Tootie is seldom a rebel against convention. Her favorite city is St. Louis, and in some respects she is the most conservative character of them all. Far from criticizing MGM's optimistic scenario, she and her sister Agnes function like the image of damaged green baize in the passage I have quoted from Sally Benson's prose: a realistic effect, they make the film's sentiment much more convincing. Minnelli himself makes a similar point in his autobiography, where he describes *Meet Me in St. Louis* as a "sentimental mood piece," and then remarks that the Halloween sequence, with its "wistful longing for horror," is "the type of fantasy that real children, raised on the grimmest of Grimm's fairy tales, would have."[6]

Like children out of Mark Twain, Tootie and Agnes are preoccupied with murder and mortality, and they provide an amusingly sinister counterpoint to the straightlaced adults. A feeling of preadolescent Grand Guignol enters the film early on, when Agnes walks through the kitchen looking for her cat: Katie teases her, claiming the animal has been tossed down the cellar stairs, where its "spine cracked on every step." Agnes flashes into anger: "If you killed her, I'll kill you! I'll stab you to death in your sleep and then I'll tie you between two wild horses till you're pulled apart!" A few minutes later, Tootie reveals a similarly morbid imagination. She is first seen riding

Figure 9. The father as a menace to the family. Joan Carroll, Harry Davenport, Mary Astor, Lucille Bremer, Leon Ames, and Judy Garland in *Meet Me in St. Louis*. (© 1944, Turner Entertainment Co., all rights reserved.)

Figure 10. The reversal of age and gender. Darryl Hickman and Margaret O'Brien in the Halloween sequence of *Meet Me in St. Louis*. (© 1944, Turner Entertainment Co., all rights reserved.)

down the street in the back of the neighborhood ice wagon, singing "Brighten the Corner Where You Are" and boasting proudly about St. Louis. Her energetic conversation with the driver, Mr. Neeley (Chill Wills), is littered with non sequiturs, but at one point she elicits a mild shock by remarking that her rag doll, Margaretha, suffers from "four fatal diseases" and "won't live through the night." As the story develops, her mischievous allusions to illness, alcoholism, violence, and death create a disconcerting contrast to MGM's lavish settings and Margaret O'Brien's own dimpled charm. To heighten this irony, the later parts of the film will revise Benson's fiction, making Tootie – not Agnes – the center of interest during Halloween.

The high point in *Meet Me in St. Louis* and one of the most striking moments in Minnelli's career, the Halloween episode follows beautifully on summertime, which ends with a spectacular shot designed to convey the season at its peak: Judy Garland singing the last notes of "The Trolley Song" while surrounded by a chorus of women in brightly colored chapeaus and beribboned costumes. Hatless and dressed in black, Garland appears to be standing in the midst of a huge floral arrangement, but almost as soon as the impression registers it fades into darkness. When the screen lightens, we see a tintype view of the Smith house in autumn. The tintype then dissolves into a nighttime shot of the house silhouetted against an inky blue sky, its "eyes" emitting an orange glow like a mountainous Jack O'Lantern. Another dissolve takes us upstairs, where Agnes and Tootie are putting the final touches on their Halloween costumes. Minnelli's camera pans across the room, beginning with a close-up of a death's-head mask and ending on the eager faces of the two girls. Lit by candlelight and dressed in old clothes from the family attic, Agnes excitedly tells Esther about the prospect of terrorizing a neighbor named Mr. Brokauff – an epic villain who is purportedly guilty of poisoning cats and burning them at midnight in his furnace. According to Tootie, Brokauff also beats his wife with a red-hot poker and fills his cellar with empty whiskey bottles. She and Agnes plan to confront him, disguised as a "drunken ghost" and a "horrible ghost."

As the girls parade through the kitchen in their costumes, Katie reacts in mock surprise: "Who are these *boys?*" she asks, causing Tootie to burst into uncontrollable laughter. Grandpa Prophater – an eternal child – advises them to wet the flour they are carrying, so it will be "harder for the victim to get off." When the girls venture outside, however, we leave the adult world partly behind, and Minnelli brilliantly exploits costume, color, and camera movement to produce a kind of neurotic beauty. Viewed from the camera crane, the scene evokes a swirling delirium and an ecstasy of potential violence. A bonfire of cast-off furniture has been set ablaze in the midst of the street, and young Darryl Hickman – his lower half dressed like a fat washerwoman, his upper half like a Bowery toughguy – stands near the inferno, directing raids on the neighborhood. "Take the Brokauffs!" he orders, but the kids back away: "Oh, no! We ain't gonna take the Brokauffs!"

A carnival or *Walpurgisnacht,* Halloween momentarily inverts the patriarchal and heterosexual values of the film, confusing genders and setting domestic property afire. Watching all this from her front porch, Tootie wears a floppy business suit, wire-rimmed glasses, and a rat's nose with long gray whiskers dangling from the nostrils; she is supposed to represent a "horrible ghost," but she looks more like a comic businessman or a parody of her father. When she and Agnes move cautiously toward the bonfire, the other children fall silent, trying to make out the two figures approaching through the gloom. Minnelli pans across a row of sinister but colorful masks, conveying the fear that hovers behind the group's bragadoccio. Agnes and Tootie, equally fearful, lower their disguises, and the tension suddenly dissolves. Greetings are exchanged, and Hickman leaps back into action, commanding the destruction of everything in sight: "Pull down their house!" he yells to a departing group. "Pull down their fence and kill 'em all!"

Tootie is the youngest figure, trying to assert her importance but always being relegated to the fringes of the action. She keeps circling the bonfire, crying, "Let me help! Let me help!" as the other kids eagerly hurl furniture into the billowing flames. Finally, desperately wanting to "kill" grownups, she volunteers for the most dangerous mission. "I'll take the Brokauffs!" she shouts. Hickman, who seems unwilling to take such a chance himself, reluctantly agrees: "All right. But if you don't hit Mr. Brokauff in the face with flour and say, 'I hate you,' the banshees will haunt you forever!"

Minnelli shows Tootie's lonely journey to the Brokauffs in a spectacular long take, with the camera tracking backward down the street, observing her unmasked face as she walks along clutching her bag of flour. The bonfire slowly recedes into the distance, becoming a companionate glow, and the windswept night closes in. A whinnying horse startles Tootie, but she keeps marching forward, terrified and courageous, until she reaches a drab house near the fringe of the neighborhood. Stepping up to the porch, she kneels beside a window and peers inside, where she can see the burly Mr. Brokauff, his bulldog, and his wife sitting in a rather cold living room. Like a youthful David, she steels herself and rings the doorbell. After a torturous pause, the door opens to reveal Mr. Brokauff in his shirtsleeves, accompanied by the bulldog. "I *hate* you, Mr. Brokauff!" Tootie cries halfheartedly, and she flings a handful of flour up at his face. "Burrr!" Mr. Brokauff growls, but after Tootie runs off, a close-up shows him wiping away the flour, shaking his head, and smiling. He then looks down at his dog, who is licking the spilled flour off of the doorsill.

The camera tracks backward at an accelerated pace as Tootie runs frantically down the street, her coattails flapping in the wind. Reaching the safety of the bonfire, she leans dizzily against a lamppost while Agnes and several other kids gather around. "I killed him!" Tootie exults, the camera craning back from her as she gazes in orgiastic wonder at the sky. Astonished, the garishly costumed crowd begins to praise her courage. "Tootie is the most powerful!" Agnes proclaims, and Hickman offers an old chair. "Here," he says, "Throw that on the fire!" Proudly, almost hysterically, Tootie adds fuel to the blaze, cheerfully shouting "I'm the most horrible! I'm the most horrible!" as the camera cranes up and away from the scene.

The sequence is much more dramatically complex and theatrical than Sally Benson's story, where Agnes's status as the "most horrible" is solemnly and quietly acknowledged by the other members of the Smith household. Like most horror movies, it reveals a dark impulse behind an innocent surface, allowing repressed violence to break garishly into a bourgeois setting. Without sacrificing its essential charm, it also suggests a deeper, more troubling critique of "normal" values. After all, the most disturbing thing about Halloween on Kensington Avenue is not Minnelli's spooky mise-en-scène, nor the fact that kids are wreaking vengeance on grownups. What makes the sequence truly unusual is its portrayal of a sinister group psychology. Despite its gentle humor and its lovely autumn colors, it shows Tootie being initiated into what Stephen Harvey has called a "savage conformity."[7]

Benson treats the story differently, centering on Agnes's strength of will when she throws flour at "Mr. Waughop." By changing the man's name to Brokauff, the film hints more strongly at xenophobia or anti-Semitism, and by making Tootie the protagonist, it emphasizes a child's need to gain approval from her community. Tootie becomes a perverse citizen, and Brokauff – a mysterious middle European who lives in a relatively barren house at the end of the street – becomes a demonic "other." In a single, wordless shot, we learn that Brokauff is in fact a rather kindly fellow who is the object of childhood fantasies; as a result, Tootie's behavior when she returns to her companions becomes troubling, and the bonfire takes on ugly implications. In 1944, audiences had seen pictures of Nazis tossing books into similar conflagrations. Not by accident, Minnelli would return to the same image later in his career; the fire in the middle of Kensington Avenue resembles another, more overtly threatening blaze in *Tea and Sympathy,* his 1956 film about middle-class prejudice.

The bonfire is a unique moment, opening the story to the kind of issues that Hollywood musicals usually avoided. But notice that Tootie also becomes a would-be murderer twice more: first when one of her Halloween pranks almost causes a trolley accident, and second when she decapitates a family of snow people in the back yard. Her behavior on these occasions is truly iconoclastic, aimed at the film's most cherished symbols; and yet both scenes are presented indirectly, as if to shield the audience from too much unpleasantness. The attack on the trolley is reported rather than shown, and when Esther learns about it, her anger at Tootie dissolves into laughter. The more disturbing assault on the snow people is also presented with a certain discretion. The scene is prompted by Judy Garland's impressive rendition of "Have Yourself a Merry Little Christmas," which is sung as a lullabye to the teary-eyed Margaret O'Brien; but Minnelli stages Tootie's frightening tantrum in a long shot, keeping us slightly removed from the child's grief and rage. Moreover, as James Agee observed when he reviewed the film on its initial release, the emotional force of her actions is somewhat diminished by the snow figures themselves, which are disappointingly fake.[18] (The winter episode as a whole lacks a believable outdoor atmosphere, probably because MGM in this period was never very good at making artificial snow; in any case, except for a few exterior shots elsewhere in the film, Minnelli seems unconcerned with the palpable effects of weather that were so important to directors like Ford or Capra, who worked at other studios.)

If the killing of the snow people is nonetheless unsettling, that is because it confronts us with a believable situation in which a child takes revenge on her family. Then, too, O'Brien's performance is highly naturalistic. Whatever one thinks of the set or the camera angles, it is difficult not to be swept away by Tootie's unrelenting tears and convulsive violence. No less than Griffith, Minnelli was alive to the powerful effects generated by an ostensibly innocent figure who suffers a severe psychological trauma, and he directed two of the most impressive weeping scenes involving child actors in the history of Hollywood. The first is here, and the next (no doubt prompted by his memory of O'Brien) is in *The Courtship of Eddie's Father* (1963), where Ron Howard becomes hysterical at the sight of a dead goldfish. In both films, the child in question is overwrought and histrionic, as if she or he were trying hard to act like an adult; in both, the performance conveys what V. F. Perkins has described as an unstable "emotional balance";[19] and in both, a barely repressed emotional life spills over its bounds, disrupting an apparently placid domestic situation.

The remarkably somber, minor-key Christmas song that precedes this scene has predicted that "next year all your troubles will be out of sight." But Tootie is unable to accept such easy consolation. A passionate admirer of St. Louis, she will brook no change, and if she must move, she will take all of her dolls with her, "even the dead ones." Standing among the broken snow people, she makes us aware of the fragility of life on Kensington Avenue. The Christmas song has alluded to a "Golden Age" which is re-ceeding as she grows up, and for a moment *Meet Me in St. Louis* becomes a true pastoral. On the surface, the child is fearful of moving to a new town; at bottom, however, she is being forced to confront a deeper fear: the inevitability of adulthood. Time and death, which have preoccupied Tootie from the beginning, have begun to acquire a new meaning.

After establishing this feeling of transience and anxiety, the film quickly banishes all sorrow, allowing the audience to regress to a more comfortable mood. The Smith family preserves their golden world, experiencing progress without fundamental change and growth without sacrifice. From an upstairs window, Mr. Smith witnesses Tootie's attack on the snow people, and suddenly recognizes the chaos he has wrought. After pondering the situation (and burning his hand while trying to light a cigar), he summons everyone into the parlor, where he irritably vows to keep the family in St. Louis "until we rot." Jubilation breaks out, and Rose's estranged beau makes a sudden entrance, angrily and impulsively declaring his love. As usual, Mr. Smith looks bewildered, but the film's only remaining problem has been neatly solved. "The First Noel" begins playing in the background, Mrs. Smith sheds tears of joy, and the family gathers around a Christmas tree as if at a homecoming.

The image once again dissolves into a new season, returning us to a circular conception of time and fulfilling the promise of the Christmas song. (All this is prefigured in the choreography at the Christmas party, where Esther waltzes off in the arms of her grandfather, only to disappear momentarily behind the Christmas tree and emerge from the other side in the arms of the boy next door.) It is now springtime, and in one of George Folsey's most lovely shots, we see the family stepping out of their house and climbing aboard a horse-drawn carriage. Wearing Easter finery and photographed in a gauzy, sunlit style that suggests an impressionist painting, they drive off to see the opening of the St. Louis exposition. As Stephen Harvey has noted, wartime restrictions on sets forced MGM to economize on the design of the fair;[20] the idyllic glow of the film's conclusion is achieved entirely through our memory of the Smith women, dressed almost as spendidly as the figures in a Ziegfield revue, descending the sloping stairs of their own front yard. But then *Meet Me in St. Louis* has always been a film about the domestication of spectacle, and its meaning lies in the way it turns a vision of home into an ideal entertainment.

Significantly, when Judy Garland finally arrives at the fair, she looks around and marvels at how the entire world has been brought to her doorstep. Don Taylor offers a counterargument, remarking that he liked the place better "when it was a swamp and there was just the two of us." (He is referring to a Rogers and Hammerstein number, "Boys and Girls Together," which Minnelli staged on an indoor set representing an undeveloped swampland. The song had been deleted from *Oklahoma!,* and for reasons of length it was also cut from *Meet Me in St. Louis.*) For Garland, however, the true Eden is more like what I have described as "third nature." She marvels that "We didn't have to come here on a train or stay in a hotel." Time and space have been conquered, and a vast display of modern commodities can be seen "right here in our home town." With this self-reflexive gesture, *Meet Me in St. Louis* neatly closes the gap between nostalgia and progress. Death is kept at bay, women remain at home, and the past is both preserved and improved upon. The world has become a theme park, and every contradiction between town and country has been resolved by the movies themselves.

4

Comedy, Patriarchy, Consumerism

Father of the Bride (1950)

A crudely oversimplified list of Great Moments in American Film Comedy might suggest that the history of the genre recapitulates the development of individuals in the society. The first important phase of comic films in Hollywood is usually associated with anarchic, polymorphous figures like Chaplin and Keaton, who worked in a period before cinema acquired speech; the second phase belongs largely to Paramount farceurs like Ernst Lubitsch and Mae West, who specialized in talking pictures about randy, barely monogamous characters; the third phase is the heyday of "screwball comedy," a subgenre that involves the rituals of courtship and marriage; and the fourth phase, occurring at the end of the classic studio system, consists mainly of "realistic" films about domesticity, foreshadowing the rise of TV sitcoms.

But this neat historical pattern is misleading. Behind the different types of comedy, most of which combine and overlap with one another in complex ways, there is a single, dominant form, running from Chaplin, Griffith, and Capra down to John Hughes and Tim Burton. It might be described as a "sentimental" or "weeping" tradition, and its origins can be traced at least as far back as the leading playwrights of early-eighteenth-century England, especially to figures like Colley Cibber and Richard Steele, who were working in opposition to the aristocratic tastes of the Restoration. These playwrights were considered "realistic" because they represented the interests of the bourgeoisie rather than those of the court; "sentimental" because they valued goodness and generosity over cleverness and trickery; and "weepy" because they elicited joyful tears in place of ribald laughter. Compared with their predecessors, they were relatively puritanical, and perhaps excessively domestic; nevertheless, we cannot condemn them without bringing ourselves under critical scrutiny. As Raymond Williams has pointed out, the Restoration wits and rakes belonged to "an artificially protected social class," whereas the dramatists who emerged in their wake lived in a world where the consequences of most actions had to be fully lived out.[1] Because we still live in such a world, the stress on good-heartedness and fellow-feeling in both sentimental comedy and most types of bourgeois melodrama has continued to shape our moral standards.

At any rate, whatever genealogy one might construct for classical Hollywood comedy, it seems clear that nearly all of Vincente Minnelli's contributions belong to a sentimental mode and to a specific historical situation. Most of his comic pictures are products of the Truman and Eisenhower years, when American entertainment was filled with idealized but increasingly precarious visions of family life. His most amusing work is centered in the home, although he deals with an entirely modern, consumerized form of domesticity. His leading characters tend to be married or widowed, inhabiting MGM's WASPish, squeaky-clean world of steadfast fathers, loving mothers, obedient children, and sumptuous material possessions. They have occasional traumas or nightmares, but in the end they remain the well-adjusted representatives of a society Minnelli would treat more neurotically in his melodramas. What gives this comic universe a distinctive tone is its unusually close proximity to both the melodrama and the musical. Minnelli deals humorously with psychic tensions inside the family, but his work seems lyricized or utopian, enlivened by full-dress parties or festive occasions. Again and again, he invests domestic settings with an air of theatricality, transforming everyday life into a show.

The definitive example of Minnelli's approach is *Father of the Bride,* a gently satiric vision of suburban Americana, somewhat reminiscent of the beautified treatment of "ordinary" folk in *Meet Me in St. Louis* and *The Clock.* Based on a popular novel by Edward Streeter (for which MGM paid the year's record price of a hundred thousand dollars), *Father* starred Spencer Tracy and Elizabeth Taylor, two of the most important celebrities of the decade. Swiftly and wittily adapted by Francis Goodrich and Albert Hackett (who had earlier worked with Minnelli on *The Pirate*), the entire film was shot in a mere twenty-eight days. It earned more than four times its investment, giving birth to a sequel, appropriately titled *Father's Little Dividend,* and then to a short-lived television series. In a variety of ways, it also influenced most of Minnelli's subsequent comedies, including *The Long, Long Trailer, Designing Woman, The Reluctant Debutante,* and *The Courtship of Eddie's Father.*

A certifiable classic of American popular culture, *Father of the Bride* has been quoted more than once by talented directors of a later generation. In

Peter Bogdanovich's *The Last Picture Show* (1971), a group of east Texas teenagers watches a rerun of the film in a dilapidated, nearly deserted theater; the teenagers are impressed with what they see, but the gulf separating their world from the one on the screen is so vast that the old MGM movie might as well have been shot on the moon. In Martin Scorsese's *Raging Bull* (1980), Jake LaMotta asks his wife where she has been all day, and she tells him she went out to see *Father of the Bride* – an allusion that calls ironic attention to Scorsese and Robert De Niro's Method-inspired naturalism. Other directors have tried a somewhat different approach, dealing with the same material as *Father of the Bride,* but treating it in demythified fashion. Consider *A Wedding* (1978), Robert Altman's cynical, improvised satire of the new rich in Chicago; or *Betsy's Wedding* (1989), Alan Alda's wry depiction of a real-estate developer in New England; or *True Love* (1990), Nancy Savoca's bittersweet, neorealist account of marriage among working-class Italians – where, for once, the story is told from the point of view of the bride rather than that of the father.

At the opposite extreme, postmodern cinema's most conservative attempt to return to *Father of the Bride* is the Disney studio's hugely successful 1991 remake, scripted by Nancy Meyers and Charles Shyer and directed by Shyer. Advertised as a "comedy about letting go," the Disney version transposes the original picture into a contemporary setting, as if the world had never changed. It retains much of the original Hackett and Goodrich script, sometimes reproducing whole sequences shot for shot; ultimately, however, it demonstrates the superior intelligence of Minnelli and his collaborators. Where the first film was superbly cast, the remake features two stars who work against the grain of their usual personae. Where the first film was quiet and gracefully underplayed, the remake is noisy and emphatic, filled with huge close-ups and schmaltzy appropriations of sixties rock and roll. Where the first film offered a mildly pointed, somewhat Freudian commentary on middle-class fatherhood, the remake tries to be as inoffensive as possible, smoothing over potential anxieties and reducing the protagonist to a cartoon.

This is not the place to undertake an extended comparison of the two versions of *Father of the Bride,* but the Disney company's awkward attempts to capture the spirit of the original picture are in certain ways instructive, revealing a good deal about the formal imperatives of Minnelli's style. To begin with, the remake helps to underline the importance of the casting of Spencer Tracy in the original movie. It seems doubtful that anyone else, then or now, could have been remotely as good in this particular role – although, surprisingly, Minnelli claims in his autobiography that the studio almost chose another actor. From the beginning it was clear that Elizabeth Taylor would play the bride; and after Hedy Lamarr rejected the role of the mother, MGM wisely chose Joan Bennett, on the grounds of her slight resemblance to Taylor. But the new production chief, Dore Schary, nearly wrecked the project by casually promising the leading part to Jack Benny, apparently because Schary thought a comic story about a man who has to pay huge sums of money for his daughter's wedding might be suitable for Benny's cheapskate persona and vaudeville talent.

The Disney company made the same decision that Schary almost made: it chose a standup comic rather than a dramatic realist. At various points in the 1991 film, Steve Martin tries to behave in subdued fashion, but at bottom he remains a professional wise guy, a specialist in send-ups of square characters. An expert at winking at the audience from behind his mask, he seems unconvincing or flat in the serious moments, and he overplays everything that calls for a delicate response. An example of his obviousness is the scene in which the father patches up a quarrel between the engaged couple and then stands uselessly in the background while they hug and kiss. Minnelli informs us that Jack Benny was tested in this scene for the original picture, and that Tracy's low-key, beautifully timed performance of the same business convinced MGM that he was better for the part. In the 1950 version, Tracy registers an attitude of comic helplessness and tries to make a discreet exit; in the corresponding moment of the remake, Steve Martin talks to himself, makes a series of exasperated faces, and pauses for at least three backward glances as he trudges up a stairway.

An even greater problem with the remake is that its central character looks fully at home in late consumer society. Spencer Tracy was a tired commuter in plain brown shoes, but Steve Martin seems more like a sneaker-wearing yuppie who likes to drive a classic sports car. The Disney producers seem not to have realized that the original Hackett–Goodrich script was about a middle-aged and essentially sedentary man who repeatedly loses his dignity; everything in the 1950 version was predicated on the breakdown of this figure's masculine control, which was threatened not only by the loss of his daughter, but also by a "feminine" world of theatricality, emotionalism, and heedless consumerism. In the remake, these issues are represented cautiously, in deference to contemporary feminism, and the father has become a youthful, southern California businessman, completely lacking the seriousness and reserve necessary to every gag Tracy was asked to perform. Tracy's earthy, sometimes clumsy simplicity added charm to his comic routines, and at the same time enhanced the overtly sentimental episodes, enabling the psychoanalytic subtext to do its work without seeming prurient or downright incestuous. Martin creates an entirely different effect. Trimly built, handsomely groomed, stylishly dressed, he looks the romantic equal of the man his daughter is about to marry. Hence the father–daughter relationship (including a series of one-on-one basketball games in the driveway) becomes unintentionally suggestive, and the film is deprived of its most important source of humor.

Tracy was in fact everywhere crucial to *Father of the Bride*'s complex ideology. As Stanley Banks, the beleaguered paterfamilias who narrates the story and performs most of the action, he demonstrates an unusual ability to negotiate seamless transitions between satire, slapstick, and sentiment. The farthest remove from the obtuse and somewhat authoritarian father played by Leon Ames in *Meet Me in St. Louis,* he seems foolish without being insensitive and helpless without being ineffectual. From the moment we first see him – slumped in a chair, emptying confetti from one of his shoes, and warning the men in the audience to beware of their daughters' weddings – he conveys a mixture of strength and self-deprecating irony. He wears a cutaway coat and is surrounded by empty champagne bottles, but he ties his shoelaces with the thick, weathered hands of the Portugese fisherman he once acted in *Captains Courageous.* He plays a conservative professional, but his sweetly humorous Irishness gives him a populist touch. Throughout the film, his sheltered and somewhat complacent daughter calls him "Pops," and hardly a scene goes by in which he does not become the butt of a joke; nevertheless, he has strength and presence, and because he balances these qualities with gentleness and an apparent lack of vanity, he helps the film negotiate a delicate compromise: the father might be a clown, but he remains the embodiment of paternalistic values.

Jack Benny would probably have conveyed the requisite dignity for the original movie, but he was a shade too effeminate, unable to communicate the gender codes that had been written into the father's role. Already possessed of a highly theatrical and comic technique, he also lacked what Minnelli described as "conviction" in the purely dramatic moments. Thus when Dore Schary offered Benny the part, Minnelli and producer Pandro Berman desperately explained to Schary that their project was "based on a real situation."[2] As Berman put it, *Father* was a " 'comedy drama about a man whose heart breaks because he loves his daughter and is about to lose her. It's not a joke. It's not a funny thing. The laughs come out of sadness and reality. We could never do it with Jack.' "[3]

To get a sense of how MGM might have treated the theme of money and marriage in a form somewhat better suited to a vaudeville and radio performer like Benny, one needs only to view the commercial videotape of

Father, which in its present version is prefaced by a "Pete Smith Specialty" entitled "Wedding Bells." Using a smirking, voice-of-God narrator, this short film tells the story of an ardent bridegroom who goes broke when he has to purchase a ring, a license, a minister, a honeymoon, and a new apartment. The impoverished hero suffers through a slapstick encounter with his rich in-laws, and when he returns from the honeymoon in Niagra Falls, all the new appliances in his apartment go berserk, spraying food around the kitchen.

Compared with Minnelli's work, "Wedding Bells" seems almost Brechtian. Indeed most forms of pure comedy have something in common with Brecht, because they induce a feeling of subversive distanciation, either through broadly expressive performance techniques or through presentational devices that put the theatrical machinery on show. Generally speaking, the favorite theme of comedy is the "failure" of performance, or the chaotic disruption of decorum and protocol. In most types of so-called high comedy, the characters are clever manipulators of social masks who peek through their roles, sharing a joke with the audience; in low comedy – as in "Wedding Bells" – they are clownishly inept or awkward, always slipping on banana peels at dignified moments. Either way, comic acting and the staging of comic material depend on a special form of expressive incoherence – a technique designed to ridicule the artificial "fronts" people maintain in both serious theater and everyday life.[4]

Stanley Banks in *Father of the Bride* is situated somewhere between the high and low extremes, but he belongs more to the second category than to the first. What complicates matters still more is that he is also a noncomic character. As I have suggested in previous chapters, all the MGM pictures to which Minnelli was assigned had a relatively shifting, mixed quality; at bottom, they were attempts to bridge disparate styles, achieving an "integrated" form. Their ultimate goal was exactly opposite from the "radical separation of elements" Brecht had proposed for the epic theater – opposite, too, from the sheer anarchy of performers like Buster Keaton, the Marx Brothers, or Monty Python. Hence the relationship between jokes and story in Minnelli's comic films is similar to the relationship between numbers and story in his musicals; everything is narrativized or plausibly motivated by the plot. By the same token, everything depends on actors who can fully inhabit their roles, so that the story will move easily from laughter to pathos. For that reason, Minnelli frequently used "serious" players like Tracy, Gregory Peck, or Glenn Ford, inserting them into sentimental dramas that were filled with slapstick situations.

Father of the Bride is a perfect instance of Minnelli's integrated approach, although it remains a comedy, chiefly because it deals with the quintessentially comic situation of failed theater. At first glance this may seem an odd claim, since the film looks like a straightforward depiction of manners in a postwar American suburb, represented in MGM's exterior shots by a street in Beverly Hills. Stanley Banks gets off a few witticisms (as when he reminds his wife that only two syllables separate "Banks" from "bankruptcy," or when he wryly notes that "trousseau" is a French word meaning "a little bundle the bride carries under her arm for her new home"), but most of the time he strikes us as a plainspoken man of the people. What makes him suitably comic – especially for Minnelli's purposes – is that he becomes involved in a kind of domestic show business. As a guest at the engagement party remarks, the Banks–Dunstan nuptials are a "big theatrical production" in which "the women take over" and the father becomes a stooge or a moneyman.

Of course, the guest is only half right. *Father of the Bride* may have been marketed for a female audience, but it rigorously upholds a male point of view, never allowing the women to "take over" for a minute. The marriage is unquestionably a "big production," calmly and expertly managed by Mrs. Banks and her daughter; once it begins, however, all the members of the family seem determined to observe the roles imposed by their social class, and their mild snobbery turns them all into producers and play actors of a sort. As a result, Minnelli is able to employ many of the skills he had perfected in the Freed unit musicals. He takes the surprising step of completely eschewing a nondiegetic music score, giving the film an exceptionally quiet, almost deadpan atmosphere; nevertheless, in his hands, *Father* becomes a vaguely self-reflexive, behind-the-scenes story of a huge, commodified spectacle. Most of the action is keyed to Spencer Tracy's dry, rather quiet style, but Stanley Banks experiences exactly the same nerve-racking expenditures, embarrassing gaffes, and ultimate triumphs as the Broadway characters in a putting-on-a-show musical like *The Band Wagon*.

Almost from the beginning, the film makes us aware of a certain theatricality in Stanley Banks's daily life. In the opening shot, the camera tracks across a living room, isolating the remnants of a spectacular party, discovering Stanley in an easy chair, his formal costume in disarray. Stanley addresses the audience directly, like an exhausted player relieved to end his performance; as he speaks, a flashback takes us to the days before the wedding, and Minnelli fills the screen with showy images of American success. Stanley is a big-city lawyer who commutes to work from what he describes as the "second-best" area of town, where he and his family "almost own" an enormous Cape Cod house. (He was a prosperous banker in the

Edward Streeter novel, but MGM thought a change of profession would make him more sympathetic to the mass audience.) A brief expository sequence illustrates his weary return home after a typical workday, and at the same time introduces us to his domestic menage, who enter the story like actors taking a bow: his attractive wife, Ellie, who says hello as she rushes off to the local garden club; his two sons, Tommy and Ben (Russ Tamblyn and Frank Orth), who appear and then vanish on teenage errands; his faithful black maidservant, Delilah (Marietta Canty), who takes his hat; and finally his beautiful daughter, Kay, who makes a dramatic entrance down a stairway, wearing jeans and a baggy shirt.

Kay is the most important of these characters, her entrance observed from Stanley's adoring point of view. She sets the plot in motion by uncharacteristically mooning about the house and announcing that she wants to marry a fellow named Buckley. Stanley immediately recalls her many suitors, who appear before us in a comic montage of male stereotypes: a clumsy teenager, a wimpy professor, and a left-wing college student. "I hope it isn't that ham with the shoulders," he thinks, as we see a laughing young man in tennis clothes (Don Taylor). Later that evening, at a genteel family dinner with his wife and daughter, Stanley is unable to shake off his anxieties. "Who is this Buckley, anyway?" he blurts out in the midst of an ice cream dessert. "And what's his last name? I hope it's better than his first one! And where the devil does he come from?" Kay tearfully informs Stanley that Buckley is not only a successful businessman but also the son of the Dunstan family, who are "as good as we are."

Stanley's anger and suspicion are prompted by a fairly obvious Freudian need to keep Kay to himself, and his attempts at maintaining respectability usually end in embarrassment. When Buckley drops by after dinner to take Kay out for a drive, Stanley hovers beside a window in the darkened living room, hoping to "get a peek at this superman" as he comes up the sidewalk. Minnelli emphasizes the theatricality of the occasion by having Tracy step out to the foyer like a player entering from the wings, hastily buttoning his coat and adopting a politely reserved attitude. Stanley remains cool throughout the encounter, and as the young couple is about to leave, he makes a calculated attempt to assert his power; noting the chilly weather outside, he advises Kay to wear her heavy coat. "Oh, Pops, I'd die in that thing!" she says. But when Buckley diplomatically agrees with Stanley, she immediately obeys, moving to the hall closet almost dreamily. "Right then I realized my day was over," Stanley remarks in his offscreen narration. "She'd still love us," he thinks (meaning, of course, himself), "but not in the old way."

In purely comic fashion, the film portrays marriage as an exchange of a female between two men; but at almost the same moment, it begins to poke fun at women, whom it depicts as giddy consumers. When the young couple exits, Ellie seems captivated by the idea that Kay wants to be married: "Oh, she'll make a beautiful bride. She has just the right coloring and figure. I know just the dress she should wear! It was in last month's *Vogue*." From this point onward, Stanley finds himself in a double crisis: as his daughter leaves his orbit, he is drawn into an expensive, increasingly public spectacle that seems to be largely controlled by women. He works hard to perform all the duties of fatherhood, but the situation becomes excruciating. He never becomes stingy or tyrannical, and the generosity of his love for both Kay and Ellie is never in doubt; still, he squirms under the pressure, and he looks increasingly foolish. Again and again, he becomes a "bad actor" who fails to impress an audience of his peers within the film.

We can observe Stanley's failed acting, and at the same time appreciate Tracy's work, if we examine a simple but representative moment. In the almost wordless scene in which Stanley tries on a dress coat left over from his own marriage ceremony, the camera is mounted on a boom, aimed slightly down at Spencer Tracy, who appears to be looking into an offscreen mirror. As Tracy takes the coat out of a box, we hear mothballs spilling onto the floor and rolling across the room. Struggling to make the garment fit, Tracy stoops slightly and makes a slow, 360-degree turn, momentarily pausing while he gingerly slips an arm into a sleeve. When he completes the turn and looks toward the mirror, his body is crouched, his arms bowed, his tongue poking ever so slightly out of his mouth. Carefully straightening himself, he pulls in his stomach, fastens a button across his waist, and proudly surveys his accomplishment.

The film treats this action somewhat differently than does the Goodrich–Hackett script, in which Stanley gets into the coat without much difficulty and Ellie indulges his self-satisfaction. In the film, Minnelli cuts away to a shot of Ellie standing in the hallway, secretly and rather disapprovingly watching Stanley's behavior. When she enters the room, she asks whether he is standing naturally, and she warns, "If that button gives way you're going to put out someone's eye." Much of the humor derives from Tracy's pantomime and Bennett's caustic delivery of her line. But the joke is enhanced by the quiet sound track and by the unmoving, Olympian viewpoint of Minnelli's camera, which tends to emphasize the slow pace of the action. Notice also a single detail of costuming, for which Minnelli can probably be credited. Before slipping on the coat, Tracy dons an elegant top hat, so that we feel a ridiculous incongruity. Without the hat, which is posed at a

Figure 11. The father–daughter romance threatened by marriage. Spencer Tracy, Joan Bennett, and Elizabeth Taylor in *Father of the Bride*. (© 1950, Turner Entertainment Co., all rights reserved.)

Figure 12. Women as consumers. Elizabeth Taylor, Joan Bennett, and Spencer Tracy in *Father of the Bride*. (© 1950, Turner Entertainment Co., all rights reserved.)

dapper, slightly rakish angle, Tracy's performance might seem mildly amusing; with it, he looks truly funny, like Mr. Hyde trying to masquerade as Dr. Jekyll.

Nearly all of the comic episodes in the film work according to this logic, implicating Stanley in a series of ludicrous attempts to play a role. I list a few of them here:

1. After a nearly sleepless night during which he wakes up Ellie by thrashing around in his bed like a wounded gorilla, Stanley becomes worried that Buckley is nothing more than a confidence man (or an actor) who "might put a bullet in the back of your head and never turn a hair." He decides to stage a man-to-man chat, hoping to discover as much as he can about the prospective bridegroom's income. First he establishes a proper front by stationing himself in a leather easy chair beside a burning hearth in his living room, lighting a pipe, and putting on a great show of paternal solicitude. Buckley arrives at the appointed moment and sits in a rigid, military posture, placing a briefcase on the coffee table and politely offering to answer any questions. Caught off guard, Stanley covers his nervousness by launching into a monologue about his own marriage and early struggles. A dissolve shows the ashtray beside his chair filling up with matches; an hour has passed, and we see Buckley struggling to stay awake while Stanley drones on, accounting for every penny he ever earned.

2. Stanley and his wife are invited to dinner with Buckley's parents, who live in a more resplendent house than Stanley's own, with a white maid. Things go reasonably well at first. The two couples exchange flattery and polite lies, but then Stanley tries to ease his tension by downing several martinis and a great deal of wine. Growing ebullient and woozy, he monopolizes conversation with long-winded stories about his daughter. When he finally gives the Dunstans an opportunity to speak, he falls asleep over his after-dinner brandy.

3. Stanley organizes a huge engagement party to announce the upcoming wedding. Laying out a tray of martinis for the arriving guests, he plans to enter the living room at an appropriate moment, ringing a silver dinner bell to call attention to his carefully prepared speech. Unfortunately, the guests begin appearing in droves, and they ask for everything but martinis. Stanley is imprisoned in the crowded kitchen for the whole afternoon, mixing drinks and spraying himself whenever he tries to open a bottle of Coke.

4. During a wedding rehearsal at the church, Stanley tries to take command of a motley group of family and friends who show up in the middle of a rainstorm. (The bride arrives late, and neither the groom nor the minister is present.) Excited and nervous, he frets about the choreography: "I'm sure you want this to come off perfect," he shouts to the scattered crowd of friends and relatives standing around in wet raingear, most of whom ignore him. "We'll stick here even if it takes all night!" Pringle, the minister's assistant, officiously and briskly runs everyone through their paces, leaving Stanley so befuddled that he can't master the art of walking down the aisle. "Step, stop! Step, stop!" Pringle commands, hiking up his pant legs to demonstrate the proper movement. Blithely dismissing the group, he turns to Stanley and remarks, "*You* must practice at home."

5. Arriving at the wedding, Stanley gets out of a car in front of the church and bumps his head, squashing his top hat over his ears at the very moment when the official photographer takes his picture.

6. At the reception after the ceremony, Stanley wanders forlornly around the periphery of the crowd and misses every important moment. Rushing up a back stairway to get a good view of his daughter tossing out her wedding bouquet, he arrives too late; shoved aside by a tidal wave of guests, he fails to see the bride and groom leave the party. As he watches the newlyweds drive off, he laments that he never had the opportunity to say goodbye to his daughter.

All these scenes require Tracy to behave in low-comic style, playing the role of a man who mistimes his entrances, misjudges his speeches, and musses up his costumes. And if Tracy's job involves the skillful portrayal of a foolish or inept player, then Minnelli's work is roughly similar. The film is filled with cleverly staged representations of theatrical chaos, showing the apparent breakdown of scenery and choreography. For example, Minnelli photographs the wedding rehearsal as if it were a musical number, using a boom-mounted camera that moves slowly down on a large set. As the camera descends, we see knots of people standing here and there, chatting with one another and halfheartedly following Pringle's directions: one of Buckley's friends (Carleton Carpenter) has trouble keeping his shoe tied, a tiny woman in a raincoat repeatedly breaks out in sneezing fits, and Stanley gesticulates hopelessly from an off-center position.

Throughout the film, Minnelli composes similar long- or middle-distance shots, many of them viewed from a crane, showing mismatched players moving around in comic patterns. At the engagement party, Stanley's kitchen overflows with strange characters who wander in and out through a swinging door, pausing to engage in animated small talk while the host wrestles with drinks. Later, in a stationary sequence shot, the front hallway of the Banks house becomes almost as busy as Pennsylvania Station in *The Clock*: Stanley answers a telephone call from Aunt Hattie, an out-of-town relative, and in the background a group of furniture movers collides with a group of interior decorators; as Stanley tells Aunt Hattie how to catch a cab, various members of the family weave through the crowd, preoccupied with their own business. Eventually, the two sets of workmen begin to threaten one another. Somebody drops a gigantic potted plant on the floor, and from offscreen comes the crash of a chandelier.

The most remarkable visualization of failed theater, however, involves a very different technique. On the eve of the wedding, in a dream sequence that parodies motifs from German expressionism and Daliesque surrealism, Stanley experiences his greatest embarrassment as a performer. This rather frightening montage is characteristic of Minnelli, who often mixed high-key entertainment with Gothic and Freudian motifs; and although it comes as something of a shock in the context of a domestic comedy, it remains subtly consistent with other aspects of the film. Notice, for example, that *Father of the Bride* makes the sublimated romance between Stanley and his daughter fairly explicit, even if it avoids an overtly psychoanalytic interpretation of their relationship. It also tells its story in flashback, rather like a film noir. In fact, the picture was photographed in black and white by John Alton, a B-unit cameraman who was also responsible for such atmospheric crime movies as *The Big Combo* and *T-Men*. In a seminal essay on noir filmmaking, Paul Schrader has bestowed special praise on Alton, describing him as "perhaps the greatest master" of the style.[5] *Father of the Bride* takes advantage of this sensibility, staging many of its scenes at night, as if the images of cheerful domesticity were being haunted by a darker mood.

Ultimately, Minnelli and Alton use the dream sequence to intensify all the social and sexual anxieties that have been running beneath the surface (Figure 13). Perhaps the most harrowing episode ever to appear in film of this type, the dream begins with an organ playing a lugubrious rendition of "Here Comes the Bride" while we see a pair of huge, vein-steaked eyes superimposed over the shadowy nave of a Gothic church. In an overhead shot that echoes the earlier scene of the wedding rehearsal, Stanley lumbers alone down the aisle, trying to execute his "step–stop" movement. One of his legs sinks into a black tile in the floor, and we cut to a spooky, wide-angle close-up of Pringle, hiding behind a latticed screen. Stanley's leg disappears up to his knee, and as he struggles to extricate himself, he tears his pants to shreds. Another wide-angle close-up shows the church organist gaping at Stanley through owlish spectacles. On his knees, Stanley attempts to crawl along the aisle, but his arms sink through the tiles and he loses the sleeves of his coat. The wedding guests – lit and photographed in a style that resembles Ingmar Bergman in the late fifties – huddle together in hideous little groups, staring aghast at Stanley's humiliation. The aisle of the church magically changes into a kind of trampoline, and as Stanley struggles forward, his remaining pant leg sticks to the floor, stretching out behind him for several yards. He now resembles a sort of plastic man, and from a low angle we see Kay in her wedding dress, clutching Buckley's arm and recoiling in horror. Stanley's trousers rip free altogether, and he stands exposed in his underwear. Buckley frowns angrily, holding Kay to his side. Kay screams, but we can't hear the sound of her voice; suddenly the scream becomes audible, shattering through the organ music and waking Stanley.

The terror of all this is heightened because we have been denied a preliminary shot of Stanley asleep. The direct cut from the end of the dream to an image of Stanley bolting out of his bed usually provokes an uneasy, almost Hitchcockian laughter; like the dreamer, audiences need a moment to reorient themselves, and they empathize when the protagonist shudders and paces around his room in a cold sweat. Clearly, the nightmare has subverted all the "daytime" imagery of the film, depicting the father as an abject incompetent, the bride and groom as grotesque apparitions, and the bourgeois community as a crowd of voyeurs garbed in expensive but funereal costumes. But it has also gone beyond anything expected of a social satire about stage fright, evoking a fear of castration and sexual abasement. Minnelli fills the sequence with shots of missing sleeves, ripped trousers, and sadistic stares; near the end, he makes the source of Stanley's anxieties explicit by confronting him with the angry gaze of his rival, Buckley, who is viewed from a low angle, clutching Kay and towering above the camera like a phallic threat.

Father of the Bride would be an even darker film if it went on to show the wedding as a comic disaster, similar to the other performances in Stanley's life. Needless to say, however, it is not a critique of bourgeois marriage, and it ends happily. In fact, it adheres to the same pattern as every MGM musical about show business, giving us a big production number that goes off without a hitch. Not long after the nightmare, we see its opposite, a

Figure 13. The father's nightmare on the eve of the wedding. Spencer Tracy, Don Taylor, and Elizabeth Taylor in *Father of the Bride*. (© 1950, Turner Entertainment Co., all rights reserved.)

perfect wedding. The upscale, vaguely Anglican ceremony is played almost in its entirety, punctuated only by Stanley's wry, offscreen commentary, which provides just enough humor to leaven the sentiment. Stanley masters his nervousness, Buckley seems haggard but loving, and both Kay and Ellie are radiantly beautiful. The result is a complete turnabout from the comic sequences – an appeal to the audience's utopian fantasies and a celebration of everything the film has mocked. In effect, the tensions raised by the plot are resolved in the fashion of a musical, where, as Jane Feuer observes, things usually end with a merger of life and art, pointing toward a "ritual marriage" of a heterosexual couple.[6]

The fictional wedding of Elizabeth Taylor, who was only seventeen when the picture was made, was one of the major cinematic events of 1950 – a year when a popular daytime TV show was broadcasting live marriage ceremonies of real couples, showering them with gifts from sponsors. Minnelli staged the wedding with his customary decorative skill, making full use of MGM's production resources and shooting much of the action from Spencer Tracy's point of view. Although a cynical guest at Kay's engagement party has warned that Stanley will be shoved out of the limelight when the big moment arrives, the gravity and poignance of the occasion seem to emerge from an unspoken drama between father and daughter. The ceremony is capped with two gigantic, diffused close-ups of Taylor and Tracy, looking into one another's eyes as if to say goodbye. The expression on Kay's face assures us that even while Stanley has "given away" one of his women, at some level he remains her ideal.

If the successful wedding allows Stanley to retain a considerable measure of authority, it also blunts the film's satire of commodity culture. Until this point, much of the comedy has resulted from the way capitalist enterprise feeds on marriage. Stanley complains that he has been forced to "put on a wedding like a Roman emperor," and when Ellie wants to purchase special dresses for the bridesmaids in a color that will suggest "wood nymphs and glades," he mutters, "Yeah, like the girl on the White Rock bottle." Early on, we see Ellie and Kay caught up in a shopping frenzy, and as the big day draws near, the house begins to overflow with presents for the bride – including silver table settings, kitchen appliances, and a kitschy statuette of the Venus de Milo with a clock in its navel. Meanwhile, hundreds of people are invited to the wedding for dubious reasons: Stanley fears that he might offend his long-standing clients, and Ellie wants the entire garden club because "they're running me for president." Stanley's secretary advises him to think of the guests as "units," each costing $3.75, and at one point Kay complains that "this isn't a wedding, it's a business convention."

106

The potentially disastrous cost of putting on a proper show becomes especially apparent when Ellie tries to employ "one of those little caterers" to arrange for the reception. This fellow, played in the snootiest possible fashion by Leo G. Carroll, is in some ways a comic surrogate for Minnelli himself – a dandified interior decorator who specializes in lavish spectaculars. Showing Ellie his sketches of a massive wedding cake intended for "the ordinary run of people," he suggests that for a bit more money he could arrange something truly elegant, such as a long table filled with cold sturgeon, topped with "a huge cake of ice with colored lights." When Ellie asks for sandwiches, he stiffens and looks down his nose: "Of course you can have anything you want, madame, but that's what we usually serve for children's parties." Later, he visits the Banks's home, which he finds impossibly small. Sporting a homburg, a frock coat, and a gilded cane, he orders his bowler-hatted, cigar-smoking "field engineer" to remove everything from the place, including the quaint but chronically inoperable French doors opening onto the back lawn.

During the actual ceremony, however, all the economic problems vanish, and the film transforms its alienated characters into rapturous artists or spectators. As in so many of Minnelli's other pictures, a happy ending is achieved through the power of sheer theatricality, with a glorious show transcending its commercial underpinnings, resolving the psychic tensions and social contradictions that preceded it. For example, just before Stanley leaves for the church, he sees his wife coming down the stairs "with all the beauty of her own wedding day on her." The shot is photographed from his angle of vision, and is designed to rhyme with a similar scene at the beginning of the picture, when he watches his daughter descend the same stairway. Ellie is wearing the perfect wedding attire for 1950, and by virtue of her costume she seems to overcome time itself, providing Stanley with a consolation for all his troubles. Her dress, like any fetish, is paradoxical; both a commodity and a work of art, it provokes anguish or desire, depending on how one looks at it. Hence the film moves easily from a satire of consumerism to a hushed appreciation of beauty.

Nowhere is the film's underlying strategy more apparent than in the next sequence, where Stanley beholds an even greater glory. Going upstairs to Kay's room, he opens the door and is stunned by the sight of his daughter, garbed in a white wedding gown and standing before a three-piece mirror, looking "like the princess in a fairy tale." The shot creates an effect common to a studio like MGM, where the image of a star frequently overwhelms the fictional context. Elizabeth Taylor had been known to the American public since childhood, and was now in the bloom of her youth – old enough to be dressed in a fashion that accounted for much of the film's box-office appeal. The shot is inscribed within a male gaze, but I suspect it was addressed primarily to readers of women's magazines; in other words, Taylor becomes at once an ideal wife and a "daddy's girl," representing both an object of masculine desire and an ideal toward which women are supposed to aspire. Just as Ellie has predicted, she's "last month's *Vogue*" come to life.

Undoubtedly Taylor stimulated various degrees of identification, envy, and regret in female spectators. Undoubtedly, too, she enhanced the market for wedding dresses. Maureen Turim has pointed out that *Father of the Bride* was a key film in the promotion of the "Sweetheart Line" of women's clothing that dominated American retail sales during the forties and fifties. By 1950, this design had come to signify a rite of passage: "Upper class, middle class, even Hollywood in its real life, everyone, that is, except the very poor engaged in this extravagant costuming to celebrate the most important social ritual of the post-war years: the wedding."[7] The image of Taylor standing in front of the mirror, admired by her fictional father, is therefore evidence of the film's cunning and almost irresistible duplicity. Minnelli and his writers have satirized women for reading *Vogue,* and now they invite those same women to stand in breathless awe of a star in the latest wedding gown; they have treated females as consumers, and now they construct a female image that can be lovingly consumed through a man's eyes. In fact, they have done this throughout the film, as we can see from the special care MGM took with all of Taylor's costumes. Figure 14 illustrates a series of clothing and hairstyle tests made at the studio, showing some of the outfits Taylor wears during the course of the story. Like a model in a fashion display, she is given costumes for every occasion, ranging from a fairly simple blouse and skirt (suitable for discussing the size of the wedding) to a black satin dress (appropriate for the scene where she almost calls off the engagement). The last image in the series is a souvenir photo, showing Taylor in her wedding gown, which was distributed by women's apparel and gift shops in towns where the movie was playing.

In the film itself, Taylor's beauty compensates for the problems Stanley has suffered, giving *Father of the Bride*'s potentially subversive satire a conservative resolution. But Spencer Tracy is even more important than Taylor in securing this happy ending. As we have seen, Tracy alternates between a comic persona and a kind of gentle wisdom, his weaknesses confirming his strength. The film makes him particularly appealing in "private" regions of the house – for example when he talks with Kay while he shaves in the bathroom, or when he listens to Kay's anxieties while eating

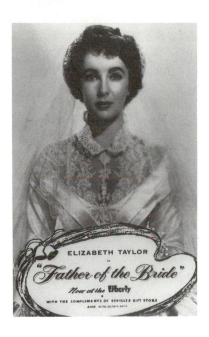

Figure 14. Elizabeth Taylor's wardrobe tests and a promotional "tie-in" for *Father of the Bride*. (© 1950, Turner Entertainment Co., all rights reserved. Photographs courtesy of the Academy of Motion Picture Arts and Sciences and the Margaret Herrick Library.)

a midnight snack in the kitchen. A father in keeping with the new Dore Schary regime at MGM, he never becomes a paragon of wisdom like L. B. Mayer's Judge Hardy; he frequently seems at a loss, and part of his attractiveness is due to the way he allows his love for his daughter and his wife to shape his role. At the party following the ceremony, he is momentarily plunged back into a comic world; but in the closing moments of the film, as he surveys the wreckage in his living room, he receives a telephone call from Kay, who assures him that he remains an important figure in her life. On his record player, he discovers an old recording of "Good Night, Ladies," and he asks Ellie to dance. (The title of the song is significant, especially given the problems women have caused Stanley throughout.) As the recording starts, Minnelli's camera tracks away from Mr. and Mrs. Banks, watching them embrace and sway to music. Discreetly exiting the house, it frames the couple through the missing French windows. Like players on a stage or figures on a wedding cake, they become symbols of a traditional marriage, moving in rhythm, acting correctly ever after.

Minnelli must have recalled *Father of the Bride* when he came to direct his 1954 film *The Long, Long Trailer,* which employs a broadly comic style appropriate to Lucille Ball and Desi Arnaz. Once again the writers were Goodrich and Hackett; once again the film centered on the consuming passions of a housewife who almost drives her husband crazy; and once again the film had a certain noir quality. The *Long, Long Trailer* is a lavishly decorated color spectacular, but it begins on a dark, rainy night, with Arnaz wearing a trenchcoat and a snap-brim hat, narrating events in flashback to the manager of a trailer park. Perhaps because of its relatively anarchic form, it occasionally has a sharper satiric edge than *Father of the Bride;* in fact, with the exception of Frank Tashlin, no other Hollywood director of the fifties expressed such malicious delight in kitsch — although in Minnelli's case the images of life on the American road were often beautiful, and the story was essentially a cozy fantasy about married love.

All of Minnelli's comedies were intended to conform to this pattern, first deflating and then honoring the American dream. Nothing Minnelli ever directed, however, was so blandly compromised as the remake of *Father of the Bride,* which deserves another brief comment by way of conclusion. As I have already suggested, the Disney company updated the story by superficially adjusting its sexual politics; it even cast Diane Keaton as Ms. Banks, giving her a career of her own. Thus when the father in the remake becomes outraged at the cost of the wedding, he directs his anger not at his wife or his daughter, but at a faceless corporation – a supermarket, which requires him to buy twelve hot dog buns instead of eight. Notice also that the Disney film replaces the nightmare before the wedding with a kind of music video: as the sentimental chords of a pop tune deluge the soundtrack, we see Steve Martin lying awake and fondly recalling images of his daughter growing up. The Freudian scenario is therefore underplayed and the women no longer seem a specific threat. Even so, the desire to consume remains a distinctly feminine trait, signified by Martin Short's flamboyant portrayal of a swishy interior decorator. In Short's performance, homosexuality comes out of the closet, only to be condescendingly treated as a joke; elsewhere the patriarchal values of the story remain unchanged, and the new version provides an even more obvious stimulant to the consumer economy than the original. The bride's wedding gown is copied from pictures of Grace Kelly's marriage to the prince of Monaco, and her accessories include a pair of lacy, rhinestone-studded sneakers. The father himself is made the object of a consumerist gaze, wearing colorful sweaters and driving an antique MG. Significantly, the supermarket in which Steve Martin throws a tantrum is unnamed, but elsewhere the film provides explicit endorsements. Unlike the studios of the fifties, who feared that the use of actual products on the screen would look like vulgar hucksterism, the Disney company seems eager to take money from advertisers: numerous brand names – including Nike sports shoes, Crate and Barrel furnishings, Krups coffee makers, Spode china, and Armani men's wear – are mentioned or shown in flattering contexts.

As I write, the same process is under way once more: a remake of *The Long, Long Trailer* has been announced, with Roseanne Barr in the starring role. One shudders to think of how many possibilities for commercial endorsements such a project could offer, and how much wit could be smothered by nostalgia. By attempting to update and replay Minnelli's comedies, Hollywood only reveals that it cannot go home again; in fact, the more we try to repeat history, the more we change for the worse.

5

Citizen Shields

The Bad and the Beautiful (1952)

This book began by comparing Minnelli with Orson Welles, and the comparison now requires some further development. Despite the obvious differences between them, the two directors had important things in common: for example, both became famous youthful directors of New York theater during the thirties; both moved to Hollywood and began making films in the early forties; and both collaborated with the talented producer John Houseman. To my knowledge, Welles never commented on Minnelli's films, but Minnelli once told interviewers at *Cahiers du Cinema* that Welles was the auteur he most respected.[1] In Minnelli's *The Band Wagon,* the comically pretentious Jeffrey Cordova, who tries to direct a musical version of *Faust,* is rather like a fictional synthesis of Welles and Minnelli himself. The two figures actually converge, however, in the movie Minnelli made immediately before *The Band Wagon: The Bad and the Beautiful,* a steamy, Academy Award–winning drama about Hollywood that was directly inspired by *Citizen Kane.*

Significantly, *The Bad and the Beautiful* originated not with Minnelli, but with Welles's former associate, Houseman, who had recently become an MGM producer. One day in 1951, Houseman was leafing through a file of submissions to the story department, looking for a project that would satisfy the demands of what he described as "an extravagant, high-powered machine created and maintained for the production of BIG pictures,"[2] when his eye fell upon a short story by George Bradshaw, entitled "Memorial to a Bad Man." This story, which had been published in the February issue of the *Ladies' Home Journal,* concerned the death of an unscrupulous Broadway director reminiscent of Jed Harris, who invites three people – an actress, a writer, and a Hollywood producer – to attend the reading of his will. The three "beneficiaries" reluctantly show up, reminiscing with a lawyer about how they were cheated and betrayed by the director at various points in their careers. Anticipating their hostility, the dead man defends himself through his will, claiming that he taught each of them important lessons and helped to make them successful. As a last request, he begs them to collaborate on the production of a play in his memory. Amused by this presumptuousness and still fascinated by a man they love to hate, the three friends agree to work on the play. The story ends on a note of ironic laughter as they contemplate the bizarre project they are about to undertake.

Bradshaw's rather slight tale was interesting chiefly because of its multiple-perspective narration, which reminded Houseman of *Kane,* a script he had nursed along and helped Welles and Herman Mankiewicz write a decade earlier. Here was an opportunity to please his new employers and at the same time return to the heady scenes of his past; here was a way of repeating history – not as farce, but as high-gloss melodrama. First, however, House-man proposed changing the setting of the story from Broadway to Holly-wood, where it would deal with a movie producer vaguely resembling David O. Selznick. In his memoirs, he says that he made this change because he was "tired of theatrical stories with protagonists patterned on Jed Harris."[3] A more compelling reason may have been his desire to avoid making a film that would be too similar to *All About Eve,* another multiple-perspective narrative about the theater, written by Herman Mankiewicz's brother Joseph, which had won the Academy Award in the previous year. In any case, Houseman's proposal was well-timed. The early fifties was a period of crisis and transition for Hollywood – the last days of what Houseman himself called "Culver City's magnificence."[4] Lowe's, Incorporated had been ordered to divest itself of its theater chains; L. B. Mayer had been replaced by Dore Schary; more than three hundred Hollywood professionals had been fired or blacklisted by the House Committee on Un-American Activities investigations; and television was changing the face of American culture. Aware of all this, the movies were beginning to examine their own past with a mixture of nostalgia and cynicism. Among the symptomatic films of the first half of the decade were *Sunset Boulevard* (1950), the remake of *A Star Is Born* (1954), *The Barefoot Contessa* (1954), and *The Big Knife* (1955). *The Bad and the Beautiful* belongs in company with these impressive productions, although it is in many ways a less troubling kind of movie, more in keeping with the conservative image of MGM.

To develop a script, Houseman engaged Charles Schnee, a former financial partner in his and Welles's Mercury Theater organization. Working with the general plot structure of "Memorial to a Bad Man" (plus a few ideas suggested by a second Bradshaw story, "Of Good and Evil," published earlier in *Cosmopolitan*), Schnee created a virtually original movie about the twenty-year history of a character named Jonathan Shields, an independent producer who has fallen upon hard times. At the beginning of this version, which was entitled *Tribute to a Bad Man,* Shields places a transatlantic call from London to three old friends — a director, an actress, and a writer — asking them to help with a new film that will enable him to make a comeback. They refuse, and when Shields's loyal assistant, Harry Pebbel, makes an appeal on his behalf, we learn why. In flashback, each of them recalls being seduced and betrayed: Shields stole the director's idea for a major production; he pretended to love the actress when he was sleeping with another woman; and he attempted to gain control over the writer's work by arranging a secret (and fatal) affair between the writer's sexy wife and the studio's Latin lover. All three of Shields's victims have since recovered and gone on to successful careers, but they claim they will never work for him again — even though, at the end of the movie, they eavesdrop on one of his telephone calls to Harry Pebbel, curious to hear what sort of project he has in mind.

With the first draft of a script in hand, Houseman approached Minnelli, who, after the recent success of *Father of the Bride* and *An American in Paris,* had become MGM's most favored director. As Houseman later remarked, Minnelli's interest in the project made it easy to mount a "BIG" production, in the manner of famous MGM blockbusters like *Dinner at Eight* or *Grand Hotel.* (The cast for the film would ultimately include Lana Turner, Kirk Douglas, Dick Powell, Gloria Grahame, Walter Pidgeon, and Gilbert Roland — names that jumped out one by one during the opening moments of the credit sequence, bombarding the audience to the rhythm of David Raksin's theme music.) But Minnelli also exerted a strong influence on the later development of the screenplay. Because it was set in the heart of the dream factory, Houseman's project afforded him an opportunity to indulge his major themes in a much more straightforward way than the Freed unit musicals had ever done. For him, *The Bad and the Beautiful* was a film about the tawdry absurdities and operatic splendors of a strangely admirable industry. Thus in the completed picture, the characters are less like Hollywood sharpies and more like frustrated dreamers, yearning for art, glamour, and sophistication. Sometimes they actually achieve moments of transforming intensity by working in Tinseltown.

Perhaps because he wanted to highlight this irony, Minnelli requested changes in the script. The original draft was a fairly straightforward hero-as-heel story, of the kind that was fashionable in the period, especially when acted by Kirk Douglas (compare *The Champion* [1949] and *Ace in the Hole*

[1951]). As Minnelli later explained in an interview, the first version "was simply about a man who was more or less of a villain, and who stepped on everybody's shoulders to get to the top. . . . He had no redeeming graces."[5] By contrast, the revised screenplay emphasizes Jonathan Shields's flamboyance, charm, and talent, all the while calling attention to his psychological problems, as if to prevent us from judging his ruthlessness too harshly. The released picture is even milder than the final draft of the script, which contained two darkly comic scenes designed to illustrate Shields's more unpleasant features. In the first of these, Shields accepts an Academy Award for *The Faraway Mountain,* paying lavish tribute to his dead father and barely acknowledging the crucial help of fledging director Fred Amiel:

CLOSE UP – AN OSCAR

held in a man's hand. CAMERA PULLS BACK to reveal Jonathan standing before the microphone on the dais, addressing the gala crowd.

Jonathan (at microphone)
It is the custom, when receiving such an honor, to thank all the people concerned. It gives me great pleasure to do so. First, I want to thank a man who devoted his life to this industry. A pioneer moviemaker. Without him, and a handful of others like him, you wouldn't be here tonight. I want to thank a man most of you hated. My father. Louis Shields.

Dead silence. Jonathan waits grimly. Finally the audience is forced to applaud. Scattered clapping, then polite applause.

Jonathan
Let me also thank Mr. Von Ellstein and Gaucho, who more than merit the honors you have awarded them tonight. And Mr. Harry Pebbel, who encouraged me to produce the picture. And Anse Chapman, the cameraman, the cutter, and all the crew, and Fred Amiel. Thank you.[6]

Although this scene was actually shot (see Figure 15), it was dropped from the final cut. The second darkly comic scene, which was apparently never filmed, occurred at the very end of the story, when we were supposed to see Shields in a Paris hotel room, aware that three people he once betrayed are eavesdropping on his call to Hollywood. Pretending to be unaware of their presence, he breaks into an elaborate apology for what he did to "three fine people that I loved." Then, in the midst of outlining "the greatest idea that's come along in years," he deliberately breaks off the connection. Lean-

Figure 15. Jonathan Shields (Kirk Douglas) accepts his first Academy Award in a scene that was cut from *The Bad and the Beautiful*. (© 1952, Turner Entertainment Co., all rights reserved. Photograph courtesy of the Academy of Motion Picture Arts and Sciences and the Margaret Herrick Library.)

ing back comfortably in his chair, he awaits a return call and explains his strategy to his press agent:

Jonathan

You love me, Syd – suppose you hated me. Think how many people there are who carry hate around for someone who's hurt them. How many of them ever get the chance to kick back – to have that person need them and come crawling – and then to have the joy of laughing in his face – It must be a lovely feeling – How can you hate after that?

(A moment. Jonathan lifts a cigarette, smiles shrewdly.)

Also, it's a great idea!

Now the phone has started to ring, and Syd starts to reach for it. Jonathan reaches out and stops him. Then he settles back in his chair.

Jonathan (smiling)
    Let it ring for a while.[7]

In the released version, the film ends on a more ambiguous and perhaps more insidiously clever note, with the three narrators gathered around a telephone in an outer office, listening to Shields's conversation with Pebbel. We never see Shields, who, like the cinema itself, remains an "absent presence" – an image mediated by memory, an overheard voice at the end of the line. And if Shields is an emblem of the movies, his collaborators are like an ideal audience; their rapt, curious expressions, framed by a dramatic spotlight and set off from the surrounding darkness, indicate how much they will always be drawn to the siren call of entertainment, and to the lure of an imaginary signifier.

Interestingly, the final change in the script was made by the MGM publicity department, who objected to Houseman's original title, *Tribute to a Bad Man*, on the grounds that it sounded too much like a cowboy movie. (*Tribute to a Bad Man* was indeed used a few years later for an MGM western starring James Cagney.) Studio executive Howard Dietz thought up *The Bad and the Beautiful*, thus contributing to a fifties vogue for such thunderous, quasi-biblical-sounding productions as *The High and the Mighty*, *The Proud and Profane*, and *The Pride and the Passion*. Houseman complained about the studio's vulgarity and bombast, but surely he was wrong; *The Bad and the Beautiful* is a perfectly appropriate description of this picture, and of Minnelli's work in general.

Throughout these relatively minor rewritings and changes, Houseman's production continued to be heavily influenced by *Citizen Kane*. It would be wrong, however, to suggest that the two movies ever had an overtly intertextual relation. *Kane* had not been shown in American theaters for over a decade, and MGM had no reason to evoke its memory. Big-city reviewers were aware that Houseman and Minnelli were alluding to Welles, and subsequent critical discussions of *The Bad and the Beautiful* have sometimes made the same point; but studio publicity never mentioned *Kane*, and Houseman was reticent about the issue – this despite the fact that he was clearly recycling his own career, adapting the controversial, politically activist work of the Mercury Theater to the demands of Hollywood. (As soon as he completed this film, he went on to produce a middlebrow version of the Mercury's greatest stage success: *Julius Caesar*, directed by Joseph Mankiewicz and starring Marlon Brando in a toga.)

117

Nowadays, of course, it seems impossible that anyone could see *The Bad and the Beautiful* without thinking of its better-known predecessor. At the most obvious level, it is a *film à clef* narrated in flashback by several characters who have intimate knowledge of a legendary figure. Jonathan Shields is based on Selznick (with a bit of Val Lewton thrown in for the benefit of cognoscenti), but he also has a few things in common with Orson Welles himself – after all, it was Welles, not Selznick, who was known as a "genius boy" (Harry Pebbel's nickname for Shields); it was Welles who prompted deep feelings of love and hate in some of his compatriots; and it was Welles who inspired many people to the greatest achievements in their careers, meanwhile (in Houseman's view) claiming most of the credit. (The casting of Kirk Douglas tends to reinforce this comparison. Douglas has little physical resemblance to Welles, but he seems a good deal younger than the other players, and he invests the character with an aura of prodigious, somewhat Wellesian theatricality.) Along similar biographical lines, Georgia Lorrison, the actress played by Lana Turner, is intended to suggest Diana Barrymore, whose alcoholism, promiscuity, and troubled relationship with her father had become public knowledge. Even some of the minor players have real-life counterparts: the two directors who work on Shields's big-budget productions are parodies of Alfred Hitchcock and Fritz Lang (the former played by Leo G. Carroll, who frequently acted in Hitchcock's films); a young woman singing in the background at a Hollywood party resembles Judy Garland; and another singer in a nightclub is reminiscent of Lena Horne.

In visual terms, too, *The Bad and the Beautiful* resembles *Kane*. It has an eerie projection-room sequence in which the shadow of a producer is cast upon a white screen; it contains a couple of Gothic houses that figure importantly in the action; it casts Paul Stewart in a minor but memorable role; and it adopts the Mercury's "curtain-call" credits, showing brief shots of the players at the end. The Gothic motif is particularly significant because Shields, like Charles Foster Kane, is something of a doomed romantic rebel. A loner afflicted by dark Oedipal compulsions, he adopts a Byronic style, rejecting bourgeois conventions. Our first glimpse of his movie studio is like a visit to Xanadu, with automobile headlights shining on a vast iron gate while David Raksin's music sounds an ominous note; and later, when we meet him in the initial flashback, he is alone in his father's deserted Hollywood castle, wearing an overcoat draped over his shoulders like a cape.

Whenever it borrows themes and visual ideas from *Kane*, however, *The Bad and the Beautiful* has different ends in mind, and it is surprising that critics have never commented on this fact. Notice, for example, a shot that

Minnelli intended as a specific reference to Welles: Georgia Lorrison, who has been carefully nurtured and coached by Shields, is shown at work, acting an emotional scene. (Minnelli lavished special attention on the movie-within-the-movie, which looks rather like the Selznick production of Garbo's *Anna Karenina* in the mid-thirties.) Wearing a discreetly tattered gown and a smudge on her cheek to represent the horrors of war, she kneels beside the unconscious body of her dying lover (Gilbert Roland, garbed in the uniform of a Czarist officer). "We're alone now," she says, sobbing and then clasping her hands as if in prayer. "Now I can tell you what I never could tell you before." She wrings her hands and reaches slowly out to touch Roland. "You must forgive me darling! You mustn't mind my crying, now that it's too late!...I love you so!" During this speech, Minnelli's camera drifts away, panning across the set to show Georgia's director and crew caught up in her performance; then it cranes up to a catwalk high in the studio, where a lighting technician looks down, smiling in admiration.

The shot is of course modeled on a famous moment in *Kane,* when the camera glides upward from Susan Alexander's opera debut to show a work-man holding his nose. But in this case, despite Minnelli's playful, campy references to the operatic quality of costume pictures, the meaning is quite the opposite. *Kane* is a satiric treatment of a media tycoon who bullies and manipulates a young woman in order to satisfy his own ego. By contrast, *The Bad and the Beautiful* is a portrait of a media tycoon who has a *good* influence, manipulating a young woman into becoming a star. In *Kane,* the judgment of the workman confirms what we see on the stage; in *The Bad and the Beautiful,* the grinning technician is there to make us believe that Lana Turner's performance, which contains every cliché in the book, is somehow great. (Minnelli reinforces the message in his autobiography, where he remarks, "This was the right assessment of the acting talent of the movie actress Lana was playing.")[8]

Here and everywhere else, *The Bad and the Beautiful* neatly reverses the politics of *Kane*. The earlier film is a psychological study of an authoritarian, protofascist male obsessed with his mother; the later film is a study of an authoritarian male's obsession with his father. (Here we might note that none of the characters in *The Bad and the Beautiful* even appear to have a mother — a change that seems ironically consistent with Houseman and Minnelli's more tolerant attitude toward established institutions.) In the earlier film, pop psychoanalysis is used in an oblique, ambiguous way, creating a disjunction between sympathy and judgment, never blunting the critique of a newspaper empire. In the later film, a patriarchal, "dollar-book" interpretation of Jonathan Shields is strongly emphasized, linking his Oedipal drama (and the similar dramas of the other characters, all of whom adopt Shields as a father-substitute) to a rationale for Hollywood.

Jonathan Shields has obvious psychological problems, including an inability to form loving relationships. It therefore seems incorrect to suggest, as Richard Dyer has done, that he is different from the three narrators in being "free of his own father."[9] Rather, he is a full-fledged neurotic who has learned to manage his inner conflicts and emulate Louis Shields. The paradox upon which the entire film rests is that his neurosis is useful, accounting for his ability to make award-winning films. In this regard, notice that, like his father, Jonathan is devoted to artistic quality as well as to commerce. As in Minnelli's previous work, art provides consolation for greed, bad behavior, and human inadequacy; in other words, the movies – especially this movie – become their own justification.

This dubious argument (roughly equivalent to a defense of Charles Foster Kane's journalism) is made clear almost from the time we first meet Jonathan Shields, at his father's funeral. A hammy minister eulogizes Shields *père* as a founder of "our great motion picture industry," while the young Fred Amiel (Barry Sullivan), who has been employed for the afternoon to act as a mourner, mutters wisecracks under his breath. When the minister praises Louis Shields as a "man of vision, an artist," Amiel sneers, "A butcher, who sold everything but the pig's whistle." The two voices make an amusing conterpoint, similar to the clash of opinions in the *Kane* newsreel, but the contradictions they establish are reconciled in the very next sequence. Fondly rubbing his hand over a medieval escutcheon emblazoned on his father's drinking mug, Jonathan Shields remarks, "He wasn't a heel. He was *the* heel. . . . But he made great pictures! So will I."

The shy, self-effacing Fred Amiel is drawn to Shields, regarding him as an ego ideal. Shields helps Amiel become a director of B movies, teaches him how to construct "cinematic" scripts, and even purchases a wedding ring for his fiancée. ("Well, children," Shields remarks, smiling paternally at the young couple as if to bless their union, "it's time you made it legal.") When Shields subsequently takes credit for Amiel's pet project and uses it as a stepping-stone in his own career, the effect is traumatic, as if a parent had abandoned a trusting child. Ultimately, however, Shields's chilling betrayal has beneficial results: Amiel is freed of an unhealthy dependency, and the practical skills he learned while working with Shields enable him to become one of the industry's most honored directors.

The same pattern is repeated in the case of Georgia Lorrison, whom Shields encounters in a Gothic house like his own, mourning the death of her father, a famous Hollywood actor. Ironically, Shields enters the decaying, apparently empty Lorrison mansion because the dead actor was his own adoptive father (Lorrison taught him about wine and women), and because he is in search of a cartoon the actor once drew, depicting the elder Shields as a devil (Figure 16). Later he will frame this cartoon and place it in his office alongside Louis Shields's photograph – a tribute Georgia can never imitate, since, according to the conventional Freudian logic of the film, she wants to *have* the Phallus, rather than to *be* it. When Shields remarks that George Lorrison was a "great actor, and a great man," Georgia replies, "He was a rat and a drunk." Shields instinctively understands this psychology, and eventually he goes to her tawdry apartment to try to save her from herself. "You're a Lorrison, all right," he sneers. "Because he was a drunk, you're a drunk. Because he loved women, you're a tramp. But you forget one thing. He did it with *style!*" Breaking a phonograph record of George Lorrison reading *Macbeth,* he announces, "That's not God talking, Georgia, that's a man!" To underline his point, he draws a mustache on her father's photograph, challenging her to do the same, and to "laugh, the way he would have laughed."

Again and again, the film excuses the sins of fathers in the name of art or "style," and it enables an authoritative male to speak the truth, even when he denies his godlike power. Thus Georgia will ultimately learn what Shields teaches – but not, as he suggests, by imitating her father. (How could she? This film would never allow a promiscuous, alcoholic woman to seem stylish.) Instead, she transfers her desire for George Lorrison to Jonathan Shields, and then discovers that Shields, too, is a cad. During their affair she behaves like a child, wearing his big overcoat, sitting on his lap, gazing at him adoringly, and promising that if they get married she "won't take up much room." Recognizing her neurosis, he chuckles, tells her that "love is for the very young," and threatens to send her to bed without any supper unless she behaves like his movie star. When she later finds him spending the night with a starlet, the shock almost kills her; but after she recovers, she becomes a more productive individual. At the beginning of the movie we see the mature Georgia – now the most celebrated star in Hollywood – doing exactly what Jonathan had once recommended: she uses her lipstick to paint a mustache on the insignia of Shields International Pictures (an insignia Shields himself took from his father's drinking mug), and, together with the other two narrators, she laughs aloud at the results (Figure 17).

The third narrator, James Lee Bartlow (Dick Powell), seems at first to be a much less immature and susceptible personality. A Sorbonne-educated "professor of medieval history," he is invited to Hollywood to adapt his own book, a "scholarly" study of the Old South that becomes a best-seller because it happens to be "liberally peppered with sex." Prompted by his youthful and restless wife (Gloria Grahame), Bartlow reluctantly agrees to work for the movies, but he feels nothing but contempt for producers. When he notices photographs of Shields's father hanging all over the studio, he studies the face and remarks, "Angry little man, wasn't he?"

Yet Bartlow, too, allows Shields to become his mentor, at one point describing him as "Professor." In return, he is betrayed twice – first by his wife, who has an affair with "Gaucho" (Roland), the studio's Latin lover, and then by Shields, who arranges the affair in order to get Bartlow to spend more time at the typewriter. The wife and Gaucho die together in a plane crash, and when Bartlow discovers that Shields knew about their relationship, he socks Shields in the jaw and walks out. Again, however, a personal trauma has salutary results. Bartlow's shock eventually passes, giving him a better understanding of his wife's character. He had imagined her as a kind of innocent, when all the while she was a frustrated housewife (the film's Emma Bovary), seductively playing a role he helped to create. His new insight, mingled with grief, desire, and anger, enables him to write a Pulitzer Prize–winning novel about the dead woman. He also becomes a major Hollywood screenwriter, owing much of his success to the lessons he learned from Jonathan Shields.

These three stories are more than a little self-serving. As *Time* magazine's review put it, *The Bad and the Beautiful* is a "big, glossily wrapped package" in which the antihero's victims regard him as "sort of lovable, for is he not responsible for the swimming pools and Oscars they have accumulated?"[10] Throughout the film, the interwoven narratives use Freudian folklore for blatantly conservative purposes: we are shown a series of people who try to resolve their ambivalent feelings toward fathers or father-substitutes, and in each case we discover that paternal influence – however neurotically managed – can lead to a productive life. The film correctly describes the old Hollywood as a patriarchy, but it suggests that the only way to personal health is through acceptance of the system, coupled with a "mature" understanding of the lessons taught by the founders of the industry. To take any other path (say, the one chosen by Welles) would be psychologically crippling or even suicidal.

In this regard, *The Bad and the Beautiful* can be described as a fairly typical Hollywood melodrama. As Robert Lang and others have pointed out, such movies usually deal with a struggle against patriarchal "Law," and they "invariably [come] down on the side of it, usually without much

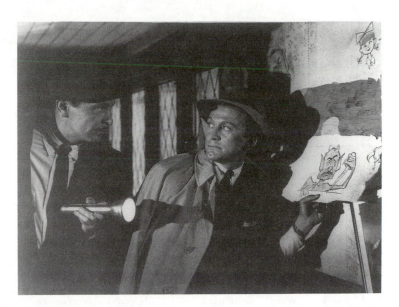

Figure 16. Jonathan Shields in search of his father's image. Barry Sullivan and Kirk Douglas in *The Bad and the Beautiful*. (© 1952, Turner Entertainment Co., all rights reserved.)

Figure 17. The three narrators deface Jonathan Shields's image and laugh at it. Barry Sullivan, Dick Powell, and Lana Turner in *The Bad and the Beautiful*. (© 1952, Turner Entertainment Co., all rights reserved.)

conviction."¹¹ What makes the film somewhat unusual is that it collapses the neat distinction between domesticity and productive labor on which the form usually depends. Like a great many of Minnelli's other pictures (especially his "show musicals"), it takes place in a liminal world of performance and theatricality, where the boundaries between the private and the public, between play and work, have become ambiguous. Because of the collaborative, almost familial nature of show business, the film can use "art" or "entertainment" as middle terms, reconciling the oppositions melodrama normally holds at bay. Thus Jonathan Shields presides over the action in three ways: as father, as tycoon, and as artist. In the last of these roles, he compensates for the tyranny of the other two. His dedication to "great pictures" – symbolized by the row of Academy Awards in his office – provides an excuse for every tension and every betrayal.

In the end, Shields is judged in roughly the same way as he judges his own father. He may be a conniving Hollywood producer, but at least he is no penny-pinching bureaucrat like his former boss, Harry Pebbel, who becomes his stooge. As a young man he recoils from *The Son of the Cat People,* a sequel to his successful horror movie, and badgers the studio into letting him adapt a "great book." Later, as head of his own production company, he refuses to release the costly Civil War epic he directed himself, on the grounds that it lacks quality. All the while he assumes a paternal role, helping three people overcome their psychological blocks to creativity.

Perhaps Minnelli, Houseman, and Schnee were trying in subtle ways to qualify this view. They make the three characters who represent the most talented people in Hollywood seem little more than stereotypes: Fred Amiel peers through a viewfinder as if he were composing photographs for a fashion magazine; Georgia Lorrison wears expensive gowns and sheds tears on cue; and James Lee Bartlow smokes a pipe and makes cynical jokes about producers. Meanwhile, Shields's movies look uniformly tacky. Most of his projects, like Selznick's, are bloated historical romances, and even his Lewton-style horror movie seems trite when we glimpse one of its sequences being filmed. By the same token, the advice Shields gives to his fellow professionals is little more than conventional Hollywood wisdom: he tells the director that people are afraid of what they cannot see on the screen, he teaches the actress to "make love" when she lights a cigarette, and he informs the writer that movies should avoid too much dialogue. For a scene in which a little old gray-haired mother is sending her son away to war, he proposes a wordless close-up: "What she's feeling," he says, "we'll leave to the audience to imagine." Unfortunately, he fails to observe this rule in his other pictures. *The Faraway Mountain,* the film he appropriates from

Fred Amiel, contains such lines as, "So, you are Teresa! And I find you just as your brother said I would – alone in the great house, proud, silent, and beautiful!"

Minnelli must have enjoyed staging the movies-within-the-movie, which involve a great deal of parody and pastiche; nevertheless, it is difficult to say exactly how much irony he intended. In the last analysis, *The Bad and the Beautiful* depends on the same glamorous costumes, melodramatic conventions, and expensive production values it occasionally satirizes. (According to a report in *Variety,* art director Ed Carfagno and set decorator Keogh Gleason prepared more than 110 sets for the film, creating designs for "English, French Provincial, Classic, Georgian, Modern, Russian, Victorian, Regency, and Early American" interiors.) Besides, as we have seen, everything hinges on our belief that Shields is a gifted producer, deserving of awards. Near the end, Harry Pebbel sounds a bit like John Houseman remembering Orson Welles: "You know, when they list the ten best pictures ever made, there are always two or three of his on the list. And I was with him when he made them."

Given all this, *The Bad and the Beautiful* might seem little more than a bespangled parade of clichés. In my view, however, it is also an immensely enjoyable movie whose very title sums up how it wants to be received – with a mixture of condescending, campy amusement and rapt fascination. In visual terms alone, it offers an unusual blending of Welles's noir expressionism with Minnelli's brightly polished, shop-window glamour, as if a Germanic mood had infiltrated a contemporary soap opera. (Minnelli later bestowed special praise on photographer Robert Surtees, remarking that *The Bad and the Beautiful* was "the best photographed black and white picture I ever directed.")[12] Then, too, the influence of *Kane* and the inherently self-reflexive nature of the story combine to promote certain kinds of distanciation. The plot is elliptical, filled with playful transitions that call attention to themselves; and the emphasis on montage, memory, and multiple viewpoints elicits a rational response, engaging the audience in analysis of the characters rather than in simple identification. Even Houseman's decision to mount a "BIG" production adds a witty dimension to the film, harmonizing with Minnelli's aestheticism and cinephilia. As Richard Dyer has shown, the casting is cleverly self-reflexive, often depending on the established images of the stars. The Georgia Lorrison character, for example, is constructed around Lana Turner's image as an insecure "clothes horse"; and if Dick Powell seems an unlikely college professor, he brings a welcome touch of Phillip Marlowe to his role, contributing significantly to the moody offscreen narration. Gloria Grahame, who was herself a great noir personality, is an appropriate companion for Powell (her very name has a Marlowesque final "e"), and when she plays a dimpled Southern coquette, it is sometimes difficult to tell whether she or the character is putting on an act.

Seen retrospectively, in the context of Minnelli's later career, the film's Freudian elements also become intriguing. All four of the "art melodramas" Minnelli made with Houseman – *The Bad and the Beautiful, The Cobweb, Lust for Life,* and *Two Weeks in Another Town* – employ a simplified version of an argument Edmund Wilson helped to popularize in his influential 1941 volume of literary criticism, *The Wound and the Bow.*[13] In each film, a character who suffers from a repressed psychic "wound" uses art as a release for thwarted libidinal energy. Sometimes art is therapeutic, and sometimes not; either way, it has a "tragic" relation to the character's personal experience. A more romantic way of formulating the same theme (and a formulation closer to the spirit of Minnelli's work) would be to say that an unbridgeable gulf separates art from life. Life is cruel, messy, and brief, whereas art, which is determined by life, is pleasurable, coherent, and outside time. Like the original romantics, Minnelli's protagonists are unable to make these two realms cohere, so they find themselves oscillating back and forth between the ecstasy of artistic inspiration and the melancholy of daily experience.

The musicals Minnelli directed for the Freed unit were of course designed to magically bridge the gulf between art and personal relationships, creating a utopian, "integrated" mise-en-scène. As many critics have shown, the classic Hollywood musical merges "story" and "number," and the plot typically ends with a spectacular song and dance in which a boy and girl, rather like Keats's figures on a Grecian urn, are suspended forever in a realm of pure "entertainment." Even in his musicals, however, Minnelli hints at loneliness or frustration: consider Judy Garland's "Have Yourself a Merry Little Christmas" in *Meet Me in St. Louis,* Fred Astaire's "By Myself" in *The Band Wagon,* or Gene Kelly's romantic desolation after the ballet in *An American in Paris.* Minnelli's nonmusical work with Houseman intensifies this sense of frustration. When the characters in these films are engaged in creative activity, they experience moments of unalienated labor and liberating, imaginative play. (Notice the montages that illustrate the process of filmmaking in *The Bad and the Beautiful* – especially the shot in which Shields and Fred Amiel dash gleefully up and down a surreal collection of stairways on the studio back lot.) But the sense of happiness and utopian fulfillment never lasts; inevitably, the characters encounter reality, and the shock of the encounter is intensified by their knowledge of what they have lost. At best, they can only stare wistfully across the space that separates life from art – like the aging actor played by Kirk Douglas in *Two Weeks in Another Town,* looking at his younger self in a private screening of *The Bad and the Beautiful,* or like Van Gogh in *Lust for Life,* leaning against a gnarled tree and putting a gun to his head, his suicide juxtaposed against the beautiful painting he has just completed.

For all its commercialism, *The Bad and the Beautiful* is an immensely effective realization of this "wounded artist" theme. No other film or novel captures so well the sense of the movie colony as a small, patriarchal family – expensively dressed, possessed of almost suburban values, and fraught with psychic tension. (To find a rough stylistic equivalent, we need to look outside of the subgenre of movies about movies to a camp television series like "Dallas.") Jonathan Shields is clearly a manic-depressive who uses filmmaking as a substitute for human relations (he confesses to Fred Amiel that a movie is like a love affair, down to the moment when the picture is finished and he feels a postcoital emptiness), but Shields is only the most flamboyant of several frustrated characters. On the surface, Fred Amiel seems a well-adjusted family man who has earned the plaudits of the industry; nevertheless, at the end of the movie he seems a shade too quiet, as if he were still suffering from a lingering insecurity. Georgia Lorrison manages to channel her morbid, forbidden obsession with her father into other paths, becoming a star; but throughout the film she remains a vulnerable, lonely character, a figure of artifice who is sad behind her glamorous exterior. James Lee Bartlow translates his passion for his wife into a successful book; but he, too, remains a loner, harboring memories of a painful infatuation.

The films we see Shields producing – most of them lavishly designed, filled with extras and complicated boom shots – are analogous to the numbers in a Minnelli musical, especially in their sense of rhythmic energy and unalienated labor. In this case, however, the "numbers" are never fully absorbed into the "story." At bottom, *The Bad and the Beautiful* is a pessimistic movie, which cannot even show us a certifiable work of art in the manner of *Lust for Life.* At best, it can only demonstrate the euphoric *process* of filmmaking, giving us moments when the characters – like Mickey and Judy in their adolescence – are swept up in the love of putting on a show. Repeatedly, it alternates between scenes of joyful play (such as the charming episode when Shields and Amiel are working on *The Doom of the Cat Men*), and scenes of traumatic *anagnorisis,* when the characters pass from innocent engagement to disillusioned alienation. What makes the series of betrayals so painful is not so much our disenchantment with Shields, but our loss of a potentially communal, relatively integrated world – a place where love and work are happily combined, and where an essentially trivial activity fully absorbs the characters' imaginations.

At another level, Minnelli's lush style calls attention to the process of moviemaking and prevents most people from taking *The Bad and the Beautiful* as a slice of life. In this sense the film is true to its own aesthetic ideals: it pushes the tension between art and life into outright conflict, with art claiming priority over nature and the signifier declaring independence from the signified. Thus in contrast to Wilder's more naturalistic *Sunset Boulevard, The Bad and the Beautiful* never shows us the actual streets of Los Angeles. Virtually every sequence is shot in the studio or on the back lot, and even though the action is spread over two decades, there is hardly any sense that the historical period has changed. Stephen Harvey has correctly observed that the film "reeks of artifice" and "parallels the sort of picture its cast of characters would make themselves, since the only reality they recognize is the kind you learn from the screen. . . . the producer-hero and his volatile crew are as prone to actorish poses as the cast of a Jonathan Shields spectacular."[14]

Minnelli himself has commented that one pitfall of the film was that "the actors could become caricatures if not properly controlled."[15] He seems to have solved the problem by immersing himself in the potentially destructive elements of the script. Everywhere *The Bad and the Beautiful* relies on a conventional imagery of Hollywood glamour, and it uses the broadest gestures of melodrama quite deliberately, thereby investing the action with romantic panache and energy. The affinity between Minnelli's style and the more general aims of the picture can be seen in the first sequence, where we see a Chapman boom rolling across a studio floor, holding a camera, two movie lights, and two men. Barely visible at the bottom edge of the screen, eight people are trotting along like galley slaves, powering the boom by hand, pressing it into a slow arc so that it begins to glide toward us. As it approaches, the gigantic arm descends, bearing down on something just below the edge of the frame. At the same moment, the scene we are watching is being photographed with a *second* craning and dollying movement. Minnelli's camera retreats at a slower pace and a slightly lower level than the diegetic apparatus, allowing it to approach and fill the screen. The two cameras stop at the same moment, and as the camera in the movie hovers in midair, Minnelli's own camera tilts down to match its angle of vision, revealing a beautiful woman reclining on a bed in a pool of studio light. The woman's head is in the foreground, and we gaze down along her

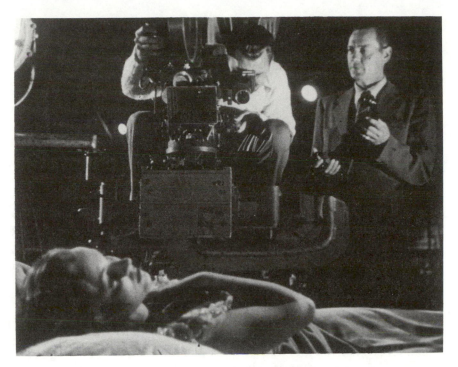

Figure 18. Fred Amiel directs. Barry Sullivan (behind the camera) in *The Bad and the Beautiful*. (© 1952, Turner Entertainment Co., all rights reserved.)

dramatically lit decolletage. The director atop the boom lifts his eye from the camera and speaks: "Say, honey, could you put that other hand up around your throat? Yeah, that's it" (Figure 18).

Minnelli's camera movement is a virtual mirror image of what we see on the screen, and it provides an obvious instance of what Jane Feuer has called "conservative self-reflexivity." Contrast this with the closing moments of *Sunset Boulevard,* where Gloria Swanson looks into the camera and offers to embrace "all those beautiful people out there in the dark." Swanson never steps out of character, but her direct mode of address slightly disturbs the dramatic illusion, establishing a less comfortable relation between the viewer and the screen. Notice also Godard's highly Brechtian movie about movies, *Contempt* (1963), which contains several references to Minnelli. In the credit sequence of that picture, we see photographer Raoul Coutard seated behind a camera, slowly tracking toward us; as he approaches, his camera slowly pans to face the screen, so that Coutard seems to be photographing the lens that photographs him. The effect is confrontational, disrupting the viewer's suspension of disbelief and creating a sense of alienation that we never feel in Minnelli's film.

I do not want to suggest that any formal technique is more progressive than any other. (It might be argued that Godard's film, which treats Brigitte Bardot in somewhat derisive fashion, is misogynistic in comparison with Minnelli's treatment of Lana Turner.) Nevertheless, it seems clear that the technique in *The Bad and the Beautiful* serves to intensify the glamour we see on the screen. The subtle pas de deux of the cameras makes for an exciting flourish, and the smoothly floating Chapman boom looks like a magnificent toy. Minnelli is captivated by the romance of Hollywood, and in showing us a vast machinery designed to create illusion, he seems to endorse the hierarchy of class and gender upon which the studio system was built. Hence he shows us a beautiful actress reclining on a bed, signifying "to-be-looked-at-ness," while an almost ludicrously phallic camera crane, guided by a male and powered by a team of laborers, rolls forward and locks her in its gaze.

A similar aestheticizing tendency is at work in the next sequence of *The Bad and the Beautiful,* where we first meet Lana Turner. A telephone rings in a star's dressing room, and a black maid (Marietta Canty) answers, looking offscreen left to announce that Jonathan Shields is calling from London. The camera pans to follow the maid's glance, and as it does so, Turner comes into view, seated before a mirrored vanity, wearing a black costume that contrasts sharply with the white-on-white decor. Just when we expect the camera to stop, it keeps moving, revealing that the image of Turner is a reflection in a mirror alongside the dressing table. As the camera slowly pans across the room, the back of Turner's "real" head floats past in the foreground, and then we see a frontal view of her face, reflected in a second mirror. At last the camera comes to a stop, framing her image as she raises a black veil from over her eyes and adjusts it for the proper effect.

Once again the careful, artfully planned shot gives us a glimpse of the division of labor in Hollywood: a black maid serves a white actress, whose job it is to provide a sexual allure for a male producer. As in the previous sequence, Minnelli constructs an enticing, fetishized image of masquerade and illusion; in fact, here and elsewhere he alludes to Sternberg's work with Dietrich, at one point costuming Turner in a powdered wig and an eighteenth-century page boy's outfit. (MGM capitalized on the scene by publishing still photos captioned "Lana Turner as a boy!") But Minnelli avoids Sternberg's perverse, almost deconstructive sophistication. Throughout, he seems fascinated with "movie magic" or with Hollywood's mythic images of itself. As Richard Dyer comments, "It is no part of *The Bad and the Beautiful* to demystify glamour by foregrounding its manufacture. Rather, the processes of manufacture themselves become fascinating and ...glamourous."[16] In this scene, for instance, the costuming, the camera movement, the lighting, and Turner's own gesture are so dazzlingly executed that they make most objections to the system seem merely puritanical.

The single most impressive instance of Minnelli's "touch" occurs midway through the picture, just after Georgia Lorrison's melodramatic confrontation with Shields on the stairway of his mansion. I have already described how Kirk Douglas grabs Turner by the hair and orders her out into the night; but the next sequence is even more spectacular, functioning as a kind of showcase for the director. It deserves a brief description, because in many ways it heightens or exaggerates the essential qualities of the entire film.

First we see Georgia stumbling outside and leaping into her car. Stunned and terrified, she drives faster and faster down the coast highway, until she goes berserk with grief. Sobbing and screaming, she completely disregards the steering wheel and the oncoming traffic, until she spins out of control and lands on the roadside, miraculously safe but dissolving in tears. Most directors would have constructed this episode as a montage, cutting between Georgia's reactions and shots of the car hurtling down the road. Minnelli shot the entire drive in one take, cutting only once to show an insert of Turner's high-heeled shoe pressing down on the accelerator. He also dispensed with music, allowing *melos* to derive from the acting, the sound effects, the flashing lights, and the movement of his camera. The car was attached to a vast turntable inside the studio, which enabled it to rock from side to side; meanwhile, the camera, mounted on a dolly, swept in little arcs around Turner, sometimes viewing the action over her shoulder and sometimes looking into her face (Figure 19). The result is an unceasing swirl of movement and the most intense performance in the film. As lights rake across the screen, Turner becomes a blur of white mink and rhinestones; she screams, closing her eyes and releasing the steering wheel as if she were trapped on a circus ride; all the while her cries are punctuated by bursts of rain on the windshield, by the stroke of the wiper blades, and by the horns of passing traffic. The car spins and rocks wildly, finally lurching to rest. More traffic goes by, and more horns. As the tumult ceases, we hear soft sobs, rain, and windshield wipers. Fade out. Fade in to a close-up of Georgia Lorrison's face, years later. Dressed in a widow's black, framed by a veil and a dark fur stole, she's lit by a ring of diffused light. "I told you I'd never work for him again," she says.

The sequence was so effective that Minnelli tried something like it a second time, in *Two Weeks in Another Town*, where Kirk Douglas takes Cyd

Figure 19. Georgia Lorrison (Lana Turner) suffers an emotional breakdown on the Pacific Coast Highway. (*The Bad and the Beautiful*, © 1952, Turner Entertainment Co., all rights reserved.)

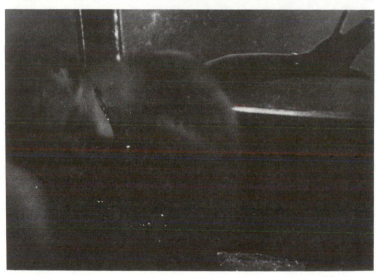

Charisse for a mad drive in a sports car. Years later, in *New York, New York* (1977), Martin Scorsese did nearly the same thing, putting Robert DeNiro behind the wheel and Liza Minnelli in the back seat. Neither of these later versions, however, is so brilliantly photographed, nor do they have the same emotional power. Albert Johnson has pointed out that the "auto hysteria" in *The Bad and the Beautiful* gains much of its strength from its context: the vaguely dizzying scene inside the mansion raises the theatrical stakes by employing what Johnson calls "silent movie technique,"[17] and the frantic drive provides a cathartic release of gathering tension. In my experience, however, present-day audiences hardly know whether to gasp or chuckle. Lana Turner's behavior, as Richard Dyer has noticed, seems "untrammeled, chaotic, violent," and at the same time she's presented as the "epitome of star artifice," visibly sitting in a studio mock-up of a car.[18] Minnelli wants the actress to produce an overflow of powerful, sexually charged feeling, but he also invites the audience to experience a sort of amused awe at Hollywood's synthetic beauty.

Whether intentionally or not, the scene in the car amounts to revealed hokum – a play of light, sound, and performance that seems both formally exciting and witty. In Andrew Sarris's phrase, it manages to transform "corn into caviar,"[19] in the process offering an implicit justification for Hollywood. Perhaps its unusual commingling of dramatic "reality" and manufactured "art" is exactly what the film as a whole is trying to achieve. In my opinion, whatever Minnelli may have intended, his greatest accomplishment in *The Bad and the Beautiful* is to make me feel toward the movie what Georgia Lorrison feels toward Jonathan Shields: the images capture my desire, but in the end I feel a need to paint a mustache across them and laugh.

6

Vincente Meets Vincent

Lust for Life (1956)

"They said Van Gogh was crazy because he killed himself. He couldn't sell a painting while he was alive and now they're worth thirty million dollars. They weren't that bad then and they're not that good now, so who's crazy?"
John Kerr to Gloria Grahame in Minnelli's *The Cobweb* (1954)

Vincent van Gogh's work is usually regarded as an important precursor of modernist art, but in many ways Van Gogh was not a modern type at all. There was nothing urban or truly bohemian in his personality, and he contributed little to what critics like T. J. Clark and Griselda Pollock have called the "mapping" of the new Paris.[1] He learned something from the impressionists, but he was ill at ease in the city and disinclined to celebrate modernity in the fashion of Manet and his followers. As John Berger and many others have pointed out, Van Gogh's chief spiritual and artistic influence was the mid-nineteenth-century painter of agricultural labor, Jean-François Millet. Repeatedly, Van Gogh chose to pitch his easel in the midst of workplaces, especially in the countryside during planting or harvesting, where he depicted labor and the natural world in a spirit of holy awe. W. H. Auden labeled him a "Religious Realist":

A realist because he attached supreme importance to the incessant study of nature and never composed pictures "out of his head"; religious because he regarded nature as the sacramental visible sign of a spiritual grace which it was his aim as a painter to reveal to others. ...He is the first painter, so far as I know, to have consciously attempted to produce a painting which should be religious and yet contain no religious iconography.[2]

135

Van Gogh's religion, however, was highly unorthodox. He was expelled by his church, and he recoiled from the behavior of nuns at the asylum at Saint-Remy, where he was briefly institutionalized. Perhaps he is better described as a Christian socialist, occupying a radicalized political and cultural terrain somewhere between William Morris and the twentieth-century avant-garde. During a period when easel painting was increasingly subject to modern technologies of production and marketing, Van Gogh ground his own paints, prepared his own canvases, and built his own frames. An ascetic, he asked only minimal support from his brother Theo, and he never aspired to riches or fame. He dreamed of establishing a communist guild of painters with its own art gallery, where members would share equally whenever a painting was sold; he even suggested a technique of collective authorship that would allow a group of artists to paint a single picture, each contributing a special expertise to the final product.

In our own time, Van Gogh is viewed quite differently – as an uncompromising individualist or a protoexpressionist whose work is susceptible to purely secular, psychological readings. His technical innovations, which were meant to enhance the effects he admired in Millet, contributed to this phenomenon. In John Berger's words, the realist tradition from which a painter like Millet had emerged offered "no formula for representing the close, harsh, patient physicality of a peasant's labor *on,* instead of *in front of* the land."[3] Van Gogh's solution to the problem was to create a painterly language of movement and energy – something closer to cinema than to still photography or dramatic pantomime – that would convey his rapport with workers and his sense of religious wonder. Ironically, his rugged brushstrokes and quick, visible gestures on the canvas became what Berger calls a "handwriting." By expressing empathy with his subject, by treating the canvas as an unorthodox iconographic surface rather than as a "window," Van Gogh created a kind of art in which, as Berger notes, the "witness had become more important than his testimony.... And the consequent crisis of meaning forced most painting to become autobiographical."[4]

Unlike the abstract expressionists, toward whom his work inevitably leads, Van Gogh was in many ways a populist: his painting was representational, decoratively colored, and devoted to commonplace subjects. But the autobiographical or psychological discourse that grew up around his work gave him another kind of popular appeal, turning him into a dramatic character. Eventually, he was known to almost everyone as the madman who cut off his ear, as the unappreciated visionary, as the romantic artist *par excellence.* He also became Millet's logical successor in a late-capitalist or postmodern environment. If, as Berger has noted, copies of Millet's *The*

Sower were reproduced in peasant households, becoming a logo for an American bank and a symbol of revolution in China, Van Gogh's bright landscapes and haunted self-portraits have adorned countless posters and T-shirts; indeed his own version of *The Sower* was once used as the climactic image in a Hollywood biopic about tormented genius.

The movie in question is of course *Lust for Life*. A number of directors – including Alain Resnais, Paul Cox, Akira Kurosawa, and Robert Altman – have depicted Van Gogh on the screen, but Vincente Minnelli's award-winning film was produced on a huge scale, giving most people of my own generation their first knowledge of the painter. In fact, for better or worse, *Lust for Life* has probably contributed more to Van Gogh's posthumous reputation than any other movie or biographical text. Guardians of high culture often mention it in passing as an example of how Hollywood vulgarizes great art, and in a sense they are correct. Given its lurid title (which is derived from Irving Stone's novel), its lavish budget, and its star performances (by Kirk Douglas as Van Gogh and Anthony Quinn as Gauguin), this film can scarcely avoid the feeling of having been concocted in the *salons* of Beverly Hills. It also contains several unintentionally funny sequences in which familiar character actors, dressed as famous painters and framed in rigid tableaux, discuss the theory of impressionism. Nevertheless, *Lust for Life* deserves to be taken seriously, both as a commentary on Van Gogh and as an instance of the "wound and the bow" theme that runs throughout Minnelli's collaborations with John Houseman. A happy marriage of Houseman's intelligence, screenwriter Norman Corwin's gift for historical narrative, and Minnelli's sensitivity to Van Gogh's medium, it remains classic Hollywood's most interesting and troubled depiction of an artistic biography. To be sure, it is a romanticized film that takes a good many dramatic liberties; nevertheless, audiences can learn something from it about Van Gogh's techniques and artistic intentions – much more than from Robert Altman's highly praised but sensationalized *Vincent and Theo* (1990), a confusing art movie that treats Van Gogh as if he were an ancestor of the punk rockers. Even if the character it portrays were shown to be a blatant distortion of the historical Van Gogh, *Lust for Life* would still have much to recommend it, especially its treatment of a certain kind of male loneliness and its implicit recognition that the practice of art (including the practice of moviemaking) can be at once heroic, neurotic, and absurd.

Minnelli once told an interviewer that *Lust for Life* was "the only time I ever asked a studio to make a picture,"[5] and he repeatedly named it as his personal favorite among all his films. His work on the production was relatively unhampered, and the completed film was essentially unchanged by studio editors. MGM hired George Cukor to reshoot a brief conversation in Theo van Gogh's apartment, and it eliminated another scene showing Gauguin arriving in Arles by the night train; otherwise, the released version was exactly what Minnelli wanted. Even so, the picture would probably never have been made except for the unexpected box-office success of *Moulin Rouge,* John Huston's 1952 film about Toulouse-Lautrec. Several other considerations also worked in Minnelli's favor: MGM's long-standing option on Irving Stone's novelized biography of Van Gogh was about to expire; Kirk Douglas was planning his own movie about the painter; Dore Schary's wife was an art lover; and, as John Houseman pointed out to the MGM brass, reproductions of Van Gogh's *Sunflowers* were hanging "in every student's dormitory in America."[6]

After recruiting Douglas and persuading the studio to film large parts of the story on location (a new experience for Minnelli, but a standard practice in the industry by this time), the principle collaborators turned the film into a relatively straightforward account of Van Gogh's short career. Corwin stripped away Irving Stone's fictional device of a seductive young woman who appears to Van Gogh in hallucinations, and, in consultation with Minnelli and Houseman, he devised a complex and much more dramatically unified psychological profile of the character. Perhaps because of the way *Moulin Rouge* had depicted Toulouse-Lautrec, *Lust for Life* makes Van Gogh a sensitive artist who craves intimacy, but who suffers rejection in all his relationships. To sharpen this conception, the film actually reverses some of the roles in the Irving Stone novel; in Stone's book, for example, Van Gogh leaves his companion Christine in order to pursue a life as a painter, whereas in the film it is Christine who leaves Van Gogh. The John Huston film, however, is preoccupied with male anxieties of castration, figured in the dwarfish Toulouse-Lautrec. By contrast, *Lust for Life* is less phallocentric, and it makes Van Gogh's neurosis seem at least partly the result of society's hostility toward sentiment and artistic idealism.

Houseman and Minnelli were also surprisingly careful not to adorn a downbeat story with "entertainment values." Unlike *Moulin Rouge, Lust for Life* shows us nothing of "naughty Paree" – only a few rooms or outdoor spaces where artists work, debate, and exhibit. It contributes somewhat to a masculine myth of the avant-garde, depicting a scruffy artist who wanders freely around Europe and meets prostitutes and *filles respecteuses;* but it also makes clear that Van Gogh was neither an exile nor a cosmopolitan *flâneur.* The man portrayed in the film sneers at Degas for painting "ballet dancers and racehorses," and the nearest he comes to a love affair is in the aforementioned interlude with Christine, a working-class prostitute who has a child to support.

In place of Parisian night life, *Lust for Life* offers the visual spectacle of Van Gogh's own work. Corwin's script, which was revised somewhat by Houseman and associate producer Jud Kinberg during filming in Europe, relied heavily on Van Gogh's letters to his brother Theo, concentrating on four stages of his life as an artist: the black-and-white drawings from the mining district of the Borinage; the "Dutch earth" drawings and paintings of rural labor in the Hague; the impressionist landscapes of fin-de-siècle Paris; and the vivid, protoexpressionist portraiture and nature paintings of the south of France. At various points in the completed film, we see montages of the original canvases, which were photographed by still cameras in museums and private collections around the world and then rephotographed in Cinemascope. Minnelli was particularly interested in bringing the audience close to the surface of Van Gogh's work, showing "all the brushstrokes and even those places where he'd squeezed paint out of the tube onto the canvas."[7] In most cases he panned his camera across the pictures or zoomed in on significant details – especially on the vortices of sunlight in the late paintings, which provided a visual correlative to all those spectacular moments in his previous films, when a swirling pattern of light or color is pushed toward a kind of hysterical excess. (The "Minnellian" feeling was heightened even more by Miklos Rozsa's music, which resembled the neurasthenic waltz he had written for the ballroom sequence in *Madame Bovary*.)

Few films in Minnelli's career involved such elaborate attention to visual style. He shot many sequences outdoors, meticulously "naturalizing" a technique he had long employed in his stage and screen musicals (most obviously in *An American in Paris*), where the mise-en-scène resembles a famous painting come to life. Nevertheless, he was constrained by the dominant technology of 1956, and posterity might have been better served had the film been made five years earlier. Because Minnelli wanted to photograph the original canvases, and because he wanted the dramatic scenes to look as much like a Van Gogh as possible, he at first argued against using the new wider-frame Cinemascope process. He and Houseman traveled to New York, where they made a special plea to Arthur Lowe, MGM's chief executive, pointing out that the old-fashioned Academy ratio was closer to the dimensions of easel painting. Lowe countered that projectionists all over the United States were likely to show the film in Cinemascope no matter how it was photographed. Minnelli eventually bowed to this logic, turning out a fairly impressive if somewhat static example of wide-screen composition; ironically, however, the film is often shown today on cable TV and videocassette in a crudely "scanned" format that cuts off the edges of the original frame and reverts everything to an approximate Academy ratio.

Even when schools, museums, and retrospective theaters can obtain a Cinemascope print of *Lust for Life*, the picture loses some of its original impact because its color has deteriorated. Like everyone in the movie business in the mid-fifties, MGM had abandoned the expensive but durable Technicolor in favor of Eastmancolor, which does not require special cameras. Minnelli disliked Eastmancolor because it was unable to register a shade of yellow appropriate to Van Gogh's palette, and he managed to obtain the studio's last remaining holdings of a related stock called Afgacolor (a variant of the German Agfacolor). With the assistance of photographers Frederick Young and Russell Harlan, he devised a color scheme to approximate the four phases of Van Gogh's career: the coal-mining scenes were dominated by slate gray, the Dutch sequences by bluish green, the Parisian episodes by splashes of bright red, and the concluding section by sunny yellow. In this form, *Lust for Life* was one of the most impressive color films ever made, indirectly confirming John Berger's argument in *Ways of Seeing* that color photography is a modern substitute for the tactile luxury of oil paint.[8] But Afgacolor was no better than the Eastman process at retaining its quality through many generations. Most prints of the film available today have a brownish orange tint, and the magnificent yellows Minnelli struggled so hard to achieve have all but disappeared.

What remains is nonetheless worthy of viewing, and is especially interesting to contemplate in theoretical terms. Throughout, Minnelli has copied Van Gogh's canvases, finding visual doubles for the original models and "enacting" such paintings as the *Potato Eaters*, the *Night Café*, and the *Portrait of Dr. Gachet*. Frequently he poses Kirk Douglas in the foreground, laboring over a cleverly forged Van Gogh that exactly duplicates what we see in the background (see, e.g., Figure 20). The implication of these shots is paradoxical: Is Van Gogh a photographic realist, or is the film trying to see the world through his eyes? Is art imitating life, or vice versa?

Such questions occur because the film's approach to the problem of representation is in many ways quite different from Van Gogh's. At first glance, *Lust for Life* seems to be based on a typically romantic or "expressive-realist" notion of art: in going outdoors to the actual locales where Van Gogh worked, and in striving for accurate period detail, it implicitly supports a literal-minded realism; meanwhile, in portraying Van Gogh as a lonely, psychologically tormented individual, it also suggests that painting is the

Figure 20. Van Gogh (Kirk Douglas) at work in Arles. (*Lust for Life*, © 1956, Turner Entertainment Co., all rights reserved.)

expression of the artist's inner life. But Minnelli's aestheticism complicates these matters. Consider Figure 21, a publicity still, which represents one of the sequences in the film. Kirk Douglas, standing next to one of Van Gogh's self-portraits, stares at his reflection in a mirror while Anthony Quinn "paints" in the background. The photo invites us to compare Douglas's made-up face with the portrait, so that we can see how faithfully the film has captured Van Gogh's likeness; it also invites us to compare the mirror with the painting. The two frames-within-the-frame *reflect* a supposed reality, and at the same time *express* Van Gogh's psychology, symbolizing his divided ego. The composition emphasizes some of the underlying assumptions of romantic art, meanwhile calling our attention to the problems Van Gogh and Gauguin have been debating earlier in the film. Is Van Gogh brooding into the mirror or reacting to the way the mirror broods at him? Is art commenting on nature, as Van Gogh believes, or simply commenting on other works of art, as Gauguin contends? We cannot know, because the film blurs such distinctions – just as it makes us puzzle over the difference between copies and originals. Because the portrait of Van Gogh used in this

Figure 21. Which is the "real" Van Gogh? Kirk Douglas and Anthony Quinn in *Lust for Life*. (© 1956, Turner Entertainment Co., all rights reserved.)

shot was a forgery, how could we possibly know what is real in the first place?

Perhaps unintentionally, *Lust for Life* deconstructs certain romantic ideas about art, and at the same time provides a complex account of a romantic personality. (Here it seems important to emphasize that Van Gogh *was* in many respects a romantic – a tragically underappreciated and dedicated figure who would not adapt to bourgeois life and who felt a religious affinity with nature and common labor.) It does not accomplish this task, however, without producing a certain incoherence. In some respects, the film's basic idea of the character can be traced back to the earliest essay on Van Gogh's art, written by his friend Albert Aurier and published in the *Mercure de France* shortly before his death:

That which characterizes all the work of Vincent Van Gogh is the excess of force, and the violence in expression. In his categorical affirmative of the essential character of things, in his often rash simplification of form, in his insolent desire to look at the sun face to face, in the passion of his drawing and color, there lies revealed a powerful one, a male, a darer who is sometimes brutal, sometimes ingeniously delicate.[9]

Lust for Life rejects the hypermasculine image described in these lines, giving Van Gogh a great many "feminine" traits and treating Gauguin's machismo unsympathetically. Even so, the film takes "violence" and "excess" as the keys to Van Gogh's behavior, depicting him as a sort of primitive who brims with good-hearted emotions. In adopting this approach, it splits the performance in two, as if it had difficulty reconciling the homespun, passionate figure played by Kirk Douglas with the articulate, lyrical voice in the letters. Strangely, whenever we hear quotations from Van Gogh's writings as narration or internal monologue, the words are spoken by James Donald, who was cast in the role of Theo. Donald was probably chosen because of his ability to portray an earnest, commonsensical businessman – the opposite of Kirk Douglas's Vincent; but each time he reads Van Gogh's letters over shots of Douglas's face, the effect is vaguely schizophrenic. On the outside, Van Gogh looks clumsy and rather American; on the inside, he has the refined soul of a British Shakespearean actor.

In his memoirs, John Houseman remarks in passing that Van Gogh's estate prohibited MGM from making any reference to the family's hereditary physical illness. Houseman does not say what the illness was, but some art historians have suggested that Vincent Van Gogh was not mentally disturbed at all; he may have suffered from what contemporary medicine describes as "temporal lobe epilepsy," and he seems to have known that his symptoms were caused by a physical disorder.[10] (In the late nineteenth century, it was not uncommon for a victim of this ailment to amputate an ear.) Perhaps because *Lust for Life* could not address the historical facts directly, it depicts the protagonist as a kind of saintly neurotic, and it concentrates on the theme of sexual loneliness. The film occasionally suggests Freudian motives for Van Gogh's behavior, especially in the scenes involving his relationship with his father, but ultimately it takes his periodic mental breakdowns as givens, leaving them unexplained. It also makes Van Gogh something of an artistic visionary and a scapegoat for established society, so that his irrationality seems bound up with his solitary drive to capture what he calls the "poetry" hidden in "a man or a woman at work, some furrows in a plowed field, or a patch of land, sea, or sky."

This last effect was implicit in Irving Stone's novel, but, more important, it was consistent with every picture that Minnelli and Houseman made together. In all of their work, the world of art is both neurotic and consoling, both irrational and therapeutic; the difference in this case is that the artist's psychological compulsion has been pushed to the breaking point. The Van Gogh we see in the film is an unstable personality, a tragic loner whose paintings function both as a release of libidinal energy and as an imaginary whirlpool, pulling him toward death. He does everything with a kind of anxious, headlong intensity, transforming the things he loves into sentimental ideals and exhausting himself with frenzied dedication to art. In a conversation with Gauguin late in the picture, he remarks that violence "sickens" him because he has so much of it inside; his barely repressed rage or "lust" conditions all his dealings with people, and whenever it threatens to erupt, he turns it further inward, to the point of self-mutilation.

Such a character was well suited to Kirk Douglas's histrionic style. Much of the vividness and emotional effect of the film derive from his crouched energy and muscular, tormented gestures, which are intended as a physical correlative for the rough, hardy surfaces of Van Gogh's paintings. Throughout, he makes Van Gogh seem both a compassionate idealist and a bumbling slob – a man who constantly oscillates between weepy sentiment and seething anger. (To create a proper posture and movement, he practiced walking with his shoes untied.) In my own view, his performance also has a vaguely Chaplinesque quality, suggesting a mixture of sensitivity, clownish athleticism, and tramplike loneliness; consider, for example, the scene in which he walks slowly away from the camera down a long corridor in an insane asylum and jumps in fear at the sound of one of the patients screaming. Although he skillfully maintains our sympathy and identification with the character, his portrayal is completely unglamorous and sometimes oppressively nerve-racked, making us aware of why so many people shy away when Van Gogh craves their friendship.

From the moment we first meet the character, Douglas makes him seem both admirable and annoying, suggesting his extreme sensitivity and ambivalence toward bourgeois authority. In the opening scene of the film, a committee of evangelicals is shown granting ordinations to a group of handsome, well-dressed young men. As the newly appointed preachers leave the room, we glimpse Van Gogh huddled outside in a corridor, looking like an anxious factory worker. The chair of the committee reports that the next case will be impossible – a "stumbling and inarticulate child" who is unable to deliver a sermon without reading from a manuscript. When Van Gogh enters, he is servile, hunched over, his hands flexing nervously but powerfully at his sides. He confesses that he could "never equal" his father, who is a respected minister, but he begs to be of some "service" to the world. Just as the committee seems on the verge of rejecting him, his cringing subservience turns into a kind of violent, angry whining: "I'll do anything, only use me!" he pleads, his voice rising in intensity like a trapped animal.

When the church reluctantly gives Van Gogh a mission in the impoverished mining district of the Borinage, his capacity for Christ-like (or masochistic) suffering becomes evident. After delivering a boring and idealistic sermon to his uncomprehending flock, he searches down a workman who has contemptuously walked out of the service. The workman describes what he has heard as "pious bilge," and Van Gogh immediately asks, "What can I do? Help me!" After being taken on a tour of the mines, where he sees consumptive children working underground, he experiences a transformation: washing dust from his face, he confronts his reflection in a mirror (an important motif), and decides to minister directly to his flock. In a series of almost hallucinatory shots that combine Minnelli's flair for camera movement, color, and massed choreography with the *topoi* of a novel like Zola's *Germinal,* we see Van Gogh covered with soot and coal, burrowing among slag heaps with the miner's wives, attending to sick children, and trying desperately to remove bodies from a collapsed mineshaft. Shambling, ape-like, appalled, he moves through the hellish world of industrial labor like an exhausted medic on a battlefield. When a delegation of church officials subsequently arrives for a visit, they are shocked to find him living in a hovel, sleeping on a bed of straw. "You have degraded the dignity of the church," one of them says, and Van Gogh reacts angrily, sounding rather like Jonathan Shields screaming at Georgia Lorrison: "I don't care to be respected! Don't worry about how I sleep!" (He kicks the straw.) "Look at the fresh graves of children!" (He gestures furiously out the window.) "Scrub floors with the women!" (He acts out the scrubbing on a tabletop.) "Get those fine clothes dirty!" (He grabs a minister's coat and flings it open.) As the delegates exit, his shouts rise to a scream: "Hypocrite! Hypocrite!"

In the subsequent episodes, we move from a public to a private world, concentrating on the character's family and love life. Dismissed from the church, an unhealthy and emotionally troubled Van Gogh takes his brother's advice and returns to the Netherlands, where he lives with his parents and begins to pursue his interest in art. His proletarian clothing and unorthodox Christianity disturb his father (Henry Daniell, a specialist in chilly and epicine characters), and at a luncheon for "cousin Kay" (Jeanette Sterke), an attractive young widow who has come for a visit, he scandalizes the entire household. Minnelli dresses Kirk Douglas in a sheepskin vest and ragged suspenders, staging his entrance into the dining room against an elaborate display of dishware arranged along a sideboard, so that he looks like a bull in a china shop. From the moment he sits down, he stares longingly across the table at the voluptuous guest, who is buttoned up to the neck in her widow's weeds; and when he makes a casual reference to her dead husband, she leaves the room in embarrassment.

Later, alone with Kay and her son at a picnic, Van Gogh suddenly declares his love. (This is one of the few scenes in the picture where a studio set represents the outdoors, but Douglas's uninhibited performance compensates for the visual awkwardness.) When Kay resists Van Gogh's proposal, he attempts to win her over with the sheer force of his desire. Douglas's insistent embrace looks at first like an attempted rape (most of his previous films had included scenes in which he treated women brutally), but then it quickly subsides into a desperate clinging. Revolted by what he has done, he falls to the ground and grovels at Kay's feet, grasping her skirts and begging for understanding until she runs away in fear.

Soon after the disastrous picnic, we see Van Gogh visiting Kay's father, the Reverend Stricker (Wilton Graff), a respectable but reasonably kindly man who grows impatient when Van Gogh cannot accept rejection. "Are you such a weakling?" he asks. "Do you have to whimper about it?" Once again Van Gogh flashes into anger, and this time his violence is directed against his own body. Thrusting his hand into a burning candle, he looks grimly at Kay's father and asks to speak with her "for as long as I can keep my hand in this flame!"

The young Martin Scorsese may have admired the image of Van Gogh holding his palm over the fire, because both *Mean Streets* and *Taxi Driver* show us characters who attempt to "purify" themselves by burning their flesh. As in Scorsese's films, the self-punishment elicits a complex feeling: Van Gogh seems oddly Christ-like or spiritual, a victim of an insensitive world, but at the same time he is clearly unbalanced and obsessed, incapable of ordinary relationships. One of the most unusual qualities of *Lust for Life* is this paradoxical, relatively dispassionate treatment of madness, which creates sympathy for the character and at the same time never allows him to become the martyred hero he sometimes resembles. (The sense of martyrdom is especially evident in a later scene in which Van Gogh leans out of a window in his house at Arles and chases off a mob that has come to see his mutilated ear: swathed in bandages and mournfully shouting, "Leave me alone," he recalls Quasimoto at his most pathetic and romantic.) The people who reject him in the early part of the film are stuffy, conventional, and more than a little neurotic themselves, but they are not exactly villains; lonely and needy as Van Gogh might be, he is never an easy companion.

The nature of Van Gogh's psychological problem remains unclear, although his lacerating anger and self-contempt are obviously prompted by a need for love. Minnelli once described the character's relationships as "asexual," and soon after the release of the film, Kirk Douglas shocked MGM executives by telling the press that he believed Van Gogh was unconsciously homosexual. Neither of these explanations, however, is adequate to the character we see on the screen. Van Gogh smothers both women and men, treating them as ego ideals and driving them away with his doglike attentiveness. More than once he is accused of being "unmanly," but the film does not support such crudely puritanical and oppressive attitudes. Ultimately, *Lust for Life* seems more interested in dramatizing the character's behavior than in explaining or justifying it; and for that reason the film achieves a delicate balance between pathos and unsentimental detachment. Van Gogh is open, generous, and passionate, but his desperate, whining pleas for companionship become excessive and sometimes annoying; he finds himself in conflict with stern patriarchs or emotionally cool personalities who have little capacity for affection, but many of his difficulties seem to be of his own making.

The scenes with the prostitute Christine, whom Van Gogh meets after his encounter with Kay's father, are especially noteworthy because of the way they balance sympathy with Van Gogh against a feeling that his artistic project is somewhat mad (Figure 22). The British actress Pamela Brown – one of Houseman's most intelligent and unorthodox strokes of casting – gives Christine a world-weary toughness and a maternal beauty without suggesting any of Hollywood's stereotypical images of womanhood. And because she is such a vivid, self-sufficient character, Van Gogh's relationship with her seems like a tragicomic fantasy. After writing a kind of ode to domestic bliss in a letter to Theo, he asks Christine to stand on a windswept beach while he paints her portrait. When the foul weather makes her walk off in disgust, he poses her for hours in their cramped room, requiring that she hold a baby in her lap like a worker's madonna. After a series of potentially violent quarrels, she leaves him, explaining cooly and forthrightly that she wants food on the table and a less slovenly existence.

Of all the failed relationships in Van Gogh's life, however, the most traumatic is with Gauguin, whom he meets in Paris and later invites to Arles. Here, too, Van Gogh seems both sympathetic and crazy, both noble and irritating. The episode is even more impressive for the way it dramatizes a failed domestic bonding between two males. From the mid-fifties onward, Minnelli's films repeatedly criticized American standards of sexual "normality," and although he never treated homosexuality directly, he flirted with the issue in *The Cobweb, Designing Woman, Tea and Sympathy, Some*

Figure 22. Van Gogh and Christine (Kirk Douglas and Pamela Brown) in
Lust for Life. (© 1956, Turner Entertainment Co., all rights reserved.)

Came Running, Home from the Hill, and *Goodby, Charlie.* In *Lust for Life,*
he depicted Van Gogh and Gauguin as what he later described as "the
original odd couple,"[11] giving homoerotic overtones to the arguments between them; he did this, however, without any suggestion of leering perversity, in the implicit recognition that the psychological tensions between
the characters were possible in any relationship.

Unlike Irving Stone's novel, the film does everything possible to make Gauguin and Van Gogh polar opposites. Gauguin is fastidious, dandified, swag-
gering, sexually confident, competitive, and contemptuous of "love." Van
Gogh is sloppy, insecure, self-effacing, idealistic about women, and hungry
for attachments. Gauguin enjoys fist fights and detests sentiment, whereas
Van Gogh is nauseated by violence and reduced to tears by *Uncle Tom's
Cabin.* The two men's attitudes toward painting are consistent with these dif-
fering personalities. Gauguin resembles Van Gogh in being an orientalist and
something of a romantic, but he is above all a coolheaded formalist who
wants to develop a personal, media-specific style. By contrast, Van Gogh is a

148

great admirer of democratic realists like Rembrandt, Millet, and Delacroix; for him, subject matter is everything, and the purpose of style is not to call attention to the canvas but to touch the heart of the viewer, communicating the holiness of nature and the "dignity of toil." It follows that Gauguin is most satisfied when he can paint inside, free of the hot sun and the punishing mistral; meanwhile, Van Gogh paces around the room, anxious to be in contact with the world. At one point, in the midst of a gale, we see Gauguin denounce the weather and give up working, just as Van Gogh begins nailing his easel down to keep it from blowing away.

The idea of these characters occupying the same cramped space is potentially comic, but Minnelli plays it for tension and menace, beginning with what he called a "Rover boys" atmosphere and ending with a deadly confrontation.[12] In order to make a vivid contrast between "strong" and "weak" personalities, and in order to heighten the feeling of impending violence, the film omits certain details from the Stone novel, such as Gauguin's illness before coming to Arles. It also emphasizes that Gauguin has fallen into an artistic dry period, and that Van Gogh is hip deep in completed work – including the paintings of sunflowers, which he hangs in Gauguin's bedroom as a gesture of friendship. From the start, Gauguin is quietly jealous of Van Gogh's art and irritated by his worshipful, smothering attentiveness. ("Mighty friendly," Anthony Quinn remarks on first seeing the sunflowers, and his reading of the line nicely conveys Gauguin's uneasiness.) In one of the most cleverly acted scenes of the film, Gauguin expresses his resentment by casually, almost contemptuously taking possession of the prostitute Rachel (Julie Robinson), who has been showing affection for Van Gogh. Just before Gauguin is introduced to this woman, she hangs one of her bracelets over Van Gogh's ear – an underplayed piece of business that Minnelli places in one corner of a busy long shot, subtly foreshadowing the bloodshed we know is coming.

In their final, nasty confrontation, Gauguin adopts the ruthless, aim-for-the-jugular style of a man who hates his companion intimately. Before exiting the yellow house in Arles, he brutally accuses Van Gogh of being a pampered, self-pitying sentimentalist: "I know all about loneliness," he says, "only I don't whine about it!" He then stalks off to the local brothel while Van Gogh, like a jilted wife in a domestic melodrama, remains at home in an agony of abandonment and self-contempt. Gauguin's speech, however, has been an unwitting echo of Kay's father, and it soon provokes a similar response. Pale, exhausted, encrusted with dirt and paint, Van Gogh seizes a razor and goes running after Gauguin, only to stop in the middle of the street. Returning home in a daze, he encounters a series of "mad," swirling lights reminiscent of the sun in his paintings, and he confronts his own tormented reflection in a mirror. After grinding his face against the glass, he steps out of the frame, and from offscreen we hear his agony as he cuts off his ear.

Art historians might lament MGM's melodramatics, but Douglas's blood-curdling scream and Miklos Rozsa's nerve-racking music have an uncommon power. The scene develops logically out of everything preceding it, confirming Van Gogh's isolation and providing one of the most agonized images of *male* emotional suffering in the history of American movies. (Such behavior is typical of movie spinsters and rejected women, especially in adaptations of Tennessee Williams's dramas, but I can think of no comparable scene in the career of any Hollywood leading man, with the qualified exception of James Stewart in such films as *Vertigo* or *It's a Wonderful Life*.) Moreover, despite the fact that Van Gogh has been treated somewhat clinically, his insane response makes him a much more sympathetic character than his ostensibly "masculine" companion: when Gauguin returns the next morning, he finds a police inspector prowling the house and Van Gogh's bloody figure sprawled face down on a bed. Without looking at his former friend, he makes an ignominious exit from Arles, as if his own life were in danger.

The breakup with Gauguin is in one sense the climax of the film, but the most spectacular and poignant moment comes later, in an almost wordless sequence after Van Gogh has been released from the asylum at Saint-Remy. As an image of individual despair, this sequence has rarely been equaled — chiefly because Minnelli staged it not in some desolate space but in a crowd, developing a counterpoint between Van Gogh's inner turmoil and a bustling, cheerful celebration of Bastille Day in the village of Auvers. Photographed on location and inspired by one of Van Gogh's paintings, the sequence is filled with vividly costumed French extras and sweeping, dramatically engineered camera movements, as if the colorful frenzy of the ballet from *An American in Paris* had been given a documentary look and a bleak purpose. Kirk Douglas winds his way through a crowd and enters a café; inside (at one corner of the Cinemascope screen), he sits hunched at a table, grasping his head in his trembling hands and disintegrating into tears. Through the window behind him, we see the communal festivity, illuminated by a cloudless sky, decked in patriotic bunting, filled with dancing couples and flag-waving kids. An attractive young waitress brings Douglas a drink, barely pausing to notice his misery. The camera remains stationary, but in the distance we can see a spinning carousel, reminiscent of all the other occasions in Minnelli's films when a character's psychological crisis is accompanied by a swirling blur of light or color: as with Emma Bovary's dance and Georgia Lorrison's ride along the Coast highway, beauty spills over into delirium, and a world of festivity or carnival becomes a friendless void.

The film draws to an end with an impressively photographed re-creation of the artist's suicide after he paints black crows rising from a blazing wheat field. True to actual events, it then shows Van Gogh on his deathbed, saying farewell to Theo. Despite all this pathos and despair, however, *Lust for Life* never seems a depressing film, probably because of its expensive production values and colorful, scenic re-creations of Van Gogh's landscapes. In the last shots, the filmmakers try to become even more positive, reprieving an earlier conversation between Van Gogh and a nun in the asylum at Saint-Remy: we hear Van Gogh describing *The Sower* as a portrait of everyman "in the bright daylight with the sun flooding everything in a light of pure gold." Finally, in a move typical of Minnelli, the camera pulls back from a huge display of Van Gogh's canvases, so that the sun becomes momentarily benign, and art provides consolation.

Even though *Lust for Life* ends on a note of sweetness and light, it does not try to expunge certain troubling ironies. Nowhere do Minnelli, Houseman, and Corwin suggest that Van Gogh's paintings have ever functioned as he intended. Van Gogh was an anticapitalist who chose art as a quasi-religious vocation; his medium, however, was easel painting, and the film makes clear that there was an unavoidable contradiction between his perhaps naive artistic purpose and the social or economic conditions under which he worked.

The major dramatic irony of the film – though it is never explicitly stated – is that Van Gogh's paintings have become the most expensive in the world. (Other, related ironies are somewhat more apparent. In one scene, Gauguin sneers at Millet for painting "calendar art," unaware that he and Van Gogh would one day themselves become the ultimate calendar artists.) Indeed the visual experience offered to the public by MGM, in which we see beautifully photographed montages of Van Gogh's canvases and dozens of undetectable forgeries spread across the sets in casual abandon, is in part a spectacle of *wealth,* roughly equivalent to the thrill of watching the costly massed extras in a DeMille epic, or the high-tech gadgets in a Schwarzenegger adventure. Nowadays, it is almost impossible to watch the sequence in which Van Gogh paints Dr. Gachet (cleverly impersonated by Everett Sloane) without being aware that in 1990 a group of Japanese bankers paid $82.5 million for the portrait. Even in 1956, Van Gogh's work was worth astonishing sums: when Kirk Douglas offered to forgo his salary on *Lust for Life* in exchange for a single Van Gogh canvas, the studio turned him down. "I can only afford to play Van Gogh," he joked. "I can't afford to own him."[3]

Why should the portrait of Dr. Gachet cost so much? The question is unanswerable because the commodity value of a painting is governed less by scarcity than by aesthetic desire. Critical discourse stimulates this desire in certain ways, but it cannot account for actual prices. Cézanne, for example, is valued less in the contemporary market than is Van Gogh, even though he has a greater critical reputation. Undoubtedly films such as *Lust for Life* boost the monetary value of paintings because they provide individual artists with celebrity, publicity, and a mythic aura; but films are simply the products of an all-pervasive commodification that extends from Van Gogh's canvases to every other art or spectacle, so that any given object in the modern world, no matter what its original purpose, can be used to promote some other object.

We can see the process at work in the marketing of *Lust for Life*. When the picture was released in New York, a host of elegant department stores – including Henri Bendel, Best and Company, Bonwit Teller, Lord & Taylor, Ohrbach's, De Pinna, Franklin Simon, Jay Thorpe, and Gimbel's – loaned MGM their windows for "the display of fashions against the backdrop of landscapes and still lifes as painted by Van Gogh."[4] We might say that in paying an honorable tribute to a painter he admired, Vincente Minnelli was simply returning to his original profession as a window decorator. But it does no good to condemn him as a mere commodifier, since his subject was already a commodity. He and Houseman were fully aware of this phenomenon, as we can tell by the dialogue from *The Cobweb* quoted as an epigraph to this chapter. Throughout *Lust for Life,* they show Van Gogh's dependence on his brother, who works for commercial dealers; and as the story progresses, they reveal a tragic, almost absurd gulf between the artist and everyone in his potential audience. The agricultural laborers in Arles do not appreciate Van Gogh's paintings (as a matter of historical fact, most of them would not pose for him) any more than the miners in the Borinage appreciate his sermons. The conservative critical establishment regards modernism as a threat to France, and even a connoisseur like the psychologist Dr. Gachet (who, significantly, treated some of the best painters of the day) seems more interested in collecting objects than in understanding the people who make them. Meanwhile, the wealthy buyers in Paris are mere investors; early on, we see a bourgeois patron in Theo's gallery studying a couple of rather academic-looking canvases and asking, "Tell me, if you were me, which would you want to have your money in?"

Under circumstances such as these, Van Gogh's desire to serve the world is quixotic, and we can hardly be surprised when he goes mad. Thus while *Lust for Life* testifies to Van Gogh's posthumous glory, it also makes us question the nature of his ultimate recognition. In its relentless exploration of the character's loneliness, in its revelation of the grinding contradictions of his art, it pushes Minnellian melodrama toward exceedingly pessimistic conclusions. The fictional Van Gogh in this film cannot fall back on the pleasures of fame or camaraderie like the show-business types in *The Bad and the Beautiful*. His passions are founded on an ideal, and he has no means of fulfilling Freud's crucial imperatives: to love and to work. The rather bureaucratic chief of the asylum at Saint-Remy tells us that "painting is beneficial, perhaps even necessary, to this patient's well being," but painting also contributes to Van Gogh's frustrations. In a capitalist world dominated by standards of "manliness," he cannot achieve *eros* or *agape;* and when he tries to communicate his feelings through art, his work seems useless, solipsistic, merely "expressive."

Minnelli must have identified with Van Gogh – not only because he treats the painter sympathetically, but also because he, too, seems to believe that art has value beyond the marketplace. *Lust for Life* is therefore his most representative achievement – the place in which he movingly confronts all the dilemmas and contraditions of his own career in the movies. Nevertheless, like all of his other films, it exemplifies many of the same problems that it criticizes. In a letter to Theo that the film does not quote, Van Gogh wrote that artists should never paint for the sake of "grandiose exhibitions," but for "people and work so that each could have in his home some pictures or reproductions which would be lessons, like the work of Millet."[15] *Lust for Life* is at best a partial fulfillment of that desire. It mechanically reproduces Van Gogh, taking him out of private collections and making him available to people in their daily lives; but in the process it also becomes a "grandiose exhibition," on a scale only Hollywood could achieve. It participates in what Peter Brook has called "the moral occult," melodramatically teaching us a few of Van Gogh's own "lessons."[16] At the same time, however, it underplays Van Gogh's political idealism and shifts the dramatic emphasis toward psychology rather than history. Ultimately, it tells the story of a gifted madman, and it turns great painting into a beautiful symptom, with no justification other than itself.

Notes

Introduction

1. Quoted in James Naremore, *The Magic World of Orson Welles* (Dallas: Southern Methodist University Press, 1989), p. 121.
2. For more recent examples of the shop-window metaphor, see the following: Charles Eckert, "The Carole Lombard in Macy's Window," in *Fabrications: Costuming and the Female Body,* ed. Jane Gaines and Charlotte Herzog (New York: Routledge, 1990), pp. 100–21; Mary Ann Doane, *The Desire to Desire: The Women's Film of the 1940s* (Bloomington: Indiana University Press, 1987), p. 24; Jane Gaines, "The *Queen Christina* Tie-Ups: Convergence of Show Window and Screen," *Quarterly Review of Film & Video,* 11, no. 1 (1989), 35–60; and Christopher Anderson, "Hollywood in the Home: TV and the End of the Studio System," in *Modernity and Mass Culture,* ed. James Naremore and Patrick Brantlinger (Bloomington: Indiana University Press, 1991), pp. 89–93.
3. "The Current Cinema," *Time* (May 14, 1945), 94.
4. For a valuable discussion of these matters in relation to modern intellectual history, see Matei Calinescu, *Five Faces of Modernity* (Durham, N.C.: Duke University Press, 1987).

1. The Aesthete in the Factory

1. Quoted in Charles Francisco, *The Radio City Music Hall* (New York: Dutton, 1979), p. 26. Minnelli himself had a good deal of influence over the interior decoration of the Music Hall; he even persuaded Georgia O'Keefe to paint designs for one of the women's rooms.
2. Theodor W. Adorno has remarked that "it was hardly accidental that the slogan *l'art pour l'art* was coined in the Paris of the first half of the nineteenth century, when literature really became large-scale business for the first time." See "Television and the Patterns of Mass Culture," in *Mass Culture: The Popular Arts in America,* ed. Bernard Rosenberg and David Manning White (New York: The Free Press, 1957), p. 475.

3. Andrew Sarris, *The American Cinema: Directors and Directions* (New York: Dutton, 1968), p. 101.

4. Vincente Minnelli and Hector Acre, *I Remember It Well* (Garden City, N.Y.: Doubleday, 1974), p. 37.

5. Ibid., p. 42.

6. Ibid., p. 45.

7. Ibid., p. 46.

8. Ibid., p. 8.

9. Robert C. Allen and Douglas Gomery, *Film History: Theory and Practice* (New York: Knopf, 1985), pp. 179–207.

10. Quoted in Stephen Harvey, *Directed by Vincente Minnelli* (New York: The Museum of Modern Art and Harper & Row, 1989), p. 28.

11. Ibid., p. 30.

12. Walter Benjamin, "Paris, Capital of the Nineteenth Century," in *Reflections*, trans. Edmund Jephcott (New York: Harcourt Brace Jovanovich, 1978), p. 146.

13. Rosalind Williams, *Dreamworlds: Mass Consumption in Late Nineteenth-Century France* (Berkeley and Los Angeles: University of California Press, 1982), p. 3.

14. Ibid., p. 3.

15. Ibid., pp. 115–16.

16. Quoted in ibid., p. 119.

17. Stephen Spender, "Moderns and Contemporaries," in *The Idea of the Modern*, ed. Irving Howe (New York: Horizon Press), p. 47.

18. Ibid., p. 47.

19. Peter Wollen, "Cinema/Americanism/the Robot," in *Modernity and Mass Culture*, ed. Naremore and Brantlinger, pp. 41–69.

20. Quoted in Stuart Ewen, *Captains of Consciousness* (New York: McGraw-Hill, 1976), p. 37.

21. Quoted in William MacAdams, *Ben Hecht: The Man Behind the Legend* (New York: Scribners, 1990), pp. 73–4.

22. Quoted in Harvey, *Directed by Vincente Minnelli*, p. 30.

23. Quoted in ibid., p. 23.

24. Minnelli and Acre, *I Remember*, p. 51. In one of his epigrammactic comments, Walter Benjamin has emphasized the connection between nineteenth-century consumer society and the surrealist movement: "The father of Surrealism was Dada; its mother was an arcade." Quoted by Susan Buck-Morss, *The Dialectics of Seeing: Walter Benjamin and the Arcades Project* (Cambridge, Mass.: MIT Press, 1989), p. 275.

25. Harvey, *Directed by Vincente Minnelli*, p. 33.

26. Stanley Green, *Ring Bells! Sing Songs! Broadway Musicals of the 1930s* (New Rochelle, N.Y.: Arlington House, 1971), pp. 12–15.

27. Norris Houghton, "The Designer Sets the Stage," *Theater Arts Monthly* (New York), 20, no. 10 (October 1936), 784.

28. Quoted in ibid., p. 785.

29. Ibid., p. 787.

30. Quoted in ibid., p. 784.

31. Harvey, *Directed by Vincente Minnelli*, p. 80.

32. For additional commentary on *The Band Wagon*'s manipulation of a high culture/pop culture distinction, see James Naremore and Patrick Brantlinger, "Six Artistic Cultures," in *Modernity and Mass Culture,* pp. 15–19.

33. Minnelli and Acre, *I Remember,* p. 33.

34. For detailed information on this and other studios, see Thomas Schatz, *The Genius of the System* (New York: Pantheon, 1988).

35. Hugh Fordin, *The Movies' Greatest Musicals* (New York: Fredrick Ungar, 1984), p. 51.

36. Ernesto Serebrinsky and Oscar Garaycochea, "Vincente Minnelli Interviewed in Argentina," *Movie* (London), 10 (June 1963), 23–8.

37. Rick Altman, *The American Film Musical* (Bloomington: Indiana University Press, 1987), chaps. 6–8. Most commentary on film genres is somewhat Aristotelian; even when it divides genres into subcategories and shows them changing over time, it assumes that we can list a set of necessary and sufficient characteristics for the various types of film. See, for example, Stephen Neale, *Genre* (London: BFI, 1983). The cognitive scientists would say that this technique belongs to the realm of "objectivist semantics," and that it has doubtful validity. Consider the following critique, from Mark Johnson, *The Body and the Mind: The Bodily Basis of Meaning, Imagination, and Reason* (Chicago: University of Chicago Press, 1987): "Objectivist semantics has tended to favor a set-theoretical view of a category as specifying necessary and sufficient conditions for membership in a given kind. But ... there is a growing body of empirical research that suggests a different view of categories as consisting of networks with prototypical members clustered in the center of the category, with less prototypical members at various distances from the central members. A category thus forms a complex radial structure, and we would need an account of the nature of these structures."

38. Thomas Elsaesser, "Vincente Minnelli," in *Genre: The Musical,* ed. Rick Altman (London: Routledge & Kegan Paul, 1981), p. 17.

39. See Leon Hunt, "E. C. on the Couch," *The Comics Journal* 133 (December 1989), 54–63. *Psychoanalysis* contained a letters column called "Id Bits," and its melodramatic stories were built around the "talking cure." We should recall that clinical psychoanalysis received widespread acceptance in the United States during the early forties. Not only popular culture, but also high criticism was affected by this development. See Chapter Five for a discussion of Edmund Wilson and Lionel Trilling's literary criticism in the period.

40. Harvey, *Directed by Vincent Minnelli,* p. 27.

41. Jane Gaines, "Costume and Narrative: How Dress Tells the Woman's Story," in *Fabrications: Costuming and the Female Body,* ed. Jane Gaines and Charlotte Herzog (New York: Routledge, 1990), p. 196.

42. James Agee, *Agee on Film,* vol. 1 (New York: McDowell, Obolensky, 1958), p. 166.

43. Joel E. Segel, "The Musicals," in Bleeker St. Cinema, *The Films of Vincente Minnelli* (New York: New York Zoetrope, 1978), p. 32.

44. Brian Henderson, *A Critique of Film Theory* (New York: Dutton, 1980), pp. 53–8.

45. Quoted in Fordin, *The Movies' Greatest Musicals,* p. 114.

46. Quoted in ibid., p. 113.

47. "The Current Cinema," *Time* (May 14, 1945), 94.

48. Barry Salt, *Film Style and Technology: History and Analysis* (London: Starword, 1983), p. 29.

49. Benjamin, "Paris, Capital of the Nineteenth Century," p. 150.

50. Ibid., p. 149. See also Emmanuelle Toulet, "Cinema at the Universal Exposition, Paris, 1900," *Persistence of Vision* 9 (1991), 10–36. Toulet notes that the techniques of the cinema and the panorama are different, but that in Paris at the turn of the century, the "terms by which the two spectacles were described or lauded are very close to the point where they could be confounded" (p. 17).

51. V. F. Perkins, *Film as Film* (New York: Penguin, 1972), p. 77.

52. Quoted in Jay Leyda, ed., *Film Makers Speak* (New York: DaCapo, 1977), p. 56.

53. Minnelli and Acre, *I Remember,* p. 164.

54. Andrew Ross, *No Respect: Intellectuals and Popular Culture* (New York: Routledge, 1989), p. 139.

55. Manny Farber, "Dream Furlough," *New Republic* (May 21, 1945), 709. Farber added: "Minnelli's work in this, and in 'Meet Me in St. Louis,' indicates that he is the most human, most skillful director to appear in Hollywood in years."

56. Agee, *Agee on Film,* p. 166.

57. Lindsay Anderson, "Minnelli, Kelly, and *An American in Paris,*" *Sequence* 14 (1952), 36.

58. Ibid., p. 38.

59. André Bazin, "On the *politique des auteurs,*" in *Cahiers du Cinema: The 1950s,* ed. Jim Hiller (Cambridge, Mass.: Harvard University Press, 1985), pp. 248–60.

60. Jean Domarchi, "Knife in the Wound," in *Cahiers: 1950s,* ed. Hiller, pp. 243–4.

61. Quoted in Jim Hiller, ed., *Cahiers du Cinema: The 1960s* (Cambridge, Mass.: Harvard University Press, 1987), pp. 2–3.

62. Quoted by T. L. French, "The Comedies," in Bleeker St. Cinema, *The Films of Vincente Minnelli,* p. 88.

63. Quoted, ibid., p. 88.

64. Quoted, ibid., p. 89.

65. Hiller, *Cahiers: 1960s,* p. 198.

66. Albert Johnson, "The Films of Vincente Minnelli," *Film Quarterly* 12 (Winter 1958), 20–35; and 13 (Spring 1959), 32–42.

67. Sarris, *American Cinema,* p. 102.

68. Ibid.

69. Michel Foucault, "What Is an Author?" (extract) in John Caughie, ed., *Theories of Authorship* (London: Routledge & Kegan Paul, 1981), pp. 287–9.

70. Ibid., p. 284.

71. James Naremore, "Authorship and the Cultural Politics of Film Criticism," *Film Quarterly,* 44, no. 1 (Fall 1990), 14–23.

72. Most criticism of this sort derived from Jean-Louis Comolli and Jean Narboni's famous *Cahiers du Cinema* editorial of 1969, "Cinema/Ideology/Criticism," reprinted in *Movies and Methods,* vol. 1, ed. Bill Nichols (Berkeley and Los Angeles:

University of California Press, 1976), pp. 22–30. Comolli and Narboni's argument helped establish the agenda for the British journal *Screen* in the seventies, especially for the writings of Colin MacCabe and Stephen Heath.

73. Elsaesser, "Vincente Minnelli," p. 12.

74. Ibid., p. 11.

75. Paul Willemen, "Distanciation and Douglas Sirk," *Screen*, 12, no. 1 (Spring 1971), 63–7. See also Willemen, "Towards an Analysis of the Sirkian System," *Screen*, 13, no. 4 (1972–3), 128–34. This critical moment is discussed at length by Barbara Klinger in her forthcoming book, *Melodrama and Meaning: History, Culture, and the Films of Douglas Sirk* (Bloomington: Indiana University Press).

76. Geoffrey Nowell-Smith, "Minnelli and Melodrama," *Screen*, 18, no. 2 (Summer, 1977), 117. In this instance, style or "excess" becomes a symptom of what Comolli and Narboni had described as an ideologically conflicted text.

77. This debate is nicely summarized in Christine Gledhill's introduction to *Home Is Where the Heart Is* (London: BFI, 1987). See also Jane Feuer, "Melodrama, Serial Form, and Television Today," in *The Media Reader*, ed. Manuel Alvarado and John O. Thompson (London: BFI, 1990), pp. 253–65.

78. Robert Lang, *American Film Melodrama* (Princeton, N.J.: Princeton University Press, 1989), pp. 224–5.

79. Quoted in Alvarado and Thompson, *Media Reader*, p. 235.

2. Uptown Folk

1. This list excludes Paramount's *Tales of Manhattan* (1942), an anthology film with one episode involving black characters, and Disney's *Song of the South* (1946), which was largely animated.

2. The package unit system began in 1955, but the end of the classic studios was in sight by 1954. See David Bordwell, Janet Staiger, and Kristin Thompson, *The Classical Hollywood Cinema: Film Style and Mode of Production to 1960* (New York: Columbia University Press, 1985), pp. 330–8.

3. All six films are discussed in two important historical surveys of African-American film: Thomas Cripps, *Black Film as Genre* (Bloomington: Indiana University Press, 1979), and Donald Bogle, *Toms, Coons, Mulattoes, Mammies, and Bucks: An Interpretive History of Blacks in American Films* (New York: Continuum, 1991). The only film to have received extensive critical treatment elsewhere is *Hallelujah!*: see, for example, Raymond Durgnat and Scott Simmon, *King Vidor, American* (Berkeley and Los Angeles: University of California Press, 1989), pp. 96–113. *Cabin in the Sky* is discussed in Harvey, *Directed by Vincente Minnelli*, pp. 40–4; see also Altman, *The American Film Musical*, which analyzes *Hallelujah!* and makes brief remarks on a few of the other black-cast musicals. Outside the context of director and genre studies or books on African-American film, the black-cast pictures are treated as if they had only technical importance. In their monumental study of the Hollywood system, Bordwell, Staiger, and Thompson make a passing reference to camera movements in *Hallelujah!* They mention *The Green Pastures* during a discussion of the focal length of camera lenses and they provide an image from *Carmen Jones* to illustrate Cinemascope. Two standard histories – David A. Cook's *A History of Narrative Film* (New York: Norton, 1990) and Gerald Mast and Bruce

Kawin's *A Short History of the Movies* (New York: Mcmillian, 1990) – mention only *Hallelujah!*, praising its use of sound.

4. For an extensive discussion of this theme in English literature, see Raymond Williams, *The Country and the City* (New York: Oxford University Press, 1973). For an analysis of how the country–city opposition structures classic Hollywood, see Robin Wood, "Ideology, Genre, Auteur," in *Film Genre Reader*, ed. Barry Keith Grant (Austin: University of Texas Press, 1986), pp. 59–73.

5. Richard Dyer, "Entertainment and Utopia," in *Genre: The Musical*, ed. Rick Altman (London: Routledge & Keagan Paul, 1981), p. 177.

6. Ibid., p. 177. A similar argument can be seen in Jane Feuer, *The Hollywood Musical* (Bloomington: Indiana University Press, 1982), pp. 67–85. Both Dyer and Feuer have something in common with Walter Benjamin, who believed that mass culture's potentially utopian, collective energy was pushed in conservative directions by capitalism. See Buck-Morss, *The Dialectics of Seeing*, pp. 523–86.

7. Dyer, "Entertainment," p. 188.

8. Robert Stam, "Bakhtin, Polyphony, and Ethnic/Racial Representation," in *Unspeakable Images: Ethnicity and the American Cinema*, ed. Lester D. Friedman (Urbana: University of Illinois Press, 1991), pp. 252–3. A similar argument can be inferred from Richard Dyer's study of Paul Robeson in *Heavenly Bodies* (London: Routledge, 1988). See also Stuart Hall, "The Whites of Their Eyes," in *The Media Reader*, ed. Alvarado and Thompson, pp. 7–23.

9. Stam, "Bakhtin," pp. 253–4.

10. Mikhail Bakhtin, *The Dialogic Imagination*, ed. Michael Holquist (Austin: University of Texas Press, 1981), p. 276.

11. I use the term "discourse" heuristically, to describe several conflicting voices surrounding and in some cases weaving themselves through the production of a single film. I do not claim that my survey of these voices is comprehensive – only that it is sufficiently broad to illustrate social conflicts in the period. It should also be noted that no discursive category is monologic. Each of the categories I have attempted to isolate could be divided into others, and these could be divided again, in a process of infinite regression. Where the response of actual historical spectators of *Cabin in the Sky* is concerned, I have relatively little to say. For an important theoretical discussion of this problem, see Manthia Diawara, "Black Spectatorship: Problems of Identification and Resistance," in *Screen* 29, no. 4 (Autumn 1988), 66–79.

12. Peter Burke, "The 'Discovery' of Popular Culture," in *People's History and Socialist Theory*, ed. Raphael Samuel (London: Routledge & Kegan Paul, 1983), p. 216.

13. See Minnelli, *I Remember*, p. 121, and Harvey, *Directed by Vincente Minnelli*, p. 41.

14. Quoted in *The Papers of the NAACP* (December 1940).

15. *The Papers of the NAACP* (April 1942).

16. Cripps, *Black Film*, p. 44.

17. Quoted in Bogle, *Toms, Coons*, pp. 136–7.

18. Quoted in Fordin, *The Movies' Greatest Musicals*, p. 74.

19. James Agee, "Pseudo-Folk," in *Agee on Film*, vol. 1, p. 407.

20. Ibid., p. 405.

21. Ibid., p. 404.

22. Ibid., pp. 406–8.

23. Adorno was a particularly hostile critic of show business. See "On the Fetish-Character in Music and the Regression of Listening" (1938), reprinted in *The Essential Frankfurt School Reader,* ed. Andrew Arato and Eike Gebhardt (New York: Continuum, 1987), where he charges that "music for entertainment" serves only to assure that people are "confirmed in their neurotic stupidity" (p. 286). See also his postwar essay, "Perennial Fashion–Jazz," in *Prisms,* trans. Samuel Weber and Shierry Weber (Cambridge, Mass.: MIT Press, 1990). Here Adorno describes jazz as a "slave" music, in which it is difficult "to isolate the authentic Negro elements" (p. 122). By its very nature, he argues, such music is subject to "standardization, commercialization and rigidification. It is not as though scurrilous businessmen have corrupted the voice of nature by attacking it from without; jazz takes care of this all by itself" (p. 122). Needless to say, James Agee's attitude toward commercial jazz and American blacks was different. He was also a contributor to *The Quiet One* (1948), a sensitive independent film about a lonely black boy, which Bogle compares favorably with Rossellini's *Paisan* (1948).

24. Quoted in Calinescu, *Five Faces of Modernity,* p. 228.

25. Agee, "Pseudo-Folk," p. 404.

26. On the relation between the Frankfurt school and Max Weber, see Arato and Gebhardt, *The Essential Frankfurt School Reader,* pp. 190–1; pp. 207–19. Fredric Jameson believes that the term "late capitalism" originated with Horkheimer and Adorno, whose conception of American society was "Weberian," involving two essential features: "1) a tendential web of bureaucratic control... and 2) the interpenetration of government and big business" (*Postmodernism, or, the Cultural Logic of Late Capitalism* [Durham, N.C.: Duke University Press, 1991], p. xvii). In what I describe as the "discourse of critical modernism," there is a strong tendency to regard the mass media as opiates or instruments of social control. Consider T. S. Eliot's conservative response to the rise of movies during the 1920s: "With the encroachment of the cheap and rapid-breeding cinema, the lower classes will drop into the same state of protoplasm as the bourgeoise" (*Selected Prose* [Harmondsworth: Penguin, 1953], p. 225).

27. Quoted in Fordin, *The Movies' Greatest Musicals,* p. 73.

28. Bogle, *Toms, Coons,* p. 132.

29. See Ethan Mordden, *The Hollywood Studios* (New York: Simon & Schuster, 1989), p. 163.

30. David Lardner, "Cinema," *New Yorker* (May 29, 1943), 117.

31. "The Current Cinema," *Time* (April 12, 1943), 91.

32. *PM Magazine* (June 1, 1943), 28.

33. Ramona Lewis, "*Cabin* Picture Called Insult," *New York Amsterdam News* (June 12, 1943), 17.

34. Bogle describes the forties as the "apex" of the "Negro Entertainment Syndrome," in which the nightclub was a recurrent setting for black performers (pp. 118–19). During the period, Ethel Waters became a major star on American radio, and Duke Ellington presented a series of forty-seven weekly hour-long broadcasts sponsored by the U.S. Treasury Department.

35. In his influential essay, Locke claimed that American blacks of the twentieth

century were involved in a "deliberate flight not only from the country to the city, but from medieval America to modern": "The pulse of the Negro world has begun to beat in Harlem. A Negro newspaper carrying news material in English, French, and Spanish, gathered from all quarters of America, the West Indies and Africa has maintained itself in Harlem for over five years.... Under American auspices and backing, three pan-African congresses have been held abroad for the discussion of common interests, colonial questions and the future co-operative development of Africa.... As with the Jew, persecution is making the Negro international." See "The New Negro," in *Black Voices*, ed. Abral Chapman (New York: Mentor Books, 1968), pp. 512–23. For an extensive discussion of the historical importance of the "New Negro," see Henry Louis Gates, Jr., "The Trope of the New Negro and the Reconstruction of the Image of the Black," *Representations* (Fall 1988), 129–55.

36. A chapter of this length cannot fully document the European fascination with Africa during the modernist period. For a discussion of the nexus of modernist aesthetics, colonial stereotypes, and obsessions about race and gender, see Marianna Torgovnick, *Gone Primitive: Savage Intellects, Modern Lives* (Chicago: University of Chicago Press, 1990), pp. 75–140. For a discussion of a similar phenomenon in European avant-garde culture between the wars, see Julian Stallabrass, "The Idea of the Primitive: British Art and Anthropology, 1918–1930," *New Left Review*, 183 (1990), 95–115.

37. Geoffrey Nowell-Smith, "On Kiri Te Kanawa, Judy Garland, and the Culture Industry," in *Modernity and Mass Culture*, ed. Naremore and Brantlinger, p. 75.

38. Quoted in Minnelli, *I Remember*, p. 58.

39. Harvey, *Directed by Vincente Minnelli*, p. 34.

40. Quoted in ibid., p. 30.

41. Altman, *The American Film Musical*, p. 273.

42. For a discussion of this strategy in other Hollywood genres, see Robert Ray, *A Certain Tendency of the Hollywood Cinema, 1930–1980* (Princeton, N.J.: Princeton University Press, 1985).

43. Altman, *The American Film Musical*, p. 292.

44. Cripps, *Black Film*, p. 92.

45. Notice, too, *Cabin*'s portrayal of a gambler named Domino Johnson (John Bubbles Sublett, the original Sportin' Life in *Porgy and Bess*), whose privileged moment is a performance of Ford Dabney and Cecil Mack's "Shine." This song (also performed by Dooley Wilson in *Casablanca* and later recorded by Bing Crosby and Frankie Laine) is one of the more uncomfortably racist moments in the film, chiefly because of its references to "curly" hair, "pearly" teeth, and fancy clothes; from the point of view of the black actor, however, it functions self-reflexively, and is the only occasion when a character is allowed to acknowledge racial difference. Moreover, while Johnson is supposed to be a villain, we are never invited to think of him as truly dangerous. Sublett's dancing makes him seem charming, and Minnelli's camera movements suggest a rapport with the figure of the black dandy.

46. Minnelli, *I Remember*, p. 121.

47. Quoted in Fordin, *The Movies' Greatest Musicals*, p. 75.

48. Joseph Shrank and Marc Connelly, *Cabin in the Sky*, mimeographed film script (September 21, 1942, revisions dated October 20, 1942), p. 21.

49. Ibid., p. 9.

50. The black performers were working against the script, but I suspect MGM wanted to "dignify" the production. In any case, the effect of dialect humor or "local color" depends on context. Consider the following speech from Langston Hughes's *Simply Heavenly* (1956): "Why, its getting so colored folks can't do nothing no more without some other Negro calling you a stereotype. Stereotype, hah! If you like a little gin, you're a stereotype.... If you wear a red dress, you're a stereotype.... Lord have mercy, honey, do-don't like no blackeyed peas and rice! Then you're a down-home Negro for true – which I is – and proud of it! I didn't come here to Harlem to get away from my people. I come here because there's more of 'em. I loves my race. I loves my people. Stereotype!" (*Five Plays by Langston Hughes*, ed. Webster Smalley [Bloomington: Indiana University Press, 1968], pp. 125–6).

51. It should be noted that the most imposing and handsome males in *Cabin* are Kenneth Spenser and Rex Ingram, who play supernatural characters. In the earthly scenes, Lena Horne is an obviously sexualized female, playing a role similar to Nina Mae McKinney's in *Hallelujah*. *Cabin* is one of the few films in which Horne functions as an agent of the narrative, and in which she moves provocatively around the set; even so, one of her singing numbers was cut because Minnelli staged it in a bubble bath.

52. Altman, *The American Film Musical*, p. 153

53. Feuer, *The Hollywood Musical*, p. 84.

54. Dyer, "Entertainment and Utopia," p. 177.

3. Third Nature

1. See, e.g., Altman, *The American Film Musical*, pp. 275–7. See also David Bordwell and Kristin Thompson, *Film Art*, 1st ed. (Reading, Mass: Addison-Wesley, 1979), pp. 268–9. The best commentary on the tension between nostalgia and modernity in the film is Alain Masson's "La douceur du foyer et le charme des soirs: *Meet Me in St. Louis*," in *Positif* 374 (April 1992), 101–3.

2. Ray, *A Certain Tendency*, pp. 82–3.

3. William Cronon, *Nature's Metropolis* (New York: Norton, 1991), pp. 1–42.

4. For a useful discussion of this term in various writings by Lukács and Adorno, see Buck-Morss, *Dialectics of Seeing*, pp. 68–70.

5. In 1903 and 1904 – the years in which the film is set – the urban labor market in the United States was flooded with women. During the first decade of the century, the number of women employed outside the home nearly doubled, and the "public sphere" was defined by their presence. The early cinema was one of the places where young, unmarried women could socialize with friends of both sexes, even though Hollywood frequently suggested that women's "natural" place was in the home. For discussion of these issues, see Kathy Peiss, *Cheap Amusements: Working Women and Leisure in Turn-of-the-Century New York* (Philadelphia: Temple University Press, 1986). See also Shelly Stamp Lindsey, "Wages and Sin: *Traffic in Souls* and the White Slavery Trade," *Persistence of Vision* 9 (1991), 90–102.

6. Minnelli, *I Remember*, p. 118.

7. For a detailed analysis of the opening sequence, see Beth Genne, "Vincente

Minnelli's Style in Microcosm: The Establishing Sequence of *Meet Me in St. Louis*," *Art Journal* (Fall 1983), 248–54.

8. Nowell-Smith, "On Kiri Te Kanawa," p. 73.

9. George Toles, "No Bigger than Zuzu's Petals: Dream Messages, Epiphanies, and the Undoing of Conventions in *It's a Wonderful Life*," *North Dakota Quarterly* (Summer 1984), 51.

10. Sally Benson, *Meet Me in St. Louis* (New York: Random House, 1942), p. 14.

11. Ibid., pp. 15–16.

12. Richard Dyer, *Heavenly Bodies*, p. 162. See also Andrew Britton, "*Meet Me in St. Louis:* Smith, or the Ambiguities," *The Australian Journal of Film Theory* 3 (1978), 7–25.

13. Robin Wood, "The American Family Comedy: From *Meet Me in St. Louis* to *The Texas Chainsaw Massacre*," *Wide Angle* 3, no. 2 (1979), 5–11.

14. Altman, *The American Film Musical*, p. 314.

15. Richard Taylor and Ian Christie, eds., *The Film Factory* (Cambridge, Mass.: Harvard University Press, 1988), pp. 260–70.

16. Minnelli, *I Remember*, p. 129.

17. Harvey, *Directed by Vincente Minnelli*, p. 53.

18. Agee, *Agee on Film*, p. 127.

19. Perkins, *Film as Film*, p. 76.

20. Harvey, *Directed by Vincente Minnelli*, p. 56.

4. Comedy, Patriarchy, Consumerism

1. Raymond Williams, *The Long Revolution* (Harmondsworth: Penguin, 1980), pp. 284–5.

2. Minnelli, *I Remember*, p. 217.

3. Quoted in ibid., p. 217.

4. These matters are discussed in greater detail in my book, *Acting in the Cinema* (Berkeley and Los Angeles: University of California Press, 1988). See especially pp. 68–82.

5. Paul Schrader, "Notes on Film Noir," *The Film Genre Reader*, ed. Barry Keith Grant (Austin: University of Texas Press, 1986), p. 174.

6. Feuer, *The Hollywood Musical*, pp. 84–5.

7. Jane Gaines, "Designing Women: The Emergence of the New Sweetheart Line," *Fabrications*, 220.

5. Citizen Shields

1. Charles Bitsch and Jean Domarchi, "Entretien avec Vincente Minnelli," *Cahiers du Cinema* 74 (August–September 1957), 12–14. Minnelli listed Welles as "one of the two or three greatest filmmakers of all time," but he also expressed admiration for a large number of other directors. Among the figures he named (sometimes at the prompting of his interviewers) were Richard Brooks, Elia Kazan, John Huston, Delbert Mann, Joseph Mankiewicz, George Stevens (as a director of comedy), Nicholas Ray, Anthony Mann, Samuel Fuller, Alfred Hitchcock, George Cukor, Wil-

liam Wyler, Ernst Lubitsch, Jean Cocteau, Jean Renoir, Max Ophuls, and Roger Vadim.

2. John Houseman, *Front and Center* (New York: Simon & Schuster, 1979), p. 371.

3. Ibid., p. 372.

4. Ibid., p. 371.

5. Serebrinsky and Garacochea, "Vincente Minnelli interviewed in Argentina," 26.

6. Charles Schnee, *Tribute to a Bad Man (The Bad and the Beautiful)*, mimeographed film script dated March 26, 1952 (Chapel Hill, N.C.: University of North Carolina Library), p. 39.

7. Ibid., p. 122.

8. Minnelli, *I Remember*, p. 255.

9. Richard Dyer, "Lana: Four Films of Lana Turner," *Movie* 25 (Winter 1977–8), 47.

10. "The Current Cinema," *Time* (January 12, 1953), 94.

11. Robert Lang, *American Film Melodrama* (Princeton, N.J.: Princeton University Press, 1989), p. 18.

12. Quoted in Bleeker Street Cinema, *The Films of Vincente Minnelli* (New York: New York Zoetrope, 1978), p. 19.

13. Edmund Wilson, *The Wound and the Bow* (New York: Random House, 1941). See also Lionel Trilling's highly influential and widely reprinted essay of the same period, "Art and Neurosis," in *The Liberal Imagination* (New York: The Viking Press, 1940).

14. Harvey, *Directed by Vincente Minnelli*, p. 213.

15. Minnelli, *I Remember*, p. 252.

16. Dyer, "Lana," 44.

17. Albert Johnson, "The Films of Vincente Minnelli, Part I," *Film Quarterly* 12 (Winter 1958), 33.

18. Dyer, "Lana," 33.

19. Sarris, *The American Cinema*, p. 102

6. Vincente Meets Vincent

1. For a discussion of early modernist painting and the social modernity of new class formations in Paris, see T. J. Clark, *The Painting of Modern Life: Paris in the Art of Manet and his Followers* (New York: Knopf, 1984). For a discussion of how Manet and his followers addressed their work to a male viewer/consumer, see "Modernity and the Spaces of Femininity," in Griselda Pollock, *Vision and Difference* (London: Routledge, 1988), pp. 50–90.

2. W. H. Auden, *Forewords and Afterwords* (New York: Vintage, 1989), p. 299.

3. John Berger, *About Looking* (New York: Pantheon, 1980), p. 77.

4. Ibid.

5. Quoted in Bleeker Street Cinema, *The Films of Vincente Minnelli*, p. 22.

6. Houseman, *Front and Center*, p. 462.

7. Minnelli, *I Remember*, p. 288.

8. "Such photography can reproduce the color and texture and tangibility of

objects as only oil paint had been able to do before. Color photography is to the spectator-buyer what oil paint was to the spectator-owner." John Berger, *Ways of Seeing* (Harmondsworth: Penguin, 1978), p. 140.

9. Quoted in Irving Stone, *Lust for Life* (New York: Longmans, Green, 1934), pp. 468–9.

10. See Bradley Collins, "Van Gogh and Gaugin on the Couch," *Art in America*, 77 (December 1989), 59.

11. Minnelli, *I Remember*, p. 293.

12. Ibid., p. 292.

13. Quoted in Bleeker St. Cinema, *The Films of Vincente Minnelli*, p. 22.

14. Houseman, *Front and Center*, p. 482.

15. Quoted in Auden, *Forewords*, p. 298.

16. Peter Brook, *The Melodramatic Imagination: Balzac, Henry James, Melodrama, and the Mode of Excess* (New Haven, Conn.: Yale University Press, 1976), p. 5. See also Lang's commentary on the "profoundly moral" qualities of melodrama in *American Film Melodrama*, pp. 18–19.

Chronology

1903	Lester Anthony Minnelli born in Chicago.
1913	The Armory show opens in New York, bringing international modernism to America.
1914–18	World War I.
1915	Premiere of D. W. Griffith's *Birth of a Nation*. The Hollywood feature film assumes hegemony over the motion picture industry. The Minnelli Brothers Tent Show closes, and Minnelli's family settles in Delaware, Ohio.
1917	Bolshevik revolution in Russia.
1920	Women's suffrage guaranteed by U.S. Constitution.
1921	Minnelli graduates from high school, moves to Chicago, and begins work as a decorator at Marshall Field.
1922–9	Heyday of international modernism: publication of Joyce's *Ulysses* and Eliot's *The Waste Land;* Buñuel and Dali's *An Andalusian Dog;* the opening of the Museum of Modern Art in New York; the Harlem renaissance; etc.
1927	Premiere of Warner Brothers' *The Jazz Singer*. Kern and Hammerstein's *Show Boat* opens on Broadway.
1925–30	Minnelli becomes a designer of "presentation shows" for the Balaban and Katz chain of movie theaters in Chicago.
1929	The Wall Street crash.
1931	Minnelli moves to New York as a designer for Paramount Publix, headquartered at the Paramount Theater.
1932	FDR's first term.
1933	Minnelli becomes a designer and director of musical shows at Radio City Music Hall.
1935	Gershwin's *Porgy and Bess* opens on Broadway. Minnelli designs and directs his first Broadway revue, *At Home Abroad*.
1936	After directing three successful revues in New York, Minnelli is offered a producer-director contract by Paramount Pictures.
1937–9	Minnelli returns to Broadway to direct musicals.

1940	Minnelli joins the Freed unit at MGM.
1941–5	U.S. involvement in World War II.
1943	Minnelli directs his first film, *Cabin in the Sky.*
1945	Minnelli marries Judy Garland.
1946	Birth of Liza Minnelli.
1948	The Paramount "consent degrees" case divests major film studios of theater chains. Dore Schary replaces L. B. Mayer as production chief of MGM.
1947–52	The House Committee on Un-American Activities investigations of Hollywood.
1951	Minnelli receives an Academy Award nomination for *An American in Paris.* Divorces Judy Garland.
1954	Supreme Court desegregates U.S. schools. Minnelli marries Georgette Magnani.
1955	Elvis Presley appears on American television. Birth of Tina Minnelli.
1956	*My Fair Lady* opens on Broadway.
1958	Minnelli wins the Academy Award for *Gigi.* Divorces Georgette Magnani. The French New Wave comes to America: Truffaut's *400 Blows,* Godard's *Breathless,* etc. The rise of auteurism. Sol Siegel becomes production chief at MGM.
1960–5	The pop art movement in America.
1960	Minnelli marries Denise Giganti.
1962	Minnelli forms Venice Productions, his own unit at MGM.
1963	The Beatles appear on American television. Assassination of JFK.
1964	Lester's *A Hard Day's Night.* Minnelli leaves MGM to direct *Goodbye, Charlie* at Twentieth Century Fox.
1968	Assassination of Martin Luther King, Jr. Assassination of Robert Kennedy. Tet Offensive in Vietnam. Election of Richard Nixon. The "Prague Spring." Student rebellion in Paris leads to a general strike. The "Langois affair." Court cases in the United States lead to the replacement of the Production Code with the Code of Self-Regulation. Minnelli directs his last major studio film, *On a Clear Day You Can See Forever,* at Paramount.
1971	Minnelli divorces Denise Giganti.
1976	Minnelli's last film, *A Matter of Time,* released by American International Pictures.
1980	Minnelli marries Margaret Lee Anderson.
1984	Minnelli receives the City of Rome Award.
1986	Minnelli receives the Order of Arts and Letters from the Legion of Honor, for contributions to French culture. He dies in Beverly Hills, California.

Filmography

Further information on Minnelli's films can be found in Stephen Harvey's *Directed by Vincente Minnelli* and François Guerif's *Vincente Minnelli*.

Apprentice work at MGM (direction or design of musical numbers)

1941
Babes on Broadway
Producer: Arthur Freed
Director: Busby Berkeley

1942
Rio Rita
Producer: Pandro S. Berman
Director: S. Sylvan Simon

1942
Panama Hattie
Producer: Arthur Freed
Director: Norman Z. McLeod

Directed by Minnelli at MGM*

1943
Cabin in the Sky
Producer: Arthur Freed
Screenplay: Joseph Schrank and (uncredited) Marc Connelly, from the musical play by Lynn Root (book), John Latouche (lyrics), Vernon Duke (music)

---

* In the United States, all of Minnelli's MGM pictures are available for 16mm rental and videotape purchase through MGM/UA.

Additional songs: Harold Arlen, E. Y. Harburg
Photography: Sidney Wagner
Art direction: Cedric Gibbons, Leonid Vasian
Sets: Edwin B. Willis, Hugh Hunt
Musical direction: George Stoll
Musical adaptation: Roger Edens
Orchestrations: George Bassman
Choral arrangements: Hall Johnson
Editor: Harold F. Kress
Costumes: Irene and Schoup
Recording: Douglas Shearer
Cast: Ethel Waters (Petunia Jackson), Eddie Anderson (Little Joe Jackson), Lena Horne (Georgia Brown), Louis Armstrong (Trumpeter), Rex Ingram (Lucias/Lucifer, Jr.), Kenneth Spencer (Rev. Green/The General), John "Bubbles" Sublett (Domino Johnson), Oscar Polk (the Deacon/Fleetfoot), Mantan Moreland (Idea Man), Bill "Poke" Bailey (Bill), Butterfly McQueen (Lily), the Hall Johnson choir
96 min.

1943
I Dood It
Producer: Jack Cummings
Screenplay: Sig Herzig, Fred Saidy, adapted from *Spring Marriage* (1928)
Photography: Ray June
Art direction: Cedric Gibbons, Jack Martin Smith
Sets: Edwin B. Willis, Helen Conway
Art direction for musical numbers: Merrill Pye
Musical direction: George Stoll
Songs: Don Raye, Gene de Paul, Lew Brown, Ralph Freed, Sammy Fain, Count Basie, Cole Porter, Vernon Duke, John Latouche, Ted Fetter, Leo Robin, Richard Meyers
Editor: Robert J. Kern
Choreography: Bob Connelly
Costumes: Irene, Irene Sharaff
Men's costumes: Gile Steele
Recording: Douglas Shearer
Cast: Red Skelton (Joseph Rivington Reynolds), Eleanor Powell (Constance Shaw), Richard Ainsley (Larry West), Patricia Dane (Suretta Brenton), Sam Levine (Ed Jackson), Lena Horne (herself), John Hodiak (Roy Hartwood), Hazel Scott (herself), Butterfly McQueen (Annette), Jimmy Dorsey and his orchestra
101 min.

1944
Meet Me in St. Louis
Producer: Arthur Freed
Screenplay: Irving Brecher, Fred Finklehoff, based on stories by Sally Benson
Photography: George Folsey

Technicolor consultant: Natalie Kalmus
Art direction: Cedric Gibbons, Lemuel Ayers, Jack Martin Smith
Sets: Edwin B. Willis, Paul Huldschinsky
Musical direction: George Stoll, Lennie Hayton
Musical adaptations: Roger Edens
Orchestrations: Conrad Salinger
Songs: Hugh Martin, Ralph Blane
Editor: Albert Akst
Choreography: Charles Walters
Costumes: Irene Sharaff
Recording: Douglas Shearer
Cast: Judy Garland (Esther Smith), Margaret O'Brien (Tootie Smith), Mary Astor (Anna Smith), Lucille Bremer (Rose Smith), Tom Drake (John Truitt), Marjorie Main (Katie), Leon Ames (Alonzo Smith), Harry Davenport (Grandpa), June Lockhart (Lucille Ballard), Henry H. Daniels (Lon Smith, Jr.), Joan Carroll (Agnes Smith), Hugh Marlowe (Colonel Darly), Robert Sully (Warren Sheffield), Chill Wills (Mr. Neeley)
113 min.

1945
The Clock
Producer: Arthur Freed
Screenplay: Robert Nathan, Joseph Shrank, from a story by Paul Gallico and Pauline Gallico
Photography: George Folsey
Art direction: Cedric Gibbons, William Ferrari
Sets: Edwin B. Willis, Mac Alper
Music score: George Bassman
Editor: George White
Special effects: A. Arnold Gillespie, Warren Newcombe
Costumes: Irene, Marion Herwood Keyes
Recording: Douglas Shearer
Cast: Judy Garland (Alice Mayberry), Robert Walker (Corporal Joe Allen), James Gleason (Al Henry), Keenan Wynn (Drunk), Marshall Thompson (Bill), Lucile Gleason (Mrs. Henry), Ruth Brady (Helen)
90 min.

1945
Yolanda and the Thief
Producer: Arthur Freed
Screenplay: Irving Brecher, based on a story by Jacques Thery and Ludwig Bemelmans
Photography: Charles Rosher
Art direction: Cedric Gibbons, Jack Martin Smith
Sets: Edwin B. Willis, Richard Pefferle
Musical direction: Lennie Hayton
Orchestrations: Conrad Salinger

Songs: Arthur Freed, Harry Warren
Editor: Albert Akst
Special effects: A. Arnold Gillespie, Warren Newcombe
Choreography: Eugene Loring
Costumes: Irene Sharaff
Lucille Bremer's gowns: Irene
Recording: Douglas Shearer
Makeup: Jack Dawn
Cast: Fred Astaire (Johnny Parkson Riggs), Lucille Bremer (Yolanda Aquaviva), Frank Morgan (Victor Budlow Trout), Mildred Natwick (Aunt Amarilla), Mary Nash (Duenna), Leon Ames (Mr. Candle), Ludwig Stossel (schoolteacher)
108 min.

1944 (released 1946)
Ziegfeld Follies
Producer: Arthur Freed
Directors of skits and musical numbers (besides Minnelli): Norman Taurog, Robert Lewis, Roy Del Ruth, Lemuel Ayres, George Sidney, Charles Walters
Photography: George Folsey, Charles Rosher, Ray June
Art direction: Cedric Gibbons, Merrill Pye, Jack Martin Smith, Lemuel Ayres
Sets: Edwin B. Willis, Mac Alper
Musical direction: Lennie Hayton
Musical adaptation: Roger Edens
Orchestrations: Conrad Salinger, Wally Heglin
Vocal arrangements: Kay Thompson
Songs: George and Ira Gershwin; Arthur Freed, Harry Warren; Ralph Blaine, Hugh Martin; Kay Thompson, Roger Edens; Philip Braham, Douglas Furber
Editor: Albert Akst
Choreography: Robert Alton, Charles Walters
Costumes: Irene Sharaff, Helen Rose
Recording: Douglas Shearer
Makeup: Jack Dawn
Cast (in order of appearance): William Powell (Florenz Ziegfield), Lucille Ball, Fred Astaire, Cyd Charisse, Virginia O'Brien, Esther Williams, Keenan Wynn, Victor Moore, Edward Arnold, Lucille Bremer, Fanny Brice, Hume Cronyn, William Frawley, Lena Horne, Red Skelton, Judy Garland, Gene Kelly, Kathryn Grayson
110 min.

1946
Undercurrent
Producer: Pandro S. Berman
Screenplay: Edward Chodorov, from a story by Thelma Strabel
Photography: Karl Freund
Art direction: Cedric Gibbons, Randall Duell
Sets: Edwin B. Willis, Jack D. Moore
Music score: Herbert Stothart
Editor: Ferris Webster

Costumes: Irene
Recording: Douglas Shearer
Makeup: Jack Dawn
Cast: Katharine Hepburn (Ann Hamilton), Robert Taylor (Alan Garroway), Robert Mitchum (Michael Garroway), Edmund Gwynn (Prof. "Dink" Hamilton), Marjorie Main (Lucy), Jayne Meadows (Sylvia Lea Burton)
116 min.

1946
Till the Clouds Roll By
Producer: Arthur Freed
Minnelli directed Judy Garland's three singing numbers in this anthology film.

1948
The Pirate
Producer: Arthur Freed
Screenplay: Albert Hackett, Francis Goodrich, from the play by S. N. Behrman
Photography: Harry Stradling
Art direction: Cedric Gibbons, Jack Martin Smith
Sets: Edwin B. Willis, Arthur Krams
Musical direction: Lennie Hayton
Orchestrations: Conrad Salinger
Songs: Cole Porter
Editor: Blanche Sewell
Choreography: Robert Alton, Gene Kelly
Costumes: Irene and Tom Keogh, executed by Karinska
Recording: Douglas Shearer
Makeup: Jack Dawn
Paintings: Doris Lee
Cast: Judy Garland (Manuela), Gene Kelly (Serafin), Walter Slezak (Don Pedro Vargas), Gladys Cooper (Aunt Inez), Reginald Owen (the Advocate), Goldsmith Brothers, Nicholas Brothers (specialty numbers)
102 min.

1949
Madame Bovary
Producer: Pandro S. Berman
Screenplay: Robert Ardrey, based on the novel by Gustave Flaubert
Photography: Robert Planck
Art direction: Cedric Gibbons, Jack Martin Smith
Sets: Edwin B. Willis, Richard Pefferle
Music: Miklos Rozsa
Editor: Ferris Webster
Special effects: Warren Newcombe
Choreography: Jack Donohue
Costumes: Walter Plunkett, Valles
Recording: Douglas Shearer

Makeup: Jack Dawn
Cast: Jennifer Jones (Emma Bovary), James Mason (Gustave Flaubert), Van Heflin (Charles Bovary), Louis Jourdan (Rodolphe Boulanger), Christopher Kent (Leon Dupuis), Gene Lockhart (J. Homais), Frank Allenby (Lhereux), Gladys Cooper (Mme. Dupuis), John Abbott (Mayor Tuvache), Henry Morgan (Hyppolite)
115 min.

1950
Father of the Bride
Producer: Pandro S. Berman
Screenplay: Albert Hackett, Francis Goodrich, based on the novel by Edward Streeter
Photography: John Alton
Art direction: Cedric Gibbons, Leonid Vasian
Sets: Edwin B. Willis, Keogh Gleason
Editor: Ferris Webster
Costumes: Helen Rose, Walter Plunkett
Recording: Douglas Shearer
Makeup: Jack Dawn
Cast: Spencer Tracy (Stanley T. Banks), Joan Bennett (Ellie Banks), Elizabeth Taylor (Kay Banks), Don Taylor (Buckley Dunstan), Billie Burke (Doris Dunstan), Leo G. Carroll (Mr. Massoula), Russ Tamblyn (Tommy Banks), Tom Irish (Ben Banks), Marietta Canty (Delilah)
93 min.

1951
Father's Little Dividend
Producer: Pandro S. Berman
Screenplay: Albert Hackett, Francis Goodrich
Photography: John Alton
Art direction: Cedric Gibbons, Leonid Vasian
Sets: Edwin B. Willis, Keogh Gleason
Music: Albert Sendry, conducted by George Stoll
Editor: Ferris Webster
Costumes: Helen Rose
Recording: Douglas Shearer
Makeup: William Tuttle
Cast: Spencer Tracy (Stanley T. Banks), Joan Bennett (Ellie Banks), Elizabeth Taylor (Kay Dunstan), Don Taylor (Buckley Dunstan), Moroni Olsen (Herbert Dunstan), Billie Burke (Doris Dunstan), Richard Rober (police sergeant), Marietta Canty (Delilah), Frank Faylen (policeman), Beverly Thompson (nurse), Donald Clarke (the Dividend)
82 min.

1951
An American in Paris
Producer: Arthur Freed

Screenplay: Alan Jay Lerner, based on his story
Photography: Alfred Gilks
Ballet photography: John Alton
Art direction: Cedric Gibbons, Preston Ames
Sets: Edwin B. Willis, Keogh Gleason
Musical direction: Johnny Green, Saul Chaplin
Music: George Gershwin
Songs: George and Ira Gershwin
Orchestrations: Conrad Salinger
Editor: Adrienne Fazan
Montage sequences: Peter Ballbusch
Special effects: Warren Newcombe, Irving Reis
Choreography: Gene Kelly, Carol Haney
Costumes: Orry-Kelly
Beaux-Arts Ball costumes: Walter Plunkett
Ballet costumes: Irene Sharaff
Recording: Douglas Shearer
Makeup: William Tuttle
Paintings: Gene Grant
Cast: Gene Kelly (Jerry Mulligan), Leslie Caron (Lise Bourvier), Oscar Levant (Adam Cook), George Guetary (Henri Baurel), Nina Foch (Milo Roberts)
113 min.

1952
The Story of Three Loves
Producer: Sydney Franklin
Minnelli directed the "Mademoiselle" episode of this three-part film.
Screenplay: George Froeschel, based on a story by Arnold Phillips
Photography: Charles Rosher, Harold Rosson
Art direction: Cedric Gibbons, Preston Ames
Sets: Edwin B. Willis
Music: Miklos Rozsa
Editor: Ralph E. Winters
Costumes: Helen Rose
Recording: Douglas Shearer
Makeup: William Tuttle
Cast: Ethel Barrymore (Mrs. Pennicott), Leslie Caron (Mademoiselle), Farley Granger (Tommy), Ricky Nelson (Tommy at age twelve), Zsa Zsa Gabor (woman at bar)
Complete film: 112 min.

1952
The Bad and the Beautiful
Producer: John Houseman
Screenplay: Charles Schnee, based on stories by George Bradshaw
Photography: Robert Surtees

Art direction: Cedric Gibbons, Edward Carfagno
Sets: Edwin B. Willis, Keogh Gleason
Music: David Raksin
Editor: Conrad A. Nervig
Special effects: A. Arnold Gillespie, Warren Newcombe
Costumes: Helen Rose
Recording: Douglas Shearer
Makeup: William Tuttle
Cast: Lana Turner (Georgia Lorrison), Kirk Douglas (Jonathan Shields), Walter Pidgeon (Harry Pebbel), Dick Powell (James Lee Bartlow), Barry Sullivan (Fred Amiel), Gloria Grahame (Rosemary Bartlow), Gilbert Roland (Victor "Gaucho" Ribera), Leo G. Carroll (Henry Whitfield), Vanessa Brown (Kay Amiel), Paul Stewart (Syd Murphy), Sammy White (Gus), Elaine Stewart (Lila), Ivan Triesault (Von Ellstein), Peggy King (singer), Francis X. Bushman (minister)
118 min.

1953
The Band Wagon
Producer: Arthur Freed
Associate producer: Roger Edens
Screenplay: Betty Comden, Adolph Green, adapted from a Broadway revue (1931) with music and lyrics by Arthur Schwartz, Howard Dietz
Photography: Harry Jackson, George Folsey
Art direction: Cedric Gibbons, Preston Ames
Sets: Edwin B. Willis, Keogh Gleason
Designer for musical numbers: Oliver Smith
Musical direction: Adolph Deutsch
Orchestrations: Conrad Salinger, Skip Martin, Alexander Courage
Editor: Albert Akst
Special effects: Warren Newcombe
Costumes: Mary Ann Nyberg
Choreography: Michael Kidd
Color stock: Ansco Color
Recording: Douglas Shearer
Makeup: William Tuttle
Cast: Fred Astaire (Tony Hunter), Cyd Charisse (Gabrielle Gerard), vocals for Charisse dubbed by India Adams, Oscar Levant (Lester Morton), Jack Buchanan (Jeffrey Cordova), Nanette Fabray (Lily Marton), Ava Gardner (herself), LeRoy Daniels (shoeshine man)
112 min.

1954
The Long, Long Trailer
Producer: Pandro S. Berman
Screenplay: Albert Hackett, Francis Goodrich, based on the novel by Clinton Twiss
Photography: Robert Surtees
Art direction: Cedric Gibbons, Edward Carfagno

175

Sets: Edwin B. Willis, Keogh Gleason
Music: Adolph Deutsch
Editor: Ferris Webster
Special effects: A. Arnold Gillespie, Warren Newcombe
Costumes: Helen Rose
Color stock: Ansco Color
Recording: Douglas Shearer
Makeup: William Tuttle
Cast: Lucille Ball (Tacy Collini), Desi Arnaz (Nicholas Carlos Collini), Marjorie Main (Mrs. Hittaway), Keenan Wynn (policeman), Gladys Hurlbut (Mrs. Bolton), Moroni Olsen (Mr. Tewitt), Burt Freed (foreman)
96 min.

1954
Brigadoon
Producer: Arthur Freed
Associate producer: Roger Edens
Screenplay: Alan Jay Lerner, based on the musical play by Lerner (book and lyrics) and Frederick Lowe (music)
Photography: Joseph Ruttenberg
Art direction: Cedric Gibbons, Preston Ames
Sets: Edwin B. Willis, Keogh Gleason
Musical direction: Johnny Green
Orchestrations: Conrad Salinger
Choral arrangements: Robert Tucker
Editor: Albert Akst
Special effects: Warren Newcombe
Choreography: Gene Kelly
Costumes: Irene Sharaff
Color stock and format: Ansco Color, Cinemascope
Recording: Dr. Wesley C. Miller
Makeup: William Tuttle
Cast: Gene Kelly (Tommy Albright), Cyd Charisse (Fiona Campbell), Van Johnson (Jeff Douglas), Elaine Stewart (Jane Ashton), Barry Jones (Mr. Lundie), Hugh Laing (Harry Beaton), Albert Sharpe (Andrew Campbell), Virginia Bosler (Jean Campbell), Jimmy Thompson (Charlie Chisolm Dalrymple)
108 min.

1955
The Cobweb
Producer: John Houseman
Associate producer: Jud Kinberg
Screenplay: John Paxton, based on a novel by William Gibson
Photography: George Folsey
Art direction: Cedric Gibbons, Preston Ames
Sets: Edwin B. Willis, Keogh Gleason
Music: Leonard Rosenmann

Editor: Harold F. Kress
Color stock and format: Eastmancolor, Cinemascope
Graphics: David Stone Martin
Recording: Dr. Wesley C. Miller
Makeup: William Tuttle
Cast: Richard Widmark (Dr. Stewart McIver), Lauren Bacall (Meg Faverson Rinehart), Charles Boyer (Dr. Douglas N. Devanal), Gloria Grahame (Karen McIver), Lillian Gish (Victoria Inch), John Kerr (Stephen W. Holte), Susan Strasberg (Sue Brett), Oscar Levant (Mr. Capp), Tommy Rettig (Mark McIver), Paul Stewart (Dr. Otto Wolff)
124 min.

1955
Kismet
Producer: Arthur Freed
Screenplay: Charles Lederer, Luther Davis, based on their musical play and the novel by Edward Knobloch
Music and lyrics: Robert Wright, George Forrest, adapted from themes by Aleksandr Borodin
Photography: Joseph Ruttenberg
Art direction: Cedric Gibbons, Preston Ames
Sets: Edwin B. Willis, Keogh Gleason
Music supervision: Andre Previn, Jeff Alexander
Orchestrations: Conrad Salinger, Alexander Courage, Arthur Morton, conducted by Previn
Vocal supervision: Robert Tucker
Musical staging and choreography: Jack Cole
Editor: Adrienne Fazan
Special effects: Warren Newcombe
Costumes: Tony Duquette
Color stock and format: Eastmancolor, Cinemascope
Recording: Dr. Wesley C. Miller
Makeup: William Tuttle
Cast: Howard Keel (Hajj), Ann Blyth (Marsinah), Dolores Gray (Lalume), Vic Damone (Caliph), Monty Woolley (Omar), Sebastian Cabot (Wazir), Jay C. Flippen (Jawan), Mike Mazurki (chief policeman), Jack Elam (Hassan-Ben)
113 min.

1956
Lust for Life
Producer: John Houseman
Associate producer: Jud Kinberg
Screenplay: Norman Corwin, based on the novel by Irving Stone
Photography: F. A. Young, Russell Harlan
Art direction: Cedric Gibbons, Hans Peters, Preston Ames
Sets: Edwin B. Willis, Keogh Gleason
Music: Miklos Rozsa

Editor: Adrienne Fazan
Costumes: Walter Plunkett
Color stock and format: Metrocolor, Cinemascope
Recording: Dr. Wesley C. Miller
Makeup: William Tuttle
Cast: Kirk Douglas (Vincent Van Gogh), Anthony Quinn (Paul Gauguin), James Donald (Theo Van Gogh), Pamela Brown (Christine), Everett Sloane (Dr. Gachet), Niall MacGinnis (Roulin), Noel Purcell (Anton Mauve), Henry Daniell (Theodorus Van Gogh), Jill Bennett (Willemien), Lionel Jeffries (Dr. Peyron), Laurence Naismith (Dr. Bosman), Eric Pohlmann (Colbert), Jeanette Sterke (Kay), Toni Gerry (Johanna), Wilton Graff (Reverend Stricker), Isobel Elson (Mrs. Stricker)
122 min.

1956
Tea and Sympathy
Producer: Pandro S. Berman
Screenplay: Robert Anderson, based on his stage play
Photography: John Alton
Art direction: William A. Horning, Edward Carfagno
Sets: Edwin B. Willis, Keogh Gleason
Music: Adolph Deutsch
Editor: Ferris Webster
Costumes: Helen Rose
Color stock and format: Metrocolor, Cinemascope
Recording: Dr. Wesley C. Miller
Makeup: William Tuttle
Cast: Deborah Kerr (Laura Reynolds), John Kerr (Tom Robinson Lee), Lief Erickson (Bill Reynolds), Edward Andrews (Herb Lee), Darryl Hickman (Al), Norma Crane (Ellie Martin), Dean Jones (Ollie), Jacqueline de Wit (Lilly Sears)
122 min.

1957
Designing Woman
Producer: Dore Schary
Associate producer: George Wells
Screenplay: George Wells, from an idea by Helen Rose
Photography: John Alton
Art direction: William A. Horning, Preston Ames
Sets: Edwin B. Willis, Henry Grace
Music: Andre Previn
Musical staging: Jack Cole
Editor: Adrienne Fazan
Special effects: Warren Newcombe
Gowns: Helen Rose
Color stock and format: Metrocolor, Cinemascope
Recording: Dr. Wesley C. Miller
Makeup: William Tuttle

Cast: Gregory Peck (Mike Hagen), Lauren Bacall (Marilla Hagen), Dolores Gray (Lori Shannon), Jack Cole (Randy Owen), Tom Helmore (Zachary Wilde), Mickey Shaughnessy (Maxie Stulz), Ned Levine (Ned Hammersmith), Chuck Conners (Johnny O.)
118 min.

1957
The Seventh Sin
Minnelli completed the shooting of this film when director Ronald Neame fell ill; in his autobiography, Minnelli says that he simply followed the original shooting script and refused to sign the film.

1958
Gigi
Producer: Arthur Freed
Screenplay: Alan Jay Lerner, from the novel by Colette
Photography: Joseph Ruttenberg
Art direction: William A. Horning, Preston Ames
Costumes, scenery, and production design: Cecil Beaton
Sets: Henry Grace, Keogh Gleason
Musical direction: Andre Previn
Music: Frederick Lowe
Orchestrations: Conrad Salinger
Lyrics: Alan Jay Lerner
Vocal supervision: Robert Tucker
Editor: Adrienne Fazan
Color stock and format: Metrocolor, Cinemascope
Recording: Dr. Wesley C. Miller
Makeup: William Tuttle, Charles Parker
Cast: Leslie Caron (Gigi), Caron's vocals dubbed by Betty Wand, Maurice Chevalier (Honore Lachaille), Louis Jourdan (Gaston Lachaille), Hermione Gingold (Mme. Alvarez), Eva Gabor (Liane d'Exelmans), Jacques Bergerac (Sandomir)
116 min.

1958
The Reluctant Debutante
Producer: Pandro S. Berman
Screenplay: William Douglas Home, from his play
Photography: Joseph Ruttenberg
Art direction: A. J. d'Eaubonne
Sets: Robert Christides
Dance music and arrangements: Eddie Warner and his orchestra
Editor: Adrienne Fazan
Wardrobe: Helen Rose, Pierre Balmain
Color stock and format: Metrocolor, Cinemascope
Sound: Guy Rophe
Makeup: Jean-Paul Ulysse

Cast: Rex Harrison (Jimmy Broadbent), Kay Kendall (Sheila Broadbent), John Saxon (David Parkson), Sandra Dee (Jane Broadbent), Angela Lansbury (Mabel Claremont)
94 min.

1958
Some Came Running
Producer: Sol C. Siegel
Screenplay: John Patrick, Arthur Sheekman, based on the novel by James Jones
Photography: William H. Daniels
Art direction: William A. Horning, Urie McCleary
Sets: Henry Grace, Robert Priestly
Music: Elmer Bernstein
Song ("To Love and Be Loved"): Sammy Cahn, James Van Husen
Editor: Adrienne Fazan
Costumes: Walter Plunkett
Color stock and format: Metrocolor, Cinemascope
Recording: Franklin Milton
Makeup: William Tuttle
Cast: Frank Sinatra (Dave Hirsh), Dean Martin (Bama Dillert), Shirley MacLaine (Ginny Moorehead), Martha Hyer (Gwen French), Arthur Kennedy (Frank Hirsh), Nancy Gates (Edith Barklay), Leora Dana (Agnes Hirsh), Betty Lou Keim (Dawn Hirsh), Larry Gates (Prof. Robert Haven French), Stephen Peck (Raymond Lanchak)
134 min.

1960
Home from the Hill (a Sol C. Siegel production)
Producer: Edmund Grainger
Screenplay: Harriet Frank, Jr., Irving Ravetch, from the novel by William Humphrey
Photography: Milton Krasner
Art direction: George W. Davis, Preston Ames
Sets: Henry Grace, Robert Priestley
Music: Bronislau Kaper
Conductor: Charles Wolcott
Editor: Harold F. Kress
Special effects: Robert R. Hoag
Costumes: Walter Plunkett
Color stock and format: Metrocolor, Cinemascope
Recording: Franklin Milton
Makeup: William Tuttle
Cast: Robert Mitchum (Wade Hunnicutt), Eleanor Parker (Hannah Hunnicutt), George Peppard (Rafe Copley), George Hamilton (Theron Hunnicutt), Luana Patton (Libby Halstead), Everett Sloane (Albert Halstead), Anne Seymour (Sarah Halstead), Constance Ford (Opal Bixby), Ken Renard (Chauncy), Ray Teal (Dr. Ruben Carson)
150 min.

1960

Bells Are Ringing

Producer: Arthur Freed
Screenplay: Betty Comden, Adolph Green, adapted from their play
Photography: Milton Krasner
Art direction: George W. Davis, Preston Ames
Sets: Henry Grace, Keogh Gleason
Musical adaptation and conducting: Andre Previn
Orchestrations: Alexander Courage, Pete King
Songs: Comden, Greene, and Julie Styne
Editor: Adrienne Fazan
Choreography: Charles O'Curran
Costumes: Walter Plunkett
Color stock and format: Metrocolor, Cinemascope
Recording: Franklin Milton
Makeup: William Tuttle
Cast: Judy Holliday (Ella Peterson), Dean Martin (Jeffrey Moss), Fred Clark (Larry Hastings), Eddie Foy, Jr. (J. Otto Prinz), Jean Stapelton (Sue), Frank Gorshin (Blake Barton), Stephen Peck (first gangster), Gerry Mulligan (Ella's blind date)
126 min.

1962

The Four Horsemen of the Apocalypse

Producer: Julian Blaustein
Screenplay: Robert Ardrey, John Gay, from the novel by Vicente Blasco Ibáñez
Photography: Milton Krasner, George Perinal
Art direction: George W. Davis, Urie McCleary, Elliot Scott
Sets: Henry Grace, Keogh Gleason
Design of four horsemen figures: Tony Duquette
Music: Andre Previn
Editors: Adrienne Fazan, Ben Lewis
Special effects: A. Arnold Gillespie, Lee LeBlanc, Robert R. Hoag
Montages: Frank Santillo
Choreography: Alex Romero
Costumes: Rene Hubert, Walter Plunkett, Orry-Kelly
Color stock and format: Metrocolor, Cinemascope
Makeup: Charles Parker, William Tuttle
Cast: Glenn Ford (Julio Desnoyers), Ingrid Thulin (Marguerite Laurier), Charles Boyer (Marcelo Desnoyers), Lee J. Cobb (Julio Madariaga), Paul Henried (Etienne Laurier), Karl Bohem (Henrich von Hartrott), Paul Lucas (Karl von Hartrott), Yvette Mimieux (Chi-Chi Desnoyers), Harriet McGibbon (Luisa Desnoyers)
153 min.

1962

Two Weeks in Another Town

Producer: John Houseman
Associate producer: Ethel Winant

Screenplay: Charles Schnee, based on the novel by Irwin Shaw
Photography: Milton Krasner
Art direction: George W. Davis, Urie McCleary
Sets: Henry Grace, Keogh Gleason
Music: David Raksin
Editors: Adrienne Fazan, Robert J. Kern, Jr.
Special effects: Robert R. Hoag
Gowns: Pierre Balmain
Color stock and format: Metrocolor, Cinemascope
Music: David Raksin
Recording: Franklin Milton
Makeup: William Tuttle
Cast: Kirk Douglas (Jack Andrus), Edward G. Robinson (Maurice Kruger), Cyd Charisse (Carlotta), George Hamilton (David Drew), Daliah Lavi (Veronica), Claire Trevor (Clara), James Gregory (Brad Byrd), Rosanna Schiaffino (Barzelli), Joanna Roos (Janet Bark), George Macready (Lew Jordan), Mino Doro (Tucino), Stefan Schnabel (Zeno), Erich von Stroheim, Jr. (Ravinski), Leslie Uggams (chanteuse)
107 min.

1963
The Courtship of Eddie's Father
Producer: Joseph Pasternak
Screenplay: John Gay, from the novel by Mark Toby
Photography: Milton Krasner
Art direction: George W. Davis, Urie McCleary
Sets: Henry Grace, Keogh Gleason
Music: George Stoll
Song ("The Rose and the Butterfly"): Victor Young, Stella Unger
Editor: Adrienne Fazan
Costumes: Helen Rose
Color stock and format: Metrocolor, Panavision
Recording: Franklin Milton
Makeup: William Tuttle
Cast: Glenn Ford (Tom Corbett), Ronny Howard (Eddie Corbett), Shirley Jones (Elizabeth Marten), Dina Merrill (Rita Behrens), Stella Stevens (Dollye Daly), Roberta Sherwood (Mrs. Livingstone), Jerry Van Dyke (Norman Jones), John La Salle Combo
117 min.

1965
The Sandpiper
Producers: Martin Ransohoff and John Calley
Screenplay: Dalton Trumbo and Michael Wilson, based on the story by Martin Ransohoff, adapted by Irene and Louis Kamp
Photography: Milton Krasner
Wildlife photography: Richard Borden
Art direction: George W. Davis, Urie McCleary

Sets: Henry Grace, Keogh Gleason
Music: Johnny Mandel
Song ("The Shadow of Your Smile"): Johnny Mandel and Paul Francis Webster
Editor: David Bretherton
Costumes: Irene Sharaff
Color stock and format: Metrocolor, Panavision
Recording: Franklin Milton
Makeup: William Tuttle
Cast: Richard Burton (Dr. Edward Hewitt); Elizabeth Taylor (Laura Reynolds); Eva Marie Saint (Claire Hewitt); Charles Bronson (Cos Erikson); Morgan Mason (Danny Reynolds); Robert Webber (Ward Hendricks); Tom Drake (Walter Robinson); James Edwards (Larry Brant); Peter O'Toole (voice)
116 mins.

Directed by Minnelli outside MGM

1964
Goodbye, Charlie
Production company: Twentieth Century Fox
Producer: David Weisbart
Screenplay: Harry Kurnitz, based on the play by George Axelrod
Photography: Milton Krasner
Art direction: Jack Martin Smith, Richard Day
Sets: Walter M. Scott, Keogh Gleason
Music: Andre Previn
Orchestration: Al Woodbury
Songs: Dory Langdon, Andre Previn
Editor: John W. Holmes
Special effects: L. B. Abbott, Emile Kosa, Jr.
Costumes: Helen Rose
Print process: Deluxe
Recording: W. D. Flick, Elmer Raguse
Makeup: Ben Nye
Cast: Tony Curtis (George Tracy), Debbie Reynolds (Charlie), Pat Boone (Bruce Minton), Walter Matthau (Sir Leopold Sartori), Joanna Barnes (Janie), Ellen MacRae (Franny), Laura Devon (Rusty), Martin Gabel (Morton Craft), Roger C. Carmel (inspector), Myrna Hansen (starlet), Michael Romanoff (patron), Michael Jackson (himself), Donna Michelle (guest on yacht)
117 min.
(Available for 16mm rental through Films, Incorporated)

1970
On a Clear Day You Can See Forever
Production company: Paramount Pictures
Producers: Howard W. Koch, Alan J. Lerner

Screenplay and lyrics: Alan Jay Lerner, based on his musical play
Photography: Harry Stradling
Production design: John De Cuir
Sets: George Hopkins, Raphael Bretton
Music: Burton Lane
Choral arrangements: Joseph J. Lilley
Music arrangements and conducting: Nelson Riddle
Editor: David Bretherton
Costumes: Cecil Beaton, Arnold Scaasi
Choreography: Howard Jeffrey
Print process: Technicolor
Recording: Benjamin Winkler, Elden Ruberg
Makeup: Harry Ray
Cast: Barbra Streisand (Daisy Gamble), Yves Montand (Dr. Marc Chabot), Bob Newhart (Dr. Mason Hume), Larry Blyden (Warren Pratt), Simon Oakland (Dr. Conrad Fuller), Jack Nicholson (Tad Pringle), John Richardson (Robert Tentrees), Pamela Brown (Mrs. Fitzherbert), Irene Handel (Winnie Wainwhistle), Roy Kinear (prince regent), Peter Cowcroft (divorce attorney), Byron Webster (prosecutor), Mabel Albertson (Mrs. Hatch), Leon Ames (Clews)
129 min.
(Available for 16mm rental through Films, Incorporated)

1976
A Matter of Time
Production company: American International Pictures
Executive producers: Samuel G. Arkoff, Giulio Sbarigia
Producers: Jack H. Skirball, J. Edmund Grainger
Production executive: Steve Previn
Screenplay: John Gay, from the novel *Film of Memory* by Maurice Druon
Photography: Geoffery Unsworth
Production design: Venerio Colasanti, John Moore
Music: Nino Oliviero
Arrangements: Carlo Esposito
Conductor: Bruno Canafora
Songs: Fred Ebb, John Kander; George Gershwin, B. G. DeSylvia
Editor: Peter Taylor
Postproduction: Salvatore Billitteri
Sound: Franca Silvi
Makeup: Christina Smith
Cast: Liza Minnelli (Nina), Ingrid Bergman (Countess), Charles Boyer (Count Sanziani), Spiros Andros (Mario Morello), Tina Aumont (Valentina), Anna Proclemer (Jeanne Blasto), Gabriele Ferzetti (Antonio Vicaria), Arnolda Foa (Pavelli), Orso Maria Guerrini (Gabriele D'Orazio), Fernando Rey (Charles Van Maar), Amadeo Nazzari (countess's admirer), Isabella Rossellini (nurse)
97 min.

Abbot and Costello Meet Frankenstein, dir. Charles Barton (Universal, USA, 1948)
Ace in the Hole (The Big Carnival), dir. Billy Wilder (Paramount, USA, 1951)
All about Eve, dir. Joseph L. Mankiewicz (Twentieth Century Fox, USA, 1950)
Anna Karenina, dir. Clarence Brown (MGM, USA, 1935)
Apartment for Peggy, dir. George Seaton (Paramount, USA, 1948)
Artists and Models, dir. Raoul Walsh (Paramount, USA, 1937)
Barefoot Contessa, The, dir. Joseph L. Mankiewicz (Figaro, USA, 1954)
Bataan, dir. Tay Garnett (MGM, USA, 1943)
Betsy's Wedding, dir. Alan Alda (Touchstone, USA, 1990)
Big Combo, The, dir. Joseph H. Lewis (Allied Artists, USA, 1955)
Big Knife, The, dir. Robert Aldrich (Columbia, USA 1955)
Blonde Venus, dir. Josef von Sternberg (Paramount, USA, 1932)
Blood of Jesus, dir. Spencer Williams (Amegro Films, USA, 1941)
Bringing Up Baby, dir. Howard Hawks (RKO, USA, 1938)
Cabaret, dir. Bob Fosse (Allied Artists, USA, 1972)
Captains Courageous, dir. Victor Fleming (MGM, USA, 1937)
Carmen Jones, dir. Otto Preminger (Twentieth Century Fox, USA, 1954)
Casablanca, dir. Michael Curtiz (Warner Brothers, USA, 1942)
Centennial Summer, dir. Otto Preminger (Twentieth Century Fox, USA, 1946)
Champion, dir. Mark Robson (Columbia, USA, 1949)
Chocolate Soldier, The, dir. Roy del Ruth (MGM, USA, 1941)
Citizen Kane, dir. Orson Welles (RKO, USA, 1941)
Contempt (Le Mépris), dir. Jean-Luc Godard (France/Italy, 1963)
Dinner at Eight, dir. George Cukor (MGM, USA, 1933)
Egg and I, The, dir. Chester Erskine (Paramount, USA, 1947)
Father of the Bride, dir. Charles Shyer (Disney, USA, 1991)
42nd Street, dir. Frank Lloyd (Warner Brothers, USA, 1933)
Gold Diggers of 1933, dir. Mervyn LeRoy (Warner Brothers, USA, 1933)
Grand Hotel, dir. Edmund Goulding (MGM, USA, 1932)
Greed, dir. Erich von Stroheim (MGM, USA, 1925)
Green Pastures, The, dir. William Keighley and Marc Connelly (Warner Brothers, USA, 1936)
Hallelujah! dir. King Vidor (MGM, USA, 1929)
Hard Day's Night, A, dir. Richard Lester (United Artists, USA/Great Britain, 1964)
Hearts in Dixie, dir. Paul Sloane (Fox, USA, 1929)
Heaven Can Wait, dir. Ernst Lubitsch (Twentieth Century Fox, USA, 1943)
High and the Mighty, The, dir. William Wellman (Warner Brothers, USA, 1954)
In the Good Old Summertime, dir. Robert Z. Leonard (MGM, USA, 1949)
In This Our Life, dir. John Huston (Warner Brothers, USA, 1942)
It's a Wonderful Life, dir. Frank Capra (Liberty Films, USA, 1946)
Ivan the Terrible, Part II, dir. Sergei Eisenstein (USSR, 1945)
Jazz Singer, The, dir. Alan Crosland (Warner Brothers, USA, 1927)
Johnny Eager, dir. Mervyn LeRoy (MGM, USA, 1941)
Last Laugh, The (Der Leste Mann), dir. F. W. Murnau (UFA, Germany, 1925)

Last Picture Show, The, dir. Peter Bogdanovich (BBS/Columbia, USA, 1971)
Lifeboat, dir. Alfred Hitchcock (Twentieth Century Fox, USA, 1944)
Life with Father, dir. Michael Curtiz (Warner Brothers, USA, 1947)
Love Me Tonight, dir. Rouben Mamoulian (Paramount, USA, 1932)
Magnificent Ambersons, The, dir. Orson Welles (RKO, USA, 1942)
Mean Streets, dir. Martin Scorsese (Warner Brothers, USA, 1973)
Mr. Blandings Builds His Dream House, dir. H. C. Potter (RKO, USA, 1948)
Moulin Rouge, dir. John Huston (United Artists, USA, 1952)
Nashville, dir. Robert Altman (Paramount, USA, 1975)
Negro Soldier, The, dir. Stuart Heisler (U.S. Army Signal Corps, USA, 1943)
New York, New York, dir. Martin Scorsese (United Artists, USA, 1977)
Oklahoma! dir. Fred Zinneman (Magna Theater Corp., USA, 1955)
Paisan, dir. Roberto Rossellini (Italy, 1948).
Pierrot le fou, dir. Jean-Luc Godard (France, 1965)
Pride and the Passion, The, dir. Stanley Kramer (United Artists, USA, 1957)
Pride and Prejudice, dir. Robert Z. Leonard (MGM, USA, 1940)
Proud and Profane, The, dir. George Seaton (Paramount, USA, 1956)
Quiet One, The, dir. Sidney Meyers (USA, 1948)
Raging Bull, dir. Martin Scorsese (United Artists, USA, 1980)
Sahara, dir. Zoltan Korda (Warner Brothers, USA, 1943)
Shadow of the Thin Man, The, dir. W. S. Van Dyke (MGM, USA, 1941)
Shall We Dance, dir. Mark Sandrich (RKO, USA, 1937)
She's Gotta Have It, dir. Spike Lee (Island, USA, 1986)
Singin' in the Rain, dir. Gene Kelley, Stanley Donen (MGM, USA, 1952)
Sitting Pretty, dir. Walter Lang (Twentieth Century Fox, USA, 1948)
Song of the South, dir. Wilfred Jackson and Harve Foster (Disney, USA, 1946)
Star Is Born, A, dir. George Cukor (MGM, USA, 1954)
State Fair, dir. Henry King (Twentieth Century Fox, USA, 1945)
Stormy Weather, dir. Andrew Stone (Twentieth Century Fox, USA, 1944)
Sunset Boulevard, dir. Billy Wilder (Paramount, USA, 1950)
Tales of Manhattan, dir. Julian Duvivier (Twentieth Century Fox, USA, 1942)
Taxi Driver, dir. Martin Scorsese (Columbia, USA, 1976)
T-Men, dir. Anthony Mann (Eagle-Lion, USA, 1947)
Torch Song, dir. Charles Walters (MGM, USA, 1953)
Tribute to a Bad Man, dir. Robert Wise (MGM, USA, 1956)
Trouble in Paradise, dir. Ernst Lubitsch (Paramount, USA, 1932)
True Love, dir. Nancy Savoca (MGM/UA, USA, 1990)
Two-Faced Woman, dir. George Cukor (MGM, USA, 1941)
Two Weeks with Love, dir. Roy Rowland (MGM, USA, 1950)
Unholy Partners, dir. Mervyn LeRoy (MGM, USA, 1941)
Vincent and Theo, dir. Robert Altman (Hemdale, Great Britain, 1990)
Wedding, A, dir. Robert Altman (Twentieth Century Fox, USA, 1978)
Wizard of Oz, The, dir. Victor Fleming (MGM, USA, 1939)
Woman of the Year, dir. George Stevens (MGM, USA, 1942)

Selected Bibliography

Adorno, Theodor W. "Television and the Patterns of Mass Culture." In *Mass Culture: The Popular Arts in America,* ed. Bernard Rosenberg and David Manning White. New York: Free Press, 1957, pp. 473–7.

Prisms. Trans. Samuel Weber and Shierry Weber. Cambridge, Mass.: MIT Press, 1990.

Adorno, Theodor W., and Max Horkheimer. *Dialectic of Enlightenment.* New York: Seabury, 1972 [1944].

Agee, James. *Agee on Film,* vol. 1. New York: McDowell, Obolensky, 1958.

"The Current Cinema." *Time* (April 12, 1943): 91.

Allen, Robert C., and Douglas Gomery. *Film History: Theory and Practice.* New York: Knopf, 1985.

Altman, Rick. *The American Film Musical.* Bloomington: Indiana University Press, 1987.

Anderson, Lindsay. "Minnelli, Kelly and *An American in Paris.*" *Sequence* 14 (1952): 34–7.

Arato, Andrew, and Eike Gebhardt, eds. *The Essential Frankfurt School Reader.* New York: Continuum, 1987.

Auden, W. H. *Forewords and Afterwards.* New York: Vintage, 1989.

Bakhtin, Mikhail. *The Dialogic Imagination.* Ed. Michael Holquist. Austin: University of Texas Press, 1981.

Bazin, André. "On the *Politique des Auteurs.*" In *Cahiers du Cinema: The 1950s,* ed. Jim Hiller. Cambridge, Mass.: Harvard University Press, 1985, pp. 248–59.

Benjamin, Walter. *Reflections.* Trans. Edmund Jephcott. New York: Harcourt Brace Jovanovich, 1978.

Benson, Sally. *Meet Me in St. Louis.* New York: Random House, 1942.

Berger, John. *About Looking.* New York: Pantheon. 1980.

Ways of Seeing. Harmondsworth: Penguin, 1978.

Bitsch, Charles, and Jean Domarchi. "Entretien avec Vincente Minnelli." *Cahiers du Cinema* 74 (August–September 1957): 12–14.

Bleeker St. Cinema. *The Films of Vincente Minnelli.* New York: New York Zoetrope, 1978.

Bogle, Donald. *Toms, Coons, Mulattoes, Mammies, and Bucks: An Interpretive History of Blacks in American Films.* New York: Continuum, 1991.

Bordwell, David, and Kristin Thompson. *Film Art,* 1st ed. Reading, Mass.: Addison-Wesley, 1979.

Bordwell, David, Janet Staiger, and Kristin Thompson. *The Classical Hollywood Cinema: Film Style and Mode of Production to 1960.* New York: Columbia University Press, 1985.

Bourget, Jean-Loup. "L'Oeuvre de Vincente Minnelli." *Positif* 310 (December 1986): 2–12.

Britton, Andrew. "*Meet Me in St. Louis:* Smith, or the Ambiguities." *Australian Journal of Screen Theory* 3 (1978): 7–25.

Brook, Peter. *The Melodramatic Imagination: Balzac, Henry James, Melodrama, and the Mode of Excess.* New Haven, Conn.: Yale University Press, 1976.

Bruno, Edoardo, ed. *Mr. Vincente: Omaggio a Minnelli.* Montepulciano, SI: Editori del Grifo, 1984.

Buck-Morss, Susan. *The Dialectics of Seeing: Walter Benjamin and the Arcades Project.* Cambridge, Mass.: MIT Press, 1989.

Burke, Peter. "The 'Discovery' of Popular Culture." In *People's History and Socialist Theory,* ed. Raphael Samuel. London: Routledge & Kegan Paul, 1983, pp. 216–40.

Calinescu, Matei. *Five Faces of Modernity.* Durham, N.C.: Duke University Press, 1987.

Campari, Roberto. *Minnelli.* Firenze: La Nuova Italia, 1977.

Carey, Gary. "Vincente Minnelli and the 1940s Musical." In *Cinema: A Critical Dictionary,* ed. Richard Roud. New York: Viking, 1980, pp. 689–96.

Casper, Joseph Andrew. *Vincente Minnelli and the Film Musical.* London: Tantivy Press, 1977.

Caughie, John, ed. *Theories of Authorship.* London: Routledge & Kegan Paul, 1981.

Clark, T. J. *The Painting of Modern Life: Paris in the Art of Manet and His Followers.* New York: Knopf, 1984.

Collins, Bradley. "Van Gogh and Gaugin on the Couch." *Art in America,* 77 (December 1989): 59.

Comolli, Jean-Louis, and Jean Narboni. "Cinema/Ideology/Criticism." In *Movies and Methods,* vol. 1, ed. Bill Nichols. Berkeley and Los Angeles: University of California Press, 1976, pp. 22–30.

Cook, David A. *A History of Narrative Film.* New York: Norton, 1990.

Cripps, Thomas. *Black Film as Genre.* Bloomington: Indiana University Press, 1979.

Cronon, William. *Nature's Metropolis.* New York: Norton, 1991.

De Cordova, Richard. "A Case of Mistaken Legitimacy: Class and Generational Difference in Three Family Melodramas." In *Home Is Where the Heart Is,* ed. Christine Gledhill. London: BFI, 1987, 255–67.

De la Roche, Catherine. *Vincente Minnelli.* The New Zealand Institute and Film Culture (USA), 1959.

Diawara, Manthia. "Black Spectatorship: Problems of Identification and Resistance. *Screen* 29, no. 4 (Autumn 1988): 66–79.

Diawara, Manthia, ed. *Wide Angle* 13, nos. 3 and 4 (July–October 1991). Special issue on black cinema.

Domarchi, Jean, and Jean Douchet. "Rencontre avec Vincente Minnelli." *Cahiers du Cinema* 128 (February 1962): 3–13.

Durgnat, Raymond, and Scott Simmon. *King Vidor, American.* Berkeley and Los Angeles: University of California Press, 1989.

Dyer, Richard. "Lana: Four Films of Lana Turner." *Movie* 25 (Winter 1977–8): 30–52.

"Entertainment and Utopia." In *Genre: The Musical,* ed. Rick Altman. London: Routledge & Kegan Paul, 1981, pp. 176–80.

Heavenly Bodies. London: Routledge, 1988.

Eckert, Charles. "The Carole Lombard in Macy's Window." In *Fabrications: Costuming and the Female Body,* ed. Jane Gaines and Charlotte Herzog. New York: Routledge, 1990, pp. 100–21.

Eliot, T. S. *Selected Prose.* Harmondsworth: Penguin, 1953.

Elsaesser, Thomas. "Vincente Minnelli." In *Genre: The Musical,* ed. Rick Altman. London: Routledge & Kegan Paul, 1981, pp. 8–27.

"Tales of Sound and Fury." In *Home Is Where the Heart Is,* ed. Christine Gledhill. London: BFI, 1987, pp. 43–69.

Ewen, Stuart. *Captains of Consciousness.* New York: McGraw-Hill, 1976.

Farber, Manny. "Dream Furlough." *New Republic* (May 21, 1945): 709.

Feuer, Jane. *The Hollywood Musical.* Bloomington: Indiana University Press, 1982.

"Melodrama, Serial Form, and Television Today." In *The Media Reader,* ed. Manuel Alvarado and John O. Thompson. London: BFI, 1990, pp. 253–65.

Fordin, Hugh. *The Movies' Greatest Musicals.* New York: Frederick Ungar, 1984.

Foucault, Michel. "What Is an Author?" (extract). In *Theories of Authorship,* ed. John Caughie. London: Routledge & Kegan Paul, 1981, pp. 287–9.

Francisco, Charles. *The Radio City Music Hall.* New York: Dutton, 1979.

Gaines, Jane, and Charlotte Herzog, eds. *Fabrications: Costuming and the Female Body.* New York: Routledge, 1990.

Gates, Henry Louis, Jr. "The Trope of the New Negro and the Reconstruction of the Image of the Black." *Representations* 24 (Fall 1988): 129–55.

Genne, Beth. "Vincente Minnelli's Style in Microcosm: The Establishing Sequence of *Meet Me in St. Louis.*" *Art Journal* (Fall 1983): 248–54.

Gledhill, Christine, ed. *Home Is Where the Heart Is.* London: BFI, 1987.

Green, Stanley. *Ring Bells! Sing Songs! Broadway Musicals of the 1930s.* New Rochelle, N.Y.: Arlington House, 1971.

Guerif, François. *Vincente Minnelli.* Paris: Edilig, 1984.

Hall, Stuart. "The Whites of Their Eyes." In *The Media Reader,* ed. Manuel Alvarado and John O. Thompson. London: BFI, 1990, pp. 7–23.

Harvey, Stephen. *Directed by Vincente Minnelli.* New York: Museum of Modern Art and Harper & Row, 1989.

Henderson, Brian. *A Critique of Film Theory.* New York: Dutton, 1980.

Hiller, Jim. ed. *Cahiers du Cinema in the 1950s.* Cambridge, Mass.: Harvard University Press, 1985.

Cahiers du Cinema in the 1960s. Cambridge, Mass.: Harvard University Press, 1987.

Houghton, Norris. "The Designer Sets the Stage." *Theater Arts Monthly* (New York), 20, no. 10 (October 1936): 776–88.

Houseman, John. *Front and Center*. New York: Simon & Schuster, 1979.

Howe, Irving, ed. *The Idea of the Modern*. New York: Horizon Press, 1967.

Hunt, Leon. "E. C. on the Couch," *Comics Journal* 133 (December 1989): 54–63.

Jameson, Fredric. *Postmodernism, or the Cultural Logic of Late Capitalism*. Durham, N.C.: Duke University Press, 1991.

Johnson, Albert. "The Films of Vincente Minnelli." *Film Quarterly* 12 (Winter 1958): 20–35; 13 (Spring 1959): 32–42.

Johnson, Mark. *The Body and the Mind: The Bodily Basis of Meaning, Imagination, and Reason*. Chicago: University of Chicago Press, 1987.

Lang, Robert. *American Film Melodrama*. Princeton, N.J.: Princeton University Press, 1989.

Lardner, David. "Cinema." *New Yorker* (May 29, 1943): 117.

Lewis, Ramona. "*Cabin* Picture Called Insult." *New York Amsterdam News* (June 12, 1943): 17.

Leyda, Jay, ed. *Film Makers Speak*. New York: DaCapo, 1977.

Lindsey, Shelly Stamp. "Wages of Sin: *Traffic in Souls* and the White Slavery Trade." *Persistence of Vision* 9 (1991): 90–102.

Locke, Alain. "The New Negro." In *Black Voices,* ed. Abraham Chapman. New York: Mentor Books, 1968.

MacAdams, William. *Ben Hecht: The Man Behind the Legend*. New York: Scribners, 1990.

Masson, Alain. *Comedie musicale*. Paris: Stock, 1981.

   "La douceur du foyer et le charme des soirs: *Meet Me in St. Louis.*" *Positif* 374 (April 1992): 101–3.

Mast, Gerald, and Bruce Kawin. *A Short History of the Movies*. New York: Macmillan, 1990.

Meyersberg, Paul. "The Testament of Vincente Minnelli." *Movie* 3 (October 1962): 10–13.

Minnelli, Vincente, with Hector Acre. *I Remember It Well*. Garden City, N.Y.: Doubleday, 1974.

Mordden, Ethan. *The Hollywood Studios*. New York: Simon & Schuster, 1989.

Naremore, James. *Acting in the Cinema*. Berkeley and Los Angeles: University of California Press, 1988.

   "Authorship and the Cultural Politics of Film Criticism." *Film Quarterly,* 44, no. 1 (Fall 1990): 14–23.

   The Magic World of Orson Welles, rev. ed. Dallas: Southern Methodist University Press, 1989.

Naremore, James, and Patrick Brantlinger, eds. *Modernity and Mass Culture*. Bloomington: Indiana University Press, 1991.

Neale, Stephen. *Genre*. London: BFI, 1983.

Nowell-Smith, Geoffrey. "Minnelli and Melodrama." In *Home Is Where the Heart Is,* ed. Christine Gledhill. London: BFI, 1987, pp. 70–4.

   "On Kiri Te Kanawa, Judy Garland, and the Culture Industry." In *Modernity and Mass Culture,* ed. James Naremore and Patrick Brantlinger. Bloomington: Indiana University Press, 1991, pp. 70–9.

Peiss, Kathy. *Cheap Amusements: Working Women and Leisure in Turn-of-the-Century New York*. Philadelphia: Temple University Press, 1986.

Perkins, V. F. *Film As Film*. New York: Penguin, 1972.

PM Magazine (June 1, 1943): 28.

Pollock, Griselda. *Vision and Difference*. London: Routledge, 1988.

Ray, Robert. *A Certain Tendency of the Hollywood Cinema: 1930–1980*. Princeton, N.J.: Princeton University Press, 1985.

Ross, Andrew. *No Respect: Intellectuals and Popular Culture*. New York: Routledge & Kegan Paul, 1989.

Salt, Barry. *Film Style and Technology: History and Analysis*. London: Starword, 1983.

Sarris, Andrew. *The American Cinema: Directors and Directions*. New York: Dutton, 1968.

Schatz, Thomas. *The Genius of the System*. New York: Pantheon, 1988.

Schnee, Charles. *Tribute to a Bad Man (The Bad and the Beautiful)*. Mimeographed film script. March 26, 1952. Chapel Hill: University of North Carolina Library.

Schrader, Paul. "Notes on Film Noir." In *The Film Genre Reader*, ed. Barry Keith Grant. Austin: University of Texas Press, 1986, pp. 169–82.

Serebrinsky, Ernesto, and Oscar Garacochea. "Vincente Minnelli Interviewed in Argentina." *Movie* 10 (June 1963): 23–8.

Shrank, Joseph, and Marc Connelly. *Cabin in the Sky*. Mimeographed film script. September 21, 1942. Revisions dated October 20, 1942. Lilly Library, Indiana University, Bloomington.

Stallabras, Julian. "The Idea of the Primitive: British Art and Anthropology, 1918–1930. *New Left Review* 183 (1990): 95–115.

Stam, Robert. "Bakhtin, Polyphony, and Ethnic/Racial Representation." In *Unspeakable Images: Ethnicity and the American Cinema*, ed. Lester D. Friedman. Urbana: University of Illinois Press, 1991, pp. 251–76.

Stone, Irving. *Lust for Life*. New York: Longmans, Green, 1934.

Taylor, Richard, and Ian Christie. *The Film Factory*. Cambridge, Mass.: Harvard University Press, 1988.

Telotte, J. P. "Self and Society: Vincente Minnelli and Musical Formula." *Journal of Popular Film and Television* 9, no. 3 (1982): 181–93.

Tobin, Yann. "La femme modele." *Positif* 307 (September 1986), 71–2.

Toles, George. "No Bigger than Zuzu's Petals: Dream-Messages, Epiphanies, and the Undoing of Conventions in *It's a Wonderful Life*." *North Dakota Quarterly* (Summer 1984): 43–60.

Torgovnick, Marianna. *Gone Primitive: Savage Intellects, Modern Lives*. Chicago: University of Chicago Press, 1990.

Toulet, Emmanuelle. "Cinema at the Universal Exposition, Paris, 1900." *Persistence of Vision* 9 (1991): 10–36.

Trilling, Lionel. *The Liberal Imagination*. New York: Viking Press, 1940.

Willeman, Paul. "Distanciation and Douglas Sirk." *Screen*, 12, no. 1 (Spring 1971), 63–7.

Williams, Raymond. *The Country and the City*. New York: Oxford University Press, 1973.

The Long Revolution. Harmondsworth: Penguin, 1980.

Williams, Rosalind. *Dreamworlds: Mass Consumption in Late Nineteenth-Century France*. Berkeley and Los Angeles: University of California Press, 1982.

Wilson, Edmund. *The Wound and the Bow*. New York: Random House, 1941.

Wood, Robin. "The American Family Comedy: From *Meet Me in St. Louis* to *The Texas Chainsaw Massacre*." *Wide Angle* 3, no. 2 (1979): 5–11.

"Ideology, Genre, Auteur." In *Film Genre Reader*, ed. Barry Keith Grant. Austin: University of Texas Press, 1986, pp. 59–73.

Index

A rebours (Huysmans), 18
Abbot and Costello Meet Frankenstein (film), 29
Ace in the Hole (film), 114
acting: Minnelli's approach to, 39–43; performances in Minnelli's films, 67, 80–1, 92–5, 98, 125–6, 128, 131, 134, 143, 144–6
Adorno, Theodor W., 1, 57, 72, 154 n2, 159–60 n23
advertising, 16, 22, 34, 108, 111, 152
aestheticism: in consumer society, 13–18; in Minnelli's personal style, 7–8, 60; in Minnelli's work, 2–4, 13–18, 34, 62, 70, 80, 125, 128–34, 141–2
aesthetique du cool, 64
Afgacolor, 140
African art, 7; *see also* Africanism; modernism
Africanism, 21–2, 24, 59–62, 66, 67, 161 n36; *see also* African art; modernism
African-American culture, 22, 59; *see also* Africanism; Harlem renaissance; "New Negro, The"
Against Interpretation (Sontag), 8
Agee, James, 34, 44, 56–7, 58, 87, 159–60 n23
Alda, Alan, 92
All About Eve (film), 113
Allen, Robert C., 11
Althusser, Louis, 47
Altman, Rick, 29, 31, 63, 64, 68, 77, 81–2
Altman, Robert, 92, 137
Alton, John, 102
Alton, Robert, 21, 26
American Cinema, The (Sarris), 46
American Communist Party, 54
American Film Melodrama (Lang), 49
American Film Musical, The (Altman), 31

American in Paris, An (film), 1, 5, 13, 18, 27, 31, 45, 114, 126, 139, 150
Ames, Leon, 74, 94
Anderson, Eddie, 51, 58, 62, 67, 70
Anderson, Lindsay, 45
Anna Karenina (film), 119
Apartment for Peggy (film), 32
arcades, 14
Arlen, Harold, 25, 58
Armstrong, Louis, 25, 55, 56
Arnaz, Desi, 32, 110
Arnold, Matthew, 46
Art Institute of Chicago, 10
art melodrama, 32, 126–7, 143–4; *see also* melodrama
art nouveau, 17–18
Astaire, Fred, 3, 7, 24, 25, 28, 35, 41, 126
Astor, Mary, 74
At Home Abroad (musical revue), 13, 19, 20–1, 60, 67
Auden, W. H., 135
Aurier, Albert, 142–3
auteur, 19–20, 29, 45, 46; *see also* auteurism; authorship
auteurism, 38–9, 45–7
authorship: critical debates over, 45–8, 49–50; in Minnelli's Broadway revues, 19–20; signs of, in Minnelli's films, 91, 114, 126–7, 139, 147–8, 150–1; *see also* auteur; auteurism
avant-garde art, 10, 17, 22, 60, 136
Ayres, Lemuel, 74, 77

Bad and the Beautiful, The (film), 1, 3–4, 27, 28, 30, 35, 37, 40–2, 45, 112–34, 153
Baker, Josephine, 60
Bakhtin, Mikhail, 53
Balaban and Katz theaters, 2, 11–12

Ball, Lucille, 32, 110
"Ballad for Americans" (song), 55, 57
ballet, 18, 21, 24, 38
Balzac, Honoré, 14, 45
Band Wagon, The (film), 1, 3, 24, 28, 29,
  30, 42, 96, 112, 126
Bardot, Brigitte, 130
Barefoot Contessa, The (film), 113
Barr, Roseanne, 111
Barrymore, Diana, 118
Barthes, Roland, 47, 73
Barton, Ralph, 10
Basie, Count, 55
Bataan (film), 55
Baudelaire, Charles, 14–15, 17
Bazin, André, 39, 45
Beardsley, Aubrey, 12, 18
Beaton, Cecil, 20
Beery, Wallace, 26
Behrman, S. N., 44, 60–1
Bells Are Ringing (film), 31
Bemelmans, Ludwig, 35
Benchley, Robert, 60
Benjamin, Walter, 10, 14, 39, 155 n24
Bennett, Arnold, 15
Bennett, Joan, 93, 98
Benny, Jack, 93–4
Benson, Sally, 72, 75, 78–9, 81, 82, 84
Berger, John, 135, 136, 140
Bergman, Ingmar, 103
Berkeley, Busby, 3, 38, 58
Berlin, Irving, 22
Berman, Pandro, 29, 94
Bertolucci, Bernardo, 1
Betsy's Wedding (film), 92
Big Combo, The (film), 102
Big Knife, The (film), 113
Black, Max, 29
black musicals, 19; see also Cabin in the
  Sky
Blane, Ralph, 76, 80
Blitzstein, Marc, 19
Blonde Venus (film), 60
Blood of Jesus (film), 64, 66
Bogdanovich, Peter, 92
Bogle, Thomas, 58
bohemianism, 14–15, 17, 135
"book" show, 19, 24
boom shot, see camera crane
Bradshaw, George, 112, 113
Brando, Marlon, 41, 117
Brecher, Irving, 72
Brecht, Bertolt, 19, 20, 35, 95
Breen Office, see Production Code
Bremer, Louise, 38, 74, 80
Breton, André, 18
Brice, Fanny, 23

Brighton Film Review, The, 48
Bringing Up Baby (film), 29
British Film Institute, 44, 48
Broadway theater: characteristics of, in
  thirties, 18–19; Freed unit's adaptation
  of, 26, 31–2; influence of, on Meet Me in
  St. Louis, 71, 73, 75; Minnelli's work in,
  7, 12, 17; treatment of black characters
  in thirties and forties by, 59–62; see also
  musical comedy
Brook, Peter, 153
Brooks, Louise, 34
Brown, Pamela, 147
Brummell, Beau, 14, 18
Buchanan, Jack, 24
Buñuel, Luis, 10, 24
Burke, Peter, 54
Burstyn, Ellen, 40
Burton, Tim, 90

Cabaret (film), 30, 34
Cabin in the Sky (film), 22, 27, 28, 31, 34,
  35, 36, 38, 42, 45, 51–70, 72
Cagney, James, 11, 21, 55, 117
Cahiers du Cinema, 45, 112
camera crane: history of, in Hollywood,
  37–8; identification of, with Minnelli's
  style, 36–9; use of, in Minnelli's films,
  41, 42, 64–6, 68, 73, 78, 86, 101–2, 119,
  127, 128–30; see also camera style; long
  take
camera style, 36–9, 41–2, 150
Cameron, Ian, 46
camp, 3, 44, 127
Canty, Marietta, 97, 130
Capra, Frank, 77, 87, 90
Captains Courageous (film), 94
Carfagno, Ed, 125
Carmen Jones (film), 51
Caron, Leslie, 34
Carpenter, Carleton, 101
Carrol, Earl, 12
Carroll, Joan, 75–6, 77
Carroll, Leo G., 107, 118
Casablanca (film), 55
Casanova's Memoirs, 12
Centennial Summer (musical), 72
Césaire, Aimé, 59
Cézanne, Paul, 152
Champion (film), 114
Chaplin, Charles, 90, 144
Charisse, Cyd, 24, 134
Chicago, 9–12, 72, 73
Chicago Theater, 11
Chocolate Soldier, The (film), 26
choreography, 19–23, 38, 101–2
Cibber, Colley, 90

Cinemascope, 33, 42, 139–40, 150
Citizen Kane (film), 4, 112–13, 117–20, 125
city versus country theme, 51, 59, 62, 63–8, 89
Clark, T. J., 135
Clock, The (film), 30, 34, 35, 37, 39, 44, 91, 102
Coburn, Charles, 26
Cobweb, The (film), 2, 27, 126, 135, 147, 152
Cocteau, Jean, 10
Cole, Nat King, 55
comedy, 29, 30, 31, 32, 74, 90–111
commodification, 3, 5; and aestheticism, 8; in "folk" musicals, 71–5, 77–80, 89; in Minnelli's style, 33–4; in modernist art, 59–60, 136–7, 151–3; in two versions of *Father of the Bride*, 93–111; *see also* costume; fashion; set design; window display
Comolli, Jean-Louis, 46
Connelly, Marc, 55, 57, 67
Conrad, Joseph, 60
consumer society, *see* commodification
Coolidge, Calvin, 16
Corwin, Norman, 137, 138, 139, 151
Cosmopolitan, 114
costume: as basis of Minnelli's style, 33, 34–6; at MGM, 28; in Minnelli's Broadway revues, 60; in Minnelli's films, 42, 63, 64, 67, 80, 84, 85, 88–9, 107–9, 131, 145; in Minnelli's "presentation" shows, 11–13
Count Bruga (Hecht), 17
Courtship of Eddie's Father, The (film), 32, 36, 39, 46, 87, 91
Coutard, Raoul, 129
Cox, Paul, 137
Cradle Will Rock, The (opera), 19
Craig, Hardin, 9
Cripps, Thomas, 55, 64
criticism, 42–50, 58
Cronon, William, 72
Crouse, Russell, 73
cubism, 22
Cukor, George, 26, 30, 138
culture industry, 1, 16, 18, 22, 57; *see also* commodification; industrialization

dada, 60
Dali, Salvador, 10, 14, 35, 102
"Dallas" (television show), 127
Dandridge, Dorothy, 55
dandyism, 3, 8, 11, 13–18; *see also* aestheticism
Daniell, Henry, 145

Daniels, Henry, 76
Daniels, LeRoy, 24
Dassin, Jules, 45
Davenport, Henry, 76
Day, Clarence, 73
De Niro, Robert, 92
Degas, Edgar, 138
Delacroix, Eugene, 149
DeMille, Cecil B., 39, 151
Demoiselles d'Avignon, Les (Picasso), 60
department stores, 1, 4, 13–16, 73, 152; *see also* Harrods, Marshall Field
Depression, *see* Great Depression
Designing Woman (film), 2, 5, 32, 91, 147
Deskey, Donald, 7
détournement, 17
Dialectic of Enlightenment (Horkheimer and Adorno), 57
Dietz, Howard, 117
Dinner at Eight (film), 114
Directed by Vincente Minnelli (Harvey), 48
discourse, 53–62, 159 n11
Disney, Walt, 55
Disney studios, 92–4, 110–11
"Distanciation in Douglas Sirk" (Willeman), 48
Domarchi, Jean, 45
Donald, James, 143
Donen, Stanley, 38, 45
Douchet, Jean, 45, 48
Douglas, Kirk, 3, 4, 41–3, 114–15, 118, 127, 131, 137–8, 140, 143–8, 150, 152
Drake, Tom, 37, 74
DuBarry, The (musical), 12
Duchamp, Marcel, 10
Duke, Vernon, 58
Dunham, Katherine, 54, 57
Duvivier, Julian, 55
Dyer, Richard, 52–3, 70, 80, 81, 120, 125, 130–1, 134

Eakins, Thomas, 35, 75
East Lynne (play), 8
Eastmancolor, 140
Eddy, Nelson, 26
Edens, Roger, 26, 58
editing, 36–7
Egg and I, The (film), 32
Eisenstein, Sergei, 1, 24, 38
Eliot, T. S., 15
Ellington, Duke, 13, 55, 56, 59, 60, 64
Elsaesser, Thomas, 31, 48
"Entertainment and Utopia" (Dyer), 52–3
Ernst, Max, 10
Erté, 12
Esquire, 13, 17, 66

ethnicity, 52; *see also* Africanism; *Cabin in the Sky*
excess, 48–9, 131–4, 139, 142–3
expressionism, 102–5, 125, 136, 139, 140–1

fairy-tale musical, 29, 68; *see also* genre; musical comedy; operetta
Famous Players-Lasky, 11
Fantazius Mallare (Hecht), 17
Farber, Manny, 44
fashion: in the figure of the dandy, 14; in Minnelli's films, 64, 72, 75, 77; in Minnelli's personal style, 17; in modern culture, 16, 22; in portrait photography, 10; *see also* commodification; costume
Father of the Bride (novel), 91
Father of the Bride (Disney film), 92–4
Father of the Bride (MGM film), 1, 27, 30, 32, 36, 42, 90–111, 114
Father's Little Dividend (film), 32, 91
fetish, 34
Feuer, Jane, 48, 68–70, 106, 129
Fieshi, Jean-André, 46
film noir, 102, 125
Film Quarterly, 46
Finklehoff, Fred
Firbank, Ronald, 18
flâneur, 10, 39, 138
Fleming, Victor, 26
Folies Bergère, 12, 22
folk musical, 29, 30, 63–4, 81–2; *see also* folklore; genre; musical comedy
folklore: in Broadway production of *Cabin in the Sky*, 54–5; in Broadway shows of the forties, 71; in cultural debates of the forties, 56; in film version of *Cabin in the Sky*, 58, 62, 64, 70; in *Meet Me in St. Louis*, 75, 77; origins of, 54; in treatment of African-American subjects, 52
Folsey, George, 37, 73
Ford, Glenn, 28, 33–4, 95
Ford, John, 36 87
Fordin, Hugh, 26, 37
Fordism, 16; *see also* industrialization
42nd Street (film), 21
Fosse, Bob, 38
Foucault, Michel, 47
Four Horsemen of the Apocalypse (film), 28, 33–4, 46
4 Saints in 3 Acts (opera), 19
Fox studios, 51
Frankfurt school, 47, 57, 160 n26; *see also* Adorno, Theodor W.; Horkheimer, Max
Freed, Arthur, 2, 3, 23, 26, 29, 30, 31, 37, 57–9, 64, 68, 70, 72, 75, 79, 96
Freed unit, *see* Freed, Arthur

Freedman, David, 23
Freud, Sigmund, 3, 60, 81, 92, 97, 102, 111, 121–2, 143, 153;; *see also* psychoanalysis
Front Page, The (Hecht), 17
Fry, Roger, 60
futurism, 22

Gaines, Jane, 34
Garbo, Greta, 26, 35, 119
Garland, Judy, 3, 34, 37, 41, 68, 72, 75, 76, 77, 80–1, 84, 87, 89, 118, 126
Garson, Greer, 81
Gauguin, Paul, 137, 141–2, 143, 147–50, 151
Gautier, Theophile, 8
gender: codes of, 93–4, 96, 143, 162 n51; female community in *Meet Me in St. Louis*, 73–4; "feminine" males, 33; in Hollywood genres, 31; male vs. female psychology in *The Bad and the Beautiful*, 121; roles in society, 162 n5; *see also* homosexuality
genre, 29–33, 48–9, 90–6, 156 n37; *see also* comedy; melodrama; musical comedy
Germinal (Zola), 145
Gershwin, George, 2, 18, 19, 22, 52
Gershwin, Ira, 2, 13
Gibson, Charles Dana, 10
Gigi (film), 1, 3, 5, 20, 31, 34–5
Gleason, Keogh, 125
Godard, Jean-Luc, 46, 129–30
Gold Diggers of 1933 (film), 11
Goldwyn, Samuel, 24
Goldwyn studios, 24
Gomery, Douglas, 11
Goodbye, Charlie (film), 28, 32, 40, 148
Goodrich, Francis, 91, 93, 98, 110
Graff, Wilton, 146
Graham, Martha, 23
Grahame, Gloria, 40, 114, 122, 126, 135
Grand Hotel (film), 114
Grapes of Wrath, The (Steinbeck), 54
Great Depression, 7, 11, 12, 54–5
Greed, 34
Green, Stanley, 18–19
Green Pastures, The (play), 54, 55
Green Pastures, The (film), 51, 56
Griffith, D. W., 90
Guys, Constantine, 10

H. M. Pulman, Esq. (film), 26
Hackett, Albert, 91, 93, 98, 110
Hall, Stuart, 49
Hallelujah! (film), 51, 58, 64
Hamilton, George, 3, 9, 41

Hammerstein, Oscar, 52, 71, 89
Harburg, E. Y., 13, 58, 64
Harlan, Russell, 140
Harlem renaissance, 22, 59; *see also* "New Negro, The"
Harpers, 3
Harris, Jed, 112, 113
Harrison, Rex, 32, 35
Harrods (Department store), 15
Harvard Lampoon, 41
Harvey, Stephen, 12, 13, 18, 30, 33, 48, 60, 86, 88, 128
Hawks, Howard, 46
Heart of Darkness (Conrad), 60
Hearts in Dixie (film), 51
Hecht, Ben, 16–17
Heisler, Stuart, 55
Hepburn, Katharine, 26
Hickman, Darryl, 85, 86
high art/low art categories, 18, 21, 24
High and the Mighty, The (film), 117
Hitchcock, Alfred, 46, 103, 118
Holiday, Billie, 67
Home from the Hill (film), 3, 5, 9, 30, 31, 33, 35, 40, 42, 148
homosexuality, 7, 147–50
Hooray for What (musical), 24
Hope, Bob, 21, 23
Horkheimer, Max, 1, 57
Horne, Lena, 22, 24, 27, 34, 51, 55, 58, 59, 62, 67, 70, 118
House Committee on Un-American Activities, 45, 113
Houseman, John, 4, 27, 29, 46, 112–14, 117–19, 124–6, 137–9, 143, 147, 151
Howard, Ron, 87
Hughes, John, 90
Hughes, Langston, 161–2 n50
Huston, John, 138
Huysmans, J. K., 18

I Dood It (film), 30
ideology: in academic film criticism, 47–9, 157 n72; in commercial entertainment, 52–4; in Minnelli's films, 62–70, 71–3, 82, 88–9, 90–1, 102–11, 119
I'll Take Manilla (film), 26
impressionist painting, 10, 11, 17–18, 88, 139
In the Good Old Summertime (film), 72
In This Our Life (film), 55
industrialization, 3, 7, 11, 14–18, 25–8, 29, 72–3; *see also* culture industry; modernity
Ingram, Rex, 54
integrated form: in "art" melodramas, 126; in Broadway revues, 20–1; in domestic

comedies, 32, 95–6; in musical films, 24, 31, 77; *see also* streamlining; unity
intertextuality, 22–4; *see also* parody; pastiche; quotation
Irish, Tom, 97
It's a Wonderful Life (film), 77, 150
Ivan the Terrible, Part II (film), 1

Jackson, Janet, 38
jazz: associated with modernity, 10, 16, 18; black performers of, 22; commodification of, 60, 64; contradictory implications of, in mass culture, 52
Jazz Singer, The (film), 52
Johnny Eager (film), 26
Johns, Jasper, 14
Johnson, Albert, 46, 134
Johnson, Hall, 38, 56
Johnson, Van, 74
Jones, Jennifer, 3, 34
Jones, Robert Edmund, 9
Jourdan, Louis, 3, 41
Joyce, James, 15
Jubilee (musical), 60
Julius Caesar (play), 117

Kant, Immanuel, 3
Keaton, Buster, 30, 90, 95
Keaton, Diane, 110
Keats, John, 126
Kelly, Gene, 18, 29, 38, 45, 126
Kelly, Grace, 111
Kendall, Jay, 35
Kern, Jerome, 24, 52
Kerr, John, 3, 41, 135
Kinberg, Jud, 139
Kismet (film), 27
Klinger, Barbara, 42
Kurosawa, Akira, 137

Lacan, Jacques, 47
Ladies' Home Journal, 112
Lamarr, Hedy, 26, 93
Lang, Fritz, 118
Lang, Robert, 49, 122–4, 165 n16
Lardner, David, 58
Last Laugh, The (film), 37
Last Picture Show, The (film), 92
Latouche, John, 55, 58
Lautréamont, Compte de (Isidore Ducasse), 17
Leadbelly, 54
Lee, Harriet, 38
Leisen, Michael, 24
leisure industry, *see* culture industry
Lerner, Alan Jay, 31
LeRoy, Mervyn, 26

Levant, Oscar, 2, 45
Lewis, Albert, 56
Lewis, Ramona, 58
Life with Father (film), 73
Lifeboat (film), 55
Light Fantastic, The (musical revue), 24
lighting, 11, 41, 43; see also photography
 (film)
Lillie, Beatrice, 13, 24
Lindsay, Howard, 73
Locke, Alain, 59
Long, Long Trailer, The (film), 32, 45–6,
 91, 110, 111
long take, 36–40, 81, 85, 131–4
Losey, Joseph, 45
Love Me Tonight (film), 25
Lowe, Arthur, 139
Lowe, Frederic, 31
Lowe's Incorporated, 25, 56, 113; see also
 Metro-Goldwyn-Mayer
Loy, Myrna, 26
Lubitsch, Ernst, 24, 32, 90
Lukács, George, 72
Lust for Life (film), 1, 3, 27, 30, 35, 42, 44,
 45, 126, 127, 135–53

MacLaine, Shirley, 34
Madame Bovary (film), 3, 30, 36, 139, 151
Madame Bovary (Flaubert), 9, 33, 122
magazins de nouveauté, see arcades
Magnificent Ambersons, The (film), 37, 73,
 78
Main, Marjorie, 26, 74
Mamoulian, Roubin, 2, 24–5
Manet, Edouard, 135
Mankiewicz, Herman, 113
Mankiewicz, Joseph, 113, 117
Marcorelles, Louis, 3
Marshall Field (Department store), 1, 9–11,
 13–14
Martin, Hugh, 76, 80
Martin, Steve, 93–4, 111
Marton, Andrew, 58
Marx, Karl, 47, 70
Marx Brothers, 95
mass culture, see culture industry
Mayer, Louis B., 25–6, 27, 58, 75, 113
McQueen, Butterfly, 67
Mean Streets (film), 146
Meet Me in St. Louis (film), 1, 10, 27, 30–
 1, 35, 37, 44, 68, 71–89, 91, 94, 126
melancholy, 8, 75
melodrama: "art" subgenre of, 32–3, 113,
 119–34, 143–53; definitions of, 29–30;
 in "folk" musicals, 81; psychoanalytic
 theories of, 48–9; relationship of, with
 domestic comedies and musicals, 31

"Memorial to a Bad Man" (Bradshaw), 112
Mépris, Le (film), 46
Mercure de France, 142
Mercury Theater, 113, 117
Method, 40–1, 75, 92
Metro-Goldwyn-Mayer (MGM), 1–3, 15,
 44, 49, 51, 68, 82, 84, 89, 117, 147;
 history of, 25–8; house style of, 87, 31–
 2; Minnelli's role in, 38–9; production of
 The Bad and the Beautiful, 112–14;
 production of Cabin in the Sky, 54–6, 59,
 62; production of Father of the Bride,
 91–7, 106–8; production of Lust for Life,
 130, 138–40, 143, 150–2; production of
 Meet Me in St. Louis, 71–80
metteur-en-scène, 45
Meyers, Nancy, 92
Meyersberg, Paul, 46
MGM, see Metro-Goldwyn-Mayer
Millet, Jean-François, 135, 136, 149, 151,
 153
Minnelli, Liza, 34, 134
Minnelli Brothers Tent Show, 8
"Minnelli and Melodrama" (Nowell-Smith),
 48
minstrel show, 22
mise-en-scène, see acting; camera style;
 costume; set design
Miss Achilles Heel (film), 26
Mr. Blandings Builds His Dream House
 (film), 32
modernism, 7, 15–18, 19, 21–3, 59–62,
 135; see also modernity
modernity, 13–18, 22, 52–3, 59, 71–3,
 135; see also industrialization;
 urbanization
Monroe, Marilyn, 28
Monty Python, 95
Moore, Grace, 12
Morris, William, 136
Moss, Carleton, 55
Motion Picture Producers Association, 55
Moulin Rouge (film), 138
Movie (journal), 46
Mule Bone (play), 54
Murnau, Fredric, 37
Museum of Modern Art, 44
musical comedy, 18–19, 24–5, 30, 31–2,
 48; see also Broadway theater; Cabin in
 the Sky; genre; Meet Me in St. Louis
My Fair Lady (film), 31

narrative: in The Bad and the Beautiful,
 119–25; in Broadway revues, 20; in
 Cabin in the Sky, 54–5, 63–4; in classic
 Hollywood, 30; in Father of the Bride,
 95–6, 112–13; in Lust for Life, 137, 140,

143; in *Meet Me in St. Louis*, 71, 73, 76–7, 82; *see also* genre
Nashville (film), 30
Nation, The, 44
National Association for the Advancement of Colored People, 55, 62
nature, theme of, 71–3, 76–7, 88–9, 149, 151
Nature's Metropolis (Cronon), 72
Negerdichte, 60
Negritude, 59
Negro Soldier, The (film), 55
"New Negro, The" (Locke), 59
New Republic, The, 44
New Yorker, The, 13, 58, 60, 72
New York City, 12–13, 18–24, 67
New York Amsterdam News, 58
New York, New York (film), 30, 134
New York Times, 55, 58
New York Daily News, 58
Night Café (Van Gogh), 140
nostalgia, 29, 44; as a theme in Minnelli's work, 53, 63, 70, 72, 77, 113
Nowell-Smith, Geoffrey, 48–9, 60, 77

O'Brien, Margaret, 75, 81, 84, 87–8
O'Neill, Eugene, 10
Objectif (journal), 45
"Of Good and Evil" (Bradshaw), 113
Of Thee I Sing (musical), 19
Office of War Information, 55
Ohio Wesleyan University, 9
Oklahoma! (musical), 71–2, 75, 89
Oklahoma! (film), 75
Oldenberg, Claes, 14
On the Town (film), 45
operetta, 18–19, 25
Ophuls, Max, 36, 37

package unit production, 51
Panama Hattie (musical), 60
panoramas, 39, 157 n50
Paramount Pictures, 11, 12, 24–5
Paramount Theater, 12
Paris, 10; film criticism in, 45–7; Minnelli's depiction of, 33–4, 138; modernity of, 8, 14–15, 17–18, 39, 135, 138
parody, 22–4, 125; *see also* intertextuality; pastiche; quotation
Partisan Review, 56
pastiche, 80, 125; *see also* intertextuality; parody; quotation
pastoral, 52, 60, 88; *see also* folklore
patriarchy, 74, 91–111, 119–25, 144–5
Peck, Gregory, 32, 95
Peppard, George, 40
Perelman, S. J., 2

performance, theme of, 96–110; *see also* acting
Perkins, V. F., 39, 46, 87
photography (film), 36–9, 57, 63, 88, 102–3, 125, 131, 139–40; *see also* camera style; Cinemascope; Eastmancolor; Technicolor
photography (portrait), 10
Picasso, Pablo, 60
Pidgeon, Walter, 26, 114
Pierrot le Fou (film), 46
Piotrovsky, Adrian, 82
Pirate, The (film), 3, 27, 28, 29, 35, 44, 45, 66, 91
PM Magazine, 58
politique des auteurs, see auteurism
Pollock, Griselda, 135
Popular Front, 54
Porgy and Bess (opera), 52
Porter, Cole, 22, 60
Portrait of Dr. Gachet (Van Gogh), 40, 51–2
postimpressionism, 17, 22, 60
postmodernism, 22, 44
Potato Eaters (Van Gogh), 140
Powell, Dick, 23, 40, 114, 121, 125–6
Powell, Eleanor, 13, 21, 26
Powell, Jane, 68
Powell, William, 26
Pride and the Passion, The (film), 117
Pride and Prejudice (film), 29
primitivism, 7, 53, 60–2; *see also* Africanism; folklore
Production Code, 3, 7, 25
proscenium, 14; *see also* window display
Proud and Profane, The (film), 117
"Pseudo-Folk" (Agee), 56
psychoanalysis, 10, 111; in criticism of Minnelli's films, 48–9; in literary criticism of the forties, 164 n13; in Minnelli's work, 3, 86–8, 102–3; 118–25, 127, 143–7; vogue for, in Hollywood, 32–3; *see also* Freud, Sigmund; surrealism
Psychoanalysis (comic book), 32, 156 n39

Quinn, Anthony, 137, 141, 149
quotation, 24, 35, 46; *see also* intertextuality; parody; pastiche

Radio City Music Hall, 2, 7, 12–13, 42, 60
Raging Bull (film), 92
Raksin, David, 114, 118
Rauschenberg, Robert, 14
Ray, Man, 14
Ray, Robert, 72
Raye, Martha, 25
reception, *see* criticism

religion, theme of, 63–6, 68, 144–5, 149, 151
Reluctant Debutante, The (film), 32, 35, 91
Rembrandt, van Rijn, 149
Renoir, Jean, 36
Republic Pictures, 55
Resnais, Alain, 137
revue musical, 19–24, 29, 34, 60, 89
Reynolds, Debbie, 28, 68
Rice, Elmer, 57
Rivette, Jacques, 45
RKO, 7, 25
Robeson, Paul, 57
Robinson, Edward G., 26
Robinson, Julie, 149
Rockefeller Center, 7
Rogers, Ginger, 3, 7, 25
Rogers, Richard, 71, 89
Roland, Gilbert, 114, 119, 122
romanticism, 5, 24; in Minnelli's films, 2–3, 118, 126–8, 140–3; in modern art, 17; and critical views of Van Gogh's work, 136–7
Romeo and Juliet, 21
Roosevelt, Franklin D., 55, 59, 71
Rosenthal, S. L., 12
Ross, Andrew, 44
Roxyettes, 12
Rozsa, Miklos, 139, 150
Russell, Rosalind, 26

Sahara (film), 55
Said, Edward, 21
St. Louis (Mo.), 72, 75
Salt, Barry, 37
Sargent, John Singer, 10
Sarris, Andrew, 8, 46, 134
Saussure, Ferdinand de, 47
Savoca, Nancy, 92
Schary, Dore, 27, 93, 94, 113, 138
Schnee, Charles, 40, 113–14, 124
Schrank, Joseph, 57–8, 67
Schwartzenegger, Arnold, 151
Scorsese, Martin, 1, 92, 134, 146
screwball comedy, 90
self-reflexivity, 22–4, 68, 80, 89, 125–34
Selznick, David, 55, 113, 119, 124
sentiment: in bourgeois comedy and drama, 90–1; in classic Hollywood, 81–2; in MGM productions, 75; in Minnelli's work, 44, 93, 95, 138, 144, 148
Sequence (journal), 44
Serena Blandish (musical), 24, 60–3
set design, 28, 34–7, 45–6, 64–8, 77–9, 107, 125; *see also* stage design
sexuality, *see* gender; homosexuality
Shadow of the Thin Man (film), 26

Shakespeare, William, 82, 143
Shall We Dance (film), 25
Sharaff, Irene, 38, 77
Shaw, George Bernard, 15
Shearer, Norma, 26
She's Gotta Have It (film), 29
Shivas, Mark, 46
Short, Martin, 111
show musical, 29, 30, 96, 103, 124; *see also* musical comedy
Show Boat (musical), 19, 52
Show Is On, The (film), 19, 21, 22, 23
Shyer, Charles, 92
Siegel, Joel E., 35
Sinatra, Frank, 3
Singin' in the Rain (film), 38
Sirk, Douglas, 48, 49
Sitting Pretty (film), 32
Skelton, Red, 30
Sloane, Everett, 151
Sloane, Paul, 10
Sloanism, 16
Smith, Jack, 37
Society of Painters and Paper Hangers, 12
Some Came Running (film), 3, 31, 34, 35, 36, 147
Song of the South (film), 55
Sontag, Susan, 8
sound recording, 77
Sower, The (Millet), 136–7, 151
Spender, Stephen, 15
Spillane, Mickey, 24
stage design, 9, 11–13, 20–1, 60–3
Stam, Robert, 53
Star Is Born, A (film), 30, 113
star system, 55, 59, 70, 80–1, 91, 92–5, 107–10, 114, 119, 125–6, 130–1, 137
State Fair (musical), 72
Steel Calvary, The (film), 26
Steele, Richard, 90
Stein, Gertrude, 19
Steinbeck, John, 54
Sterke, Jeanette, 145
Stevens, George, 26
Stevens, Rise, 26
Stewart, Elaine, 4, 41, 42
Stewart, James, 150
Stewart, Paul, 118
Stone, Irving, 137, 138, 143, 148, 149
Stormy Weather (film), 51, 55
streamlining, 7, 21, 72; *see also* integrated form
Streeter, Edward, 91
Sturges, Preston, 32
style, 3–4, 13; control of, by departments at MGM, 28; in Minnelli's Broadway shows, 20–3; in Minnelli's films, 33–42,

60–70, 77–88, 91–5, 101–6, 119, 121, 127–34, 139, 150–1; *see also* authorship
suburbia, 64, 71, 74, 91, 96, 127
Sullivan, Barry, 120, 129
Summer Holiday (musical), 72
Sunflowers (Van Gogh), 138
Sunset Boulevard (film), 113, 128, 129
surrealism, 10; Minnelli's uses of, 24, 25, 62, 102–3, 126; and modernity, 17–18, 155 n24
Surtees, Robert, 125
Swanson, Gloria, 129

Tales of Manhattan (film), 55
"Tales of Sound and Fury" (Elsaesser), 48
Tamblyn, Russ, 97
Tashlin, Frank, 110
Taxi Driver (film), 146
Taylor, Don, 89, 97
Taylor, Elizabeth, 91, 93, 106, 107–09
Taylor, Robert, 26
Tea and Sympathy (film), 3, 30, 33, 87, 147
Technicolor, 23, 140
television, 32, 74, 90, 91, 106, 113, 127
Thalberg, Irving, 25
Theater Arts, 20
Threepenny Opera, The (opera), 19
Thulin, Ingrid, 33, 34
Tiller Girls, 12–13
Time magazine, 2, 37, 58, 122
Times Square (film), 25
Tin Pan Alley, 26, 52
T-Men (film), 102
Toles, George, 78
Torch Song (film), 30
Totem and Taboo (Freud), 60
Toulouse-Lautrec, Henri, 138
Tracy, Spencer, 26, 32, 41, 91–6, 98–102
Tribute to a Bad Man (film), 114, 117
Trouble in Paradise (film), 21
True Love (film), 92
Turim, Maureen, 108
Turner, Lana, 3, 4, 26, 35, 42, 114, 118, 119, 125, 130–4
Twain, Mark, 82
Twentieth Century Fox, 32, 51, 56
Two-Faced Woman (film), 26
Two Weeks in Another Town (film), 27, 37, 46, 126, 127, 131, 134
Two Weeks with Love (film), 68

Ulysses (Joyce), 15
Undercurrent (film), 30
Unholy Partners (film), 26
unity, 19–21; *see also* integrated form
urbanization, 16–17, 52, 59, 62–3, 71–4,

135, 162 n5; *see also* industrialization; modernity; suburbia
utopian entertainment: art treated as utopian force, 33; Benjamin's attitude toward, 159 n6; Dyer's analysis of, 52–3; in Minnelli's films, 59, 68–70, 75, 91, 106, 126

Van Gogh, Vincent, 35, 127, 135–53
Van Dyke, W. S., 26
Vanities (stage show), 12
Vanity Fair, 3, 10
Variety, 12, 125
vaudeville, 11, 19, 94
Vertigo (film), 150
Very Warm for May (musical), 24
Vidor, King, 26, 58, 64
Vogue, 3, 98, 108
von Sternberg, Josef, 24, 34, 60, 130

Walsh, Raoul, 25
Walters, Charles, 38
Wanger, Walter, 55
Warhol, Andy, 14
Warner, Sidney, 36
Warner Brothers, 38, 51, 52, 59
Waste Land, The (Eliot), 15
Waters, Ethel, 13, 24, 36, 51, 59, 60, 62, 64, 67, 70
Ways of Seeing (Berger), 140
Wedding, A (film), 92
"Wedding Bells" (short film), 95
"weeping" comedy, 90
Weil, Kurt, 19, 25
Weissmuller, Johnny, 26
Welles, Orson, 1, 37, 73, 78, 112, 113, 117–18, 123, 125
Wells, H. G., 15
West, Mae, 90
Whistler, James McNeill, 10–11
White, Walter, 55
Wilder, Billy, 32
Willeman, Paul, 48
Williams, Raymond, 90–1
Williams, Rosalind, 14
Williams, Spenser, 64–6
Williams, Tennessee, 150
Willkie, Wendell, 55, 58
Wills, Chill, 84
Wilson, Dooley, 58
Wilson, Edmund, 126
window display, 1, 9–10, 13–14, 33–5, 73, 152
Wizard of Oz, The (film), 26, 57, 72, 80
Wollen, Peter, 16
Woman of the Year (film), 26
Wood, Robin, 81

Works Progress Administration, 54, 55, 56

World War II, 32, 72, 86; effect on black performers, 53, 55–6, 59; effect on Hollywood, 25; effect on Minnelli's Broadway revues, 20

Wound and the Bow, The (Wilson), 126, 137

Yellow Book (journal), 17

Yolanda and the Thief (film), 27, 35, 66

Young, Frederick, 140

Young, Robert, 26

Zanuck, Daryl, 55

Ziegfield, Florenz, 19, 23, 89

Ziegfield Follies (film), 29, 38, 80–1

Ziegfield Follies of 1936, The (stage show), 19, 20, 23, 60

Zinneman, Fred, 75

Zola, Emile, 145

Zukor, Adolph, 24